Liberal Religion:
Principles and Practice

Liberal Religion:
Principles and Practice

A POPULAR THEOLOGY

Frank G. Opton

Prometheus Books
700 East Amherst St.   •   Buffalo, New York 14215

Published 1982 by Prometheus Books
700 East Amherst Street, Buffalo, New York 14215

Library of Congress Card Number: 81-81129
ISBN: 0-87975-155-X

Printed in the United States of America

To Eva

Contents

7

Preface

A Matter of Moral Passion

A full page in *The New York Times* solicited potential advertisers for *Playboy* magazine. The advertisement depicted an attractive young man at the wheel of a car, and the headline read: "When I read *Time,* I am thinking of the world. When I read *Playboy,* I am thinking about me." The message is clear: if you want to influence me, make me think of myself, not of the world around me. While some idealists care about the environment, the *Playboy* man or *Playgirl* woman does not. The individual is only interested in self, absorbed in self.

Playboy and *Playgirl* have grown up in a culture which was, for several thousand years, permeated by pious preachments that preferred one way of life and tolerated another. Liberal Religion is different because it closely interrelates one's spirituality and intelligence with the environment and with the realities of life. Life around us is part of Liberal Religion; the two are inseparable. Liberal Religion requires everybody to think of himself or herself as part of the whole. It does not tolerate a way of life which differs from what it postulates.

Society today seems to be bogged down in a morass of inflation, unemployment, declining productivity, and crime waves. But this is not the root of the social disarray. The root of the evil is apathy and indifference. Philosophers and theologians tell us that this is so because people are estranged from society and from God. This is what existentialism teaches. One derives little comfort (and no hope) from such philosophical and theological explanations.

Ours has been called the age of anxiety. Anxiety means irresolution. Irresolution is related to apathy, and one wonders which is cause and which is effect, or whether both are two sides of the same coin. It matters little.

11

Obviously, individuals cannot rid themselves of irresolution or apathy unless they will it; and one is not likely to master such willpower unless one has the desire or the impulse to do so. Such desire or impulse has a religious or religion-like nature. Indeed, the current vogue of charismatic and evangelical religion aims at diverting attention away from anxieties. The vogue appeals to a sentimental abandon of good feeling and to a dulling of the intellect. It is another form of the same old traditional, other-worldly religion which has failed mankind. Those who accept and absorb Liberal Religion feel no anxiety and are able to help overcome the disarray of society.

Not everybody drifts aimlessly, but many do and they set the tone of contemporary living. These people, epitomized by the *Playboy* advertisement, do not care what happens around them, where they are going, and what is going to happen. Civil servants do not think of the welfare of the public they are supposed to serve; teachers are not devoted to the task of raising a generation of educated citizens; plumbers respond only weeks after a leak is reported; physicians make no house calls; landlords provide no heat; the consumer is thrown not to the wolves, but to the equally mindless computer; waiters cannot boil an egg when the egg machine is out of order; the United States intelligence apparatus does not supply adequate intelligence — the list is endless. If one complains, one is answered with a shrug of the shoulders or a sneering "get with it."

We live in a time of high unemployment, and yet it is very difficult to fill many jobs. This is true not only of many menial positions which go begging because people prefer to starve or accept welfare payments rather than dirty their hands. It applies also to jobs requiring skill and experience. The explanation of the paradox is that many persons prefer to "do their own thing," or starve, rather than accept regular work with a view of earning money and furthering their careers. "Money is not everything," becomes a blight on human growth rather than an expression of lofty idealism. It is as if the statement "In the sweat of thy face shalt thou eat bread" is felt to be the curse Biblical authors intended.

Work is not a curse nor is it a cause for despair or unhappiness. To work purposefully is fulfilling if the purpose is more than self gratification. What is called for is a spiritual purpose and principle. The person of commitment to principle is not to be laughed at. America became a strong and healthy country because her pioneers knew what they wanted and were imbued by a purpose larger than self. The famed Protestant work ethic and the New England conscience, which are held to be largely responsible for the strength and growth of America, are dead or, at least, inoperative. The lack of motivating power must be replaced by passion, that moral passion which Bernard Shaw calls the only real passion. This is not a new religious idea. Long ago, Søren Kierkegaard (1813–1855) said that our age does not lack reflection but passion. Apathy can be overcome by moral passion and passionate commitment. The Hitler holocaust has demonstrated the importance of a passionate attitude. Traditional Religion did not approve of Hitler. Where it resisted him, both inside and outside of Germany, it did so with prudence and without passion.

The moral passion which this book reflects is a passion for the beliefs of Liberal Religion. These are the beliefs of those who, often unfairly and stupidly, have been scorned as unbelievers. This assault has driven Liberal Religion into a defensive position which neglects to state its positive beliefs and values. One tends to overlook the fact that today Liberal Religion is the only religion which can flourish equally well among people whose ancestors limited their worship to Moses, Jesus, Mohammed, Buddha, Krishna, Zoroaster, or any of the other traditional divinities.

Liberal Religion makes men and women turn their faces to the world and gain inspiration in the affirmation of the reality of the world. The imperfections of this reality are not glossed over. Nevertheless, Liberal Religion scorns the cynic who preaches that a mere human cannot improve reality. It is a religion which, if pursued with moral passion, promises to create what is known in popular language as the Kingdom of God on earth.

PART ONE

PRINCIPLES

1

Introduction to Liberal Religion

It is of the utmost importance to establish the unique identity of Liberal Religion. It is different from all other religions, as different as modern chemistry from ancient alchemy.

This book attempts to clarify what Liberal Religion means when it speaks of religion, God, Jesus, sin, salvation, immortality, truth, and related subjects. Part II discusses the application of these concepts to some concrete problems. The task requires frequent reference to what is called in this book Traditional Religion, which is the opposite of Liberal Religion. Juxtaposing these viewpoints will shed light on the meaning and character of Liberal Religion.

The phrase "Traditional Religion" is a collective term for many nonliberal religions found in the Judeo-Christian tradition, as well as religions in other traditions. That substantial differences separate these religions is a fact which cannot be denied. But the similarities outweigh the differences. These religions are grounded on similar, mostly supernatural, premises; they are scripture-based. An Englishman described the religious scene in America in these words: "A Methodist is a Baptist who has been to high school; a Presbyterian is a Methodist who has been to college; an Episcopalian is a Presbyterian who has gotten into society; and a Catholic is an Episcopalian who has gotten religion."[1] The term "Traditional Religion" also embraces the so-called secular American religion characterized by a devotion to Americanism which is not liberal and has the earmarks of Traditional Religion. In this book, the phrase "Traditional Religion" also includes Russian Marxism, i.e., Marxism as interpreted by Lenin and his followers.

17

The first step towards a proper understanding of Liberal Religion is a liberation from the fetters of old-time language. Western culture has become encrusted with a religious language which has been thoughtlessly perpetuated. Words such as "religion," "God," "sin," "salvation," and "immortality" have acquired meanings which have no application to Liberal Religion. Liberal Religion is built on what contemporary budget makers call a "zero basis," which means that Liberal Religion is not wedded to old-time concepts and words in the religious dictionary. Nor is it wedded to tradition, sentimentality, and mysticism, which almost suffocate Traditional Religion.[2] This does not mean that Liberal Religion abjures tradition, sentimentality, or mysticism, but it insists on evaluating them in light of scientific knowledge and what they have to offer to the religiously liberal mind. Unfortunately, Liberal Religion has not been able to create a new language. The vocabulary remains the same, but the meanings of the words are not the same as in Traditional Religion. This makes Liberal Religion fresh and vital. The ancient concepts have frequently degenerated into mumbo jumbo uttered parrot-like in a manner that deadens rather than lifts men's spirit.

The Liberal Religion expounded in this book is an affirmative faith which shuns indifference. It therefore must be distinguished from a religious attitude which, out of indifference, is so broadminded that its identity is jeopardized.

There are at least three kinds of such pseudo-religious liberals. First, there are those who do not take religion seriously. They like to go to worship services occasionally, but it does not matter to them whether the service is Methodist, Unitarian, Roman Catholic, or Jewish. They have some vague beliefs, but these beliefs play no part in their daily life. An example of such pseudo-liberalism is the lady who said that, after her death, she wanted her body to stay in a church for twenty-four hours before burial, and she did not care what kind of church.

The second kind of pseudo-liberal religion is represented by a person who, out of a sense of allegiance, attends worship services on certain high holidays, but has no use for, or interest in, religion during the rest of the year.

The third and largest group of pseudo-liberal religionists consists of those who discard some of the rituals and beliefs of the ancient faith. According to current polls and published statistics, the memberships of evangelical and charismatic churches have been increasing while so-called liberal churches have been losing members. The churches designated as liberal in these polls are those which have a loose religious discipline and are easygoing on their members. In truth, they are holding on to Traditional Religion; they are only pseudo-liberal and no part of Liberal Religion. Some Roman Catholic theologians (for instance Eduard Schillebeeckx and Hans Küng) have been censored by the Vatican because they do not accept the Gospels as the unquestioned word of God. They question the doctrines of the Virgin Birth and papal infallibility. They emphasize the humanity of Jesus rather than his divinity, and tend to be nonconformists in other ways. Nevertheless, the so-called liberal Catholics remain firmly wedded to trinitarian doctrine and adhere to Traditional Religion.

When the rebel theologian Father Küng was forbidden by Rome to continue as a professor of Roman Catholic theology, the press referred to him as "the liberal theologian Küng." This is a misnomer. Father Küng is a liberal only in the sense that he questions certain Roman Catholic doctrines. Unlike Martin Luther, Father Küng has reaffirmed his allegiance to Roman Catholic religion. He is not, nor does he claim to be, a Religious Liberal. His church has neither excommunicated nor defrocked him. The conflict in the church, of which Father Küng is the most prominent contemporary example, is that between traditionalists and modernists. Modernists are not liberals who seek to make the traditional context of religion more palatable for modern taste. Küng writes that, "Contemporary theology is not striving to cook up new systems of man-made precepts, but to awaken a living consciousness of the word of God as witnessed in Scripture."[3]

The late Episcopal Bishop Pike was censured for denying the doctrine of the Virgin Birth. He did not recant, but neither did he leave his church. In 1979, Mrs. Sonia Johnson of Virginia was excommunicated from the Mormon Church because she was a militant lobbyist for the Equal Rights Amendment to the American Constitution. Equality of men and women violated a tenet of the Mormon religion. Mrs. Johnson protested but did not wish to alter her religious affiliation.

Reform Judaism, the most modern of the three branches of Judaism, also belongs into this category of pseudo-liberal religions. Reform Jews, as a rule, are easygoing and not dogmatic; but they still adhere to the basic tenets of the Old Testament and to traditional prayers. There are also Jews whose only connection with Judaism is an emotional allegiance to the history of their persecuted ancestors. This is understandable and noble, but it cannot be considered a religion.

Liberal Religion is not vague; it is a positive religion. Its value system is as rigorous as that of many conservative religions. The rigor of Liberal Religion rejects various forms of indifference to religious matters such as apathy and easygoing toleration. It rejects Sunday school programs which have no religious content and merely degenerate into weekend playpens where the children are occupied with biblical coloring books. It rejects the activity of those who attend services only because the children must be picked up from Sunday school.

Not all Traditional Religionists adhere to their religion. These deviations must be ignored in a book of this type which refers to Traditional Religion merely as a backdrop to a discussion of Liberal Religion and takes Traditional Religion at its word. To the extent that traditionalists do not practice what their religion teaches, they are living proof of the vitality of at least one principle of Liberal Religion, namely, freedom of belief.

The deviationists in Traditional Religion are an impediment to the flourishing of Liberal Religion. If confronted with some irrational or obscure doctrine in Traditional Religion, some deviationists will smile and say: "Of course, I do not believe that. I just disregard this piece of religious superstition." However, most of these deviationists still affirm their inherited religious affiliation and will not turn to Liberal Religion. This attitude may be motivated by inertia, sentimentality, or by stubbornness. Another important factor is that many people do not think religion is sufficiently important to be troubled by doctrines, beliefs, or practices that they might find unacceptable. They would rather wear stained clothes than go to the trouble of changing clothes. Tradition and habit are very powerful.

Traditional Religion is an utter failure because its religious message has not substantially elevated the conduct of people during the past five thousand years. It cannot be denied that Traditional Religion has gained millions of adherents. This, however, cannot be regarded as a religious success. Anybody who counts the number of adherents as a measure of success should be reminded that the best selling newspapers are those emphasizing crime, sex, and scandals. The level of what millions of people like to read, hear, or believe is, unfortunately, rather low. The low level of religious achievement attained by Traditional Religion is exemplified by the following citation from *A Tale of Two Cities*. Speaking of France in 1775, Charles Dickens wrote, "Under the guidance of Christian pastors, she entertained herself with such human achievements as sentencing a youth to have his hands cut off, his tongue torn out with pincers, and his body burned alive, because he had not kneeled down in the rain to do honor to a dirty procession of monks which passed within his view. . . ." It is the same today. One can read in contemporary newspapers how Catholics and Protestants murder each other in Ireland; in the Middle East devout Moslems terrorize Jews, and devout Jews kill Moslems; political dissidents in China, Russia, and Southeast Asia are brutally exterminated. African tribal chiefs do the same: five million persons in Africa are refugees from their homeland. The holocaust in Hitler's Germany could not have happened if the Christian religion had been more than a surface label. The lynch mobs in the United States consisted mostly of so-called good Christians. In the Republic of South Africa, the Dutch Reformed Church is the backbone of the hateful doctrine of apartheid.

Traditional Religion has demonstrated its inability to establish a spiritual order that shuns violence and brutality, and one that promotes friendship, peace, and what is called Christian love. The failure of Traditional Religion is responsible for the pervasive low morality in the world. And yet, many contemporaries believe, or are led to believe, that morality can be elevated by greater emphasis on the so-called old values which include Biblical religion. This hankering for, and pandering to, values and concepts that have consistently failed mankind is truly astonishing, if not repulsive. It is time to do away with the hollow idols and to progress to the principles and precepts of Liberal Religion. Adoption of these principles and precepts would lead to better living conditions. The obstacle thereto is that the ineffectual old religious traditions are ingrained in Western civilization. Entrenched habits, concepts, and practices die hard. Even when the old ways have failed, many people cling to the familiar, seeking solace from the old and fearing the new. But, more and more people seem to be ready, and even eager, to scuttle the old traditions without wishing to abandon religion. Liberal Religion offers them a desirable and viable alternative.

Liberal, as well as Traditional, Religion exists in all parts of the world. This book deals primarily with Western religion in general and more narrowly with religion in the United States. The core of Liberal Religion in the United States is constituted by societies that make up the Unitarian Universalist Association, the Ethical Culture Movement, and some Jewish, Methodist, and Quaker groups. Many Liberal Religionists are at the present time unorganized and, as the phrase goes, "unchurched." They are included here even though most of them have an almost visceral aversion to anything that smacks of church. It is hoped that this book will help harness the devotion, the talents, and the goodwill of some of these unorganized people into what, for convenience, is called the Liberal Church.

Of course, the Liberal Church does not exist as an organized entity. It is an open-ended community of free spirits from very diverse backgrounds. Few of them profess adherence to a Christian church or a Jewish Temple because Liberal Religion extends far beyond the Judeo-Christian base. Many traits of Liberal Religion are found in ancient Stoicism, which believed in an all-embracing brotherhood of men and women, individual responsibility for personal virtue or the lack thereof, and which was indifferent to the apparatus of public worship.

The members of the Liberal Church come from all corners of the spiritual world. Those in the first generation have been mostly "come outers," and they enjoy their freedom so much that they incline toward being very permissive. But, as John Hayward has pointed out:

> Permissive religion, like permissive education, or permissive methods of child rearing, has a temporary appeal to anyone who feels that he has previously been restricted by an authoritarian in his culture. But, once the change of bondage has been completely discarded, and once a second generation has been reared in the vacuum of freedom for its own sake, the question of the substance of faith is again brought forward.[4]

The "come outers" are generally driven by a spirit of rebellion against the doctrines and practices of Traditional Religion. This spirit of rebellion remains alive in Liberal Religion. At times, it has expressed itself as rebellion against all religion, but this is not what Liberal Religion stands for. Liberal Religion has positive religious principles.

There is a good deal of diversity of beliefs among Religious Liberals. Although Liberal Religion is based on rationalism, there is not one truth to which everyone must subscribe. This pluralism is described in the slogan: "We do not all think alike but we all alike agree to think!"

Nobody can presume to speak for all Religious Liberals or even for any other. The statements in this book are therefore merely the conceptions of one Liberal Religionist. However, there is a great deal of commonality among Religious Liberals. Most of the author's statements reflect that commonality. They are not intended to suggest a liberal dogma. A dogma is a fixed and immutable set of beliefs and is different from a creed. As the author has said elsewhere, "creed" is not a dirty word.[5] The often repeated proclamation that ours is a creedless religion is just not true. For instance, all Religious Liberals believe in freedom of thought and the democratic process, and that is a creed. True Liberal Religion is not wedded forever to this creed. Such is its freedom of thought and its belief in the democratic process that Liberal Religion will abandon it if, at some future time, it should become convinced that thought should not be free or that there should be no democratic process. This flexibility is, in itself, part of the creed. To say that Liberal Religion is creedless — that it has no beliefs — is not only untrue, it is a statement of weakness which misrepresents the nature of Liberal Religion. This misrepresentation is the reason why many persons are not attracted to Liberal Religion. The frequent statement that Liberal Religion has standards but no creed, rests on a rather meaningless distinction.

Liberal Religion is exciting: it arouses as much passion and emotion as Traditional Religion with its contemporary offshoots in various cults and charismatic sects. The difference is that the passion and emotion of Liberal Religion are based upon rationality. It is a widespread error that a reasonable person cannot be emotional or passionate. The devotion of Liberal Religion to rationality is pure: it is not induced by rituals or symbols, nor is it communicated by myths or sentimental traditions that have little relevance to modern man.

Liberal Religion is a child of the Enlightenment, that period beginning in the late eighteenth century when Western culture began to break up the pattern of rigid medieval religiosity. This does not mean that Liberal Religion abjures what transpired before that time. On the contrary, Liberal Religion draws on the wisdom and the inspiration of all ages.

This is all part of the evolutionary process. Liberal Religion today is based on the doctrine of evolution which includes physical as well as cultural evolution and therefore, of necessity, religious evolution. The end of evolution is not in sight, therefore Liberal Religionists consider themselves to be participating co-creators of the Universe.

Traditional Religion does not expect mortals to participate in the building of the future, which, in any event, lies in another world. The future of Liberal Religion is in this world. Russian Marxism also envisages a better future in this world. What Russian Marxism has in common with Traditional Religion is its rigidity; it sees the future as foreordained in a fixed pattern.

The commitment to the Universe has lately been strengthened by the general interest in the human environment. It could be said that, in the United States, the so-called Protestant ethic has been replaced as a dominant factor by the environmental ethic. Devoted as it is to the physical and cultural evolution of the Universe, Liberal Religion is a strong supporter of the environmental ethic.

The biblical injunction to have dominion over the earth and its creatures, which Traditional Religion has used to justify exploitation, is reinterpreted as a command to stewardship and conservation. Liberal Religion demands that the Creation and its natural balance be nurtured and protected against incursions, that no incursion be allowed unless required in the public interest, not only of the present, but also of future generations. Situations of this kind arise, for instance, when it is proposed to use a natural wilderness area for industrial purposes, to start surface (strip) mining, to utilize wetlands, or to deal with an endangered species of animals.

The key word of the environmental ethic is "integration." This goes beyond the physical integration of man and nature. In Liberal Religion it denotes the effort of every individual to conduct himself or herself as a part of the Universe, and to recognize that all other individuals, regardless of race, nationality, religion, social status, or sex, share equally in this enterprise.

Proceeding further with an explanation of the term "Liberal Religion," it seems appropriate to say a few words about the term "liberal." It is often used in a pejorative sense. Liberals in America are depicted as un-American, soft on communism, pinkos, or they are denounced as ruthless exploiters of an economic *laissez faire* system. The truth is that liberalism has a very honorable tradition in the United States. It is the fountainhead of Americanism. Jefferson, Adams, Madison, Monroe, Franklin and most other promoters of the American Revolution were flaming liberals. All great developments, from the Declaration of Independence to the Civil War, from the Emancipation to the Civil Rights Movement, are one continuous forward surge toward the realization of the American liberal idea. Liberals believe in the perfectability of life, and they are hospitable to innovations and reforms.

By contrast, the conservative takes a low view of every part of the human action, as Ralph Waldo Emerson pointed out in his lecture on "The Conservative." In the concluding paragraph of this lecture, Emerson said: "It is a happiness for mankind that innovation has got on so far and has so free a field before it. . . . It (the system) predicts that amidst a planet peopled with conservatives, one reformer may yet be born." To James Luther Adams, the leading contemporary liberal theologian, the concept of liberalism is not quite simple. He discerns ambiguities. Although Adams is firmly committed to the Liberal Church, his uneasiness seems to stem from the depth of his devotion to Judeo-Christian tradition and Liberal Christianity. His Religious Liberalism is built upon what he calls the five smooth stones of Liberalism.[6] Frederick May Eliot, the late president of the American Unitarian Association, wrote in 1935, "The test of any man's liberalism is his refusal to employ coercion on his fellow man."[7] This is a litmus test by which the liberalism of a person's religion may be determined. Liberals are in danger of being duped by charlatans like the late Reverend Jim Jones who shrewdly played upon liberal and progressive sentiments, advocated social activism, denounced racism and militarism, and who, at the horrible end in Guyana in 1978, was able to force his followers into a mass killing.

The word "liberal," in the present context, denotes liberation from Traditional Religious teaching; it has no political connotation. Liberal Religion is embraced by political conservatives as well as political liberals. For instance, President William Howard Taft was not only a staunch Republican, but also prominent in the American Unitarian Association. The politically conservative Chamberlain family in England were members of the Unitarian Church. Religious Liberals sit on both sides of the aisle in the United States Congress. The Americans for Democratic Action are an outspoken liberal political group, but many Religious Liberals are opposed to them. The Liberal Party of New York has many members who pray on Traditional altars. In short, the word "liberal," in the present context, has no special political connotation even though, like many other citizens, Religious Liberals are generally interested in the political life of their nation. The political involvement of Religious Liberals will be discussed later in Chapter 18.

Some excuse must be made for the use of the word "theology" in the title of this book. The excuse is necessary because many Liberal Religionists, and probably some potential members of the Liberal Church, disdain the word. They disdain it because the term is frequently associated with old-time religion, doctrinaire attitudes, and pettifogging controversies. This is an unsupportable prejudice. "Theology" does not mean merely the study of God. Rather, the word embraces the broad study of all aspects of religion and the exposition of general principles of religion. As Max Stackhouse says in his introduction to James Luther Adams's essays, *On Being Human Religiously,* "All profound theology is directly pertinent to the genuinely human, all that is genuinely human is pertinent to theology."[8] Where as in Liberal Religion, the evolutionary process is at the center of religion, one sometimes uses the phrase, "process theology."[9] Henry Nelson Wieman, who was a professor of the philosophy of religion, drew a distinction between theology and philosophy of religion.[10] That scholarly distinction is worth mentioning, but it has no relevance here.

What will be attempted here is an ordered outline of theological views common to most members of the Liberal Church. If Liberal Religion tries to avoid this, it jeopardizes its religious identity and subjects itself to the criticism which Robert Hemstreet levels at the Unitarian Universalists: "At the present time, our movement has no recognizable theological shape. Our liberalism is formless."[11] Some years ago, an article in the *London Economist* suggested that there is a vertical and a horizontal theology. Vertical theology is based on a monarchical relationship between God and man. Horizontal theology is grounded in the idea of brotherhood, with God being the big brother. If one accepts this proposition, one can hardly avoid classifying Traditional Religion as vertical theology and Liberal Religion as horizontal theology.

The phrase "popular theology" in the title of this book denotes a distinction from professional theology. Professional theologians are learned scholars; they frequently speak and write in esoteric language which young people and the ordinary layperson find hard to understand. This is one of the reasons for the aversion to theology and a frequent failure to appreciate the substance of the Liberal faith. This author is not equipped to deal with esoteric problems. The present approach shuns recondite learning while emphasizing the pragmatic and the experimental. Sometimes, this method results in what may appear to be logical inconsistencies, and, in addition, it exposes ambiguities. Where this happens, it merely reflects the human condition.

The famous five points of the Unitarians illustrate the problem. The points merit space in this chapter for several reasons. Mention was made before of the aversion of Unitarian Universalists to any creed, which aversion the late Paul Carnes, as early as 1963, called a fear "that is irrational to the point of being dogmatic."[12] Nevertheless, in 1943, a committee of the then American Unitarian Association formulated a statement of five principles which appeared to be a good theological basis for a common belief. These five principles are: (1) Individual Freedom of Belief, (2) Discipleship to Advancing Truth, (3) The Democratic Process in Human Relations, (4) Universal Brotherhood, and (5) Allegiance to the Cause of a United World Community. Although these five points have come into disuse, the General Assembly of the Unitarian Universalist Association adopted consensus resolutions in the mid-sixties on the United Nations and on race relations. This is as far as the Liberal Church has gone.

It will be noted that the last three of the five points are affirmative statements of religious belief which are irreconcilable with the first two points. For instance, a person may not believe in the democratic process (point 3). If that excludes him from the Liberal Church, then there is no freedom of belief (point 1). And yet, the five points represented then, and still do represent, what Liberal Religion stands for. What this demonstrates is that freedom of belief is not absolute even in the Liberal Church, and it is an error to assume that one can believe just anything and still be counted as an adherent to Liberal Religion.

As mentioned at the beginning of this chapter, language impedes the ingathering of religious liberals. Some of them will not enter any place where the word "God" is spoken. The paucity of the language is such that no substitute has been found for this ancient word which signifies the reverence and the emotion the Religious Liberal feels in the presence of an overwhelming experience, commonly known as a religious experience.

In his book *Honest to God* the Anglican Bishop Robinson suggested that this language barrier might be overcome by suspending for a while the use of the word "God."[13] The proposal has not been accepted. It is suggested that this Christian Bishop's language generosity could be matched by accepting the word "God" for a while until a substitute has been found, provided the word is used sparingly and without cloying piety.

Liberal Religion finds it difficult to avoid the expression "Kingdom of God" even though it seeks that kingdom in this life in contradistinction to Traditional Religion.

Another language difficulty arises because of the word "religion." The next chapter is devoted to that concept. Some Liberal Religionists reject the word. It has been said that it is impossible to formulate any kind of consensus for Liberal Religion because, while Liberal Religionists share common values, they disagree on religious language, on words to be used to describe their common devotion. This diversity is supposed to be a virtue, something to be proud of. The truth is that language is the most effective, even if inadequate, means of communication among human beings. Without such communication, no conviction or belief could thrive. Fear of language is a poor excuse for the failure to verbalize a theology for the Liberal Church.

Another language impediment has been the proposition that Liberal Religion is not religion at all, but merely a method of behavior. This, it would appear, is merely a linguistic quibble. If it is more than a quibble, then it should be said that the Method is a valid doctrine for stage actors to whom it is a theory of how to do things. What we need to know, however, is not how to believe, but what to believe—what it is that unites Liberal Religion.

The fear of language is unworthy of Liberal Religion. Like everything in the Universe, language is alive and it evolves. What Paul, Luther, and Calvin meant when they spoke of "God" is not the same as what Plato meant when he used the word. Liberal Religion infuses the word with its own meaning. As Humpty-Dumpty said to Alice, "Words mean what I want them to mean."[14]

"Freedom" is such a word. There is hardly any religious movement that does not claim freedom as one of its ideals. But how different these ideals are! In Liberal Religion "freedom" means freedom from any fetters of tradition, from doctrine, and from authoritative direction. "Freedom" means a method of reaching conclusions and beliefs about the meaning of life, about the human destiny, the relationship between individuals and other individuals in the Universe. Every individual is free to, and even expected to, think for himself or herself. Individual conclusions and beliefs may not be in accordance with the tenets of Liberal Religion, no matter how broad they might be. It would be false, as was said before, to state that, in Liberal Religion, everybody is free to believe what he or she likes. Freedom is not an idol but a tool.

A word should be said about ambiguity. No matter how precise one tries to be in one's expression of religious beliefs, a residue of ambiguity remains in all matters of religion. This should not be a cause for satisfaction by anti-religionists, because they, too, cannot escape ambiguity.

Our lack of precision and certitude is the result of limited powers of human reason. What lies beyond the frontiers of knowledge is beclouded by uncertainty. Traditional Religion covers this cloudy field with myths and hand-me-down superstitions. Liberal Religion prefers the scientist's search for truth, which is based on self-correcting hypotheses.

Traditional Religion rests on a limited picture of the Universe, as our ancestors and the Scripture writers knew it. Liberal Religion, on the other hand, endeavors to push the frontiers of knowledge forward and outward, fired by a faith that this is possible as well as desirable. The result is a religious faith commanding allegiance and devotion while evoking emotion and even passion.

James Luther Adams wrote that before a Religious Liberal can go anywhere he must study roadmaps.[15] This book tries to be such a roadmap and guide. As a rule, Liberal Religionists are too reticent about their religion. Sometimes they envy the ease with which Traditionalists can present their religious position by citing dogmas, fixed creeds, and doctrines. In contradistinction, religious liberals tend to be vague, if not unsure, about their religious identity. At times, they even revel in their vagueness. Actually, there is a unity in the fellowship of the Liberal Church which is not as apparent and certainly not as compelling as the dogmas of Traditional Religion. Therefore, it often escapes attention and even eludes the Liberal Religionists themselves.

The ultimate purpose of this book, therefore, is to pierce the vagueness and to lend greater substance and cohesion to the peculiar identity of the Liberal Church, with a view towards spreading its good news. The aim is to do this in simple, direct language without allegories and metaphors. In pursuing this aim, the author cannot claim the concurrence of all Religious Liberals. Some of them are attached to metaphors and to myths. (Myths are discussed in Chapter 7.)

In addition to the pseudo-liberal religionists who were mentioned at the beginning of this chapter, there is a religious group which might be called, "halfway" Liberal Religionists. These folk abjure supernaturalism and they profess rationalism, but they will not allow scientific truth to interfere with their religion. Thus, Peter Fleck writes in his book *The Mask of Religion* that science and religion belong to different realms, "science to the realm of the real, the material, the world; religion to the realm of the true, the unseen, the beyond";[16] "We no longer believe that truth remains truth when it is unveiled";[17] "the naked truth is a contradiction in terms."[18] This is a halfway and very unsatisfactory approach to the unveiled, nonmythical Liberal Religion expounded in this book.

2

Religion

Joy and Happiness

Religion is serious but not stern. The psalmist in the ancient temple sang, "Make a joyful noise unto the Lord"[1] or, as modern translators put it, "come into God's presence with songs of joy." Vincent Silliman, the contemporary poet and hymnwriter, wrote:

> Let religion be to us life and joy
> Let it be a voice of renewing challenge to the best
>   we have and may be
> Let it be a call to generous action. . . .[2]

Semi-darkness and dusty odors are alien to the places of worship of Liberal Religion. The pursuit of happiness is an inalienable right not only in the American Declaration of Independence but for all adherents of the Liberal Church. The Liberal Church rejects the Puritan tradition which leaves no room for joy, beauty, and intellect.

One of the greatest successes of Traditional Religion is that it has instilled in oppressed and wretched people the faith that they would be rewarded in heaven if they bear their yoke on earth patiently and faithfully. No wonder that the Irish cleric, Jonathan Swift, author of *Gulliver's Travels,* defined happiness as a perpetual state of being deceived. What the Liberal Church strives for is happiness—undeceived happiness—in one's lifetime on earth. Liberal Religion is an earthbound religion which accepts the words of Moses,

29

"that it may go well with thee . . . and that you mayeth prolong thy days upon the earth" (Deut. 4:40). If the phrase "Kingdom of God" has any meaning, it means the Kingdom of God on earth. In Liberal Religious services, Schiller's *Ode to Joy,* which is the concluding part of Beethoven's Ninth Symphony, is often sung. As with other works of art, Liberal Religionists do not mind traditional imagery, but they become exuberant when they sing the closing lines:

> Ever singing march we onward
> Victors in the midst of strife
> Joyful music lifts us sunward
> In the triumph song of life

Traditional Religion has thrown a pall over this joy. St. Augustine and Calvin despised the earth, thought its inhabitants depraved, and had no faith in man's ability to distinguish good from evil. The Puritans in New England even disapproved of the Christmas festivities as frivolous. The Princeton historian Thomas Jefferson Wertenbaker, in his book *The First Americans,* devotes a chapter to "The Rule of Conduct" imposed by the Puritan leaders of the day.[3] A few excerpts illuminate their concepts of religion, some of which still prevail:

> To the Puritan, this world . . . seemed a place of temptation and danger. On trial before an exacting God he was constantly subjected to the wiles of Satan and his minions. . . . Nor was the Puritan content with maintaining this rigid standard for himself, he insisted that his neighbors should conform to it also. Sin and worldliness, dread diseases of the soul, are no less contagious than diseases of the body. . . .

> Laws for the observance of the Sabbath were everywhere rigidly enforced. In Massachusetts a law was passed in 1653 which made it a misdemeanor to waste time by taking walks on the streets or by visiting ships in the port on Sunday.

> In New London, John Lewis and Sarah Chapman were brought before the court in 1670 for sitting together, on the Lord's Day, under an apple tree in Mr. Chapman's orchard. . . . Massachusetts prohibited shuffleboard and bowling, and fined innkeepers who permitted their guests to indulge in these games. From time to time, laws were passed in various New England colonies against observing Christmas, indulging in mixed dances, playing cards or performing on certain musical instruments. God's time must not be frittered away. . . .

The pall which Traditional Religion cast over the land was also observed by Mrs. Trollope in 1832: "I never saw a population so totally divested of gaiety: there is no trace of this feeling from one end of the Union to the other."[4] In Europe, the composer Haydn (1732-1809) was severely criticized because the music in his Masses was cheerful.

All this in the name of religion, and all out of what Bertrand Russell called an irrational fear of happiness.[5] This is not the place to inquire into the psychology of guilt feelings which were, and are, apparently at the bottom of this fear of earthly happiness and hope for happiness in the afterlife. Suffice it to say that Liberal Religion is not burdened with any such guilt feelings. Nor is it burdened with anxiety (or Angst). Fear or Angst of the unknown power of the Universe inspired primitive religions and persists in Traditional Religion. As Alan Watts points out, Christianity is a religion in which anxiety plays a greater part than faith.[6] Traditional Religion fosters fear and trembling. In Genesis, God is quoted as worrying that man might become as smart as Himself (Gen. 3:5 and 4:22). Liberal Religion has overcome fear and Angst. It is in tune with the Universe. It loves the world.

One need not even delve into psychology in order to understand Traditional Religion's anti-worldliness. The theology of Traditional Religion is based on world hostility. As the Apostle John wrote in one of his epistles (I John 2:15): "Love not the world, neither the things that are in the world. If any man love the world, the love of the Father is not in him." This attitude is related to the Christian belief in man's innate depravity and to the Islamic contempt for the pleasurable aspect of life, the Hindu ideal of asceticism, and the Buddhist striving for Nirvana. In the West, those who do not share John's anti-worldliness are often denounced as materialists. If materialism means love of the world and "the things that are in the world," then Liberal Religion is a materialistic religion.

It is probably true that most people do not merit the good life they enjoy. This, however, is no reason for gloom and teeth gnashing. Rather, it should be a spur to greater worthiness and spirituality.

The happiness of Liberal Religion is not the superficial happiness which one observes, for instance, on television commercials. It is the happiness of the womb, of feeling at peace with the world and the environment.

Some find joy and happiness in solitary and contemplative religion. Such a hermit-like attitude is not favored by Liberal Religion. Liberal Religion seeks and teaches the joy of a caring community and the happiness of participation. It is therefore clear that Liberal Religion does not approve of the cult of peace of mind or a religiosity which merely seeks release from anxiety. While peace of mind and release from anxiety are not the aim of Liberal Religion, its adherents are likely to experience such release. This is so because Liberal Religion is in harmony with human experience. Unlike Traditional Religion, Liberal Religion does not torment a thinking person by the discrepancy between known reality and religious doctrine.

Definitions

When people in the Western world speak of religion they generally speak of the Judeo-Christian tradition. They overlook that this tradition prevails only in a small part of the world. To think of religion in terms of that tradition bespeaks a narrow and parochial outlook. It is one of the characteristics of Liberal Religion that it has a broadly universal outlook. It encompasses, for instance, the Oriental tradition and the tradition of the American Indians, both of which were untouched by the Judeo-Christian tradition.

Some seemingly smart critics regard religion as an anachronism, believing that religious people live in the clouds. What the modern age demands, they will tell us, is a hard headed, empirical, and pragmatic approach to the spiritual problems of the world. They do not know that this is exactly the approach of Liberal Religion.

Definitions help to establish the focus of the subject matter under discussion, but they are seldom precise. The free spirit of Liberal Religion precludes and, indeed, rebels against any precision. None is claimed here.

Someone once said that all religions say the same thing in the sense that all mountaineers climb mountains. That does not mean that all ascents are the same, but it does mean that all ascents are about going up. The climbing routes differ. While we are here primarily concerned with what is common to all religions, it would be a mistake to assume, as some people do, that all religions are essentially the same. There is great variety in the detail of doctrine, ritual, and philosophy.

The common usage of the words "religion" and "religious" does not reflect any deep analytical thought. Both friends and foes of religion are guilty of superficial thoughtlessness. Religions differ on such fundamental issues as: the origin of the Creation, the concept of God, the idea of one god versus several or many gods, the nature of sin, the role of women, and the position of the minister. These examples suffice to show that it is inappropriate to disregard the differences.

Generally, the abstract concepts of religion are only understood if expressed or exemplified in concrete terms. One of the best known examples are the Ten Commandments which constitute a concrete expression of the religious concepts during the days of Moses. The same book of the Bible which contains the Ten Commandments, also contains detailed directions on how to offer an animal sacrifice and how to build a sanctuary. All these directions are regarded as concrete expressions of the Will of God and therefore of religion. Jesus conveyed the abstract concepts of religion by telling parables, stories designed to explain abstract principles. The church later developed a veneration for the cross and other tangible symbols. Men are taught to revere the saints, to observe rituals, and to attend worship services on prescribed days. Moslems bow toward Mecca. All such forms are designed to convey to the believers the abstract ideas of religion. The trouble is that most adherents of Traditional Religion exalt form over substance and, in doing so, they forget and neglect substance. The devout·theologian Dietrich Bonhoeffer sought a return to pure religion by postulating "Christianity without Religion."[7] He regarded religion as an undesirable garment of Christianity. To Liberal Religion, this makes little sense because it regards religion as a matter of substance, not as a garment. Liberal Religion's response to Bonhoeffer (if he had not been hanged by the Nazis) would be that, instead of Christianity without religion, it would prefer religion without Christianity.

Professor Joseph Fletcher, a former Episcopal priest, wrote that he used to celebrate communion as a man of faith and as a theologian, but that he was never a religious man.[8] Apparently, for Professor Fletcher, religion is merely a matter of rituals.

Liberal Religion has the opposite difficulty. It concentrates on the substance and sometimes neglects the form which many people crave in order to express their religious faith. The chapter on worship and prayer (Chapter 19) is addressed to this aspect of Liberal Religion.

The uplifting nature of Liberal Religion, its very transport, is summarized by Duncan Howlett, a great contemporary Religious Liberal: "Religion, in its widest dimension, lifts a man off his knees, draws him out of his armchair or away from his desk and flings him into the midst of life with commitments that not merely guide him, but may even drive him in what he does."[9]

Some people say that they are not religious. Upon further inquiry, one finds that they say this because they do not attend services at a church or temple; they do not pray; they do not care for rituals or dogmas; or they do not believe in God. To Liberal Religion, none of these matters is a test of whether or not a person is religious. What matters to Liberal Religion is whether a person is concerned with what happens around him or her. If a person feels responsible for the well-being of his or her environment, he or she is a religious person imbued with the spirit of religion. Such people may not always, or only infrequently, yield to this spirit of religion much the same as Traditional Religionists may skip sabbath services. These instances of weakness do not have any bearing upon the concept of religion. Sometimes the only facet of religion experienced by many people is when they stand in awe before a snowcapped mountain, are humbled by the manifestations of heredity, or marvel at the constancy in the habits of migratory birds. A contemporary novel about Australia describes it thus: "Sometimes they spent days on end in the saddle, miles away from the homestead, camping at night under a sky so vast and filled with stars, it seemed they were a part of God."[10] Or, to quote a classic philosopher for this kind of religious experience, Kant concluded in his *Critique of Practical Reason* that, "Two things fill the mind with ever increasing wonder and reverence, . . . the starry heavens above me and the moral law within me." To put it simply, religion is the human striving for integration into the Universe.

The fundamental concept of religion is that of spiritual unity with the Universe. Albert Einstein searched, during his life at Princeton, for a unified field theory which would bring together in a series of mathematical equations the great physical morass that governs the Universe: electromagnetism, gravity, and nuclear power. He had a hunch that such overriding unity existed, but he could not prove it scientifically. Liberal Religion claims such a unified field theory of all religious values and forces. This pragmatic approach to the concept of religion was also used by the United States Supreme Court when, in the early religious liberty decisions, it found it necessary to define religion. In the words of one of these decisions, the term religion "has reference to one's views of his relations to the Creator and the reverence for his being and character."[11] If one substitutes the word "creation" for "creator" one arrives at a broad definition which reflects Liberal Religion's view.

The urge to reduce all things to one seems to be as old as philosophy and science. The ancient Greek, Thales of Miletus (640–546 B.C.), regarded water as the basic principle to which everything could be reduced. Einstein and Thales were monists. If one explains monism as the view that there is only one fundamental reality, obviously there is a kinship between monism and monotheism—the belief that there is only one God. What Liberal Religion has in common with Einstein, Thales, monism, and monotheism is its faith that every person is part of the Universe. The Liberal Religionist feels bound to the Universe, loves it, wants to perfect it, and to be a collaborator in the Creation. As the poet of the Rockingham Hymn says, "Creation's Lord we give thee thanks, that this thy world is incomplete . . . that work awaits our hands and feet." Or in Longfellow's words of another hymn, "All are architects of fate." Fate does not just happen: man makes it happen, and Liberal Religion demands that what happens must be for the good of all fellow creatures.

Religion grows out of the urge to come to terms with the Universe. Therefore, it is the manifestation or expression of one's attitude toward the Universe. At times this attitude is one of complete submission, and sometimes it is one of integrative cooperation. The former is typical of Traditional Religion; the latter is representative of Liberal Religion, where the individual regards himself and other individuals as reverent co-creators of the Universe. This, then, leads to the definition of religion as the rational and emotional urge to integrate into the Universe.

The Liberal theologian Henry Nelson Wieman (1884–1975) defined religion as creative interchange. This is an appealing concept which Wieman himself has elaborated, and it is being further developed and explained by contemporary students of Wieman's theology.[12] A long chapter could be devoted to how Wieman defines Religion. In *The Wrestle of Religion with Truth,* we read, "Religion is man's acute awareness of the realm of unattained possibility and the behavior that results from that awareness."[13] In the introduction to the same book Wieman says, "Religion is man's endeavor to adapt himself to the facts of existence."[14] In the introduction to his book *Man's Ultimate Concern,* Professor Wieman seems to disagree with Tillich's definition of religion as man's ultimate concern. Wieman says, "Philosophy is ultimate concern, religion is ultimate commitment."[15]

Religion is a human instinct. As the great jurist Benjamin Cardozo puts it, "Something intuitively apprehended as great and noble."[16] Just as one does not have to be a scholar to have a philosophy of life and to be a philosopher, so man needs no book, no teacher, and no theology to be religious. A thinking person may not like to admit that religion is a matter of instinct. Those who insist that they are not religious and have an aversion to religion are prone to construe intellectual arguments against religious instincts. All this flies in the face of common experience. The original instinct of primitive man was fear and awe of the overpowering forces of nature as manifested by such phenomena as thunderstorms and lightning. That fear has not altogether vanished. Primitive man, and his contemporary counterpart, responds by seeking to propitiate and then to assimilate this awesome power by seeking integration with it. An old American Indian prayer begins, "Oh, Great Spirit, whose voice I hear in the winds, and whose breath gives life to all the world, hear me." Felix Adler, the founder of the Ethical Culture Movement, puts it this way, "In our nature, we have not only a mind that reasons . . . but also a tendency for striving toward completeness, toward wholeness of life and being."[17]

An instinct is a mixture of genetic and cultural heritage. It has become more refined in the course of time. Then came the systematizers and the exploiters who, with not necessarily sinister motives, added dogmas, rituals, mysteries, and rules and channeled the religious instincts into a variety of religions. This is the history of Traditional Religion. Liberal Religion then strove, and still strives, to liberate religion from the barnacles with which Traditional Religion has encrusted and encumbered the wholesome religious instincts of human beings.

What organized religion—both Traditional and Liberal—can and will do is to sort out the religious instincts and mold them into a coherent religious system.

Instead of speaking of instinct, some prefer the term "intuition." Thus, religion has been defined as people manifesting a collective concern for the ultimate meaning and purpose of life—a shared intuition of, and commitment to, transcendent life.

Religion is more than mere ideology; it does not spring only from the brain, as ideology does. Moses, Jesus, Mohammed, and Buddha spoke to everyone. Plato and Hegel—eminent ideologists—spoke only to a few. The distinction between religion and ideology is often blurred. Thus, when people join in a public demonstration, for instance, to protest the building of a nuclear power plant, they are moved by concern for the environment. All of them will agree that this is an ideological concern. In many, if not all, instances it is also a religious concern. The demonstrators are driven by that moral passion which was called for in the preface to this book.

It has also been said that ideology is rational, whereas religion does not relate to rationality. That is not correct, as far as Liberal Religion is concerned. As will be discussed in Chapter 4, Liberal Religion is eminently rational.

Religion, according to Victor Murray, is not a system "which we apply to particular circumstances; it is a system which emerges from a survey of certain events in which religious factors are at work."[18] Such events are discussed in the second part of this book, which deals with topics like democracy, human dignity, justice, social concern, politics, religious liberty, and other manifestations of Liberal Religion.

George Fox, the founding father of the Quakers (The Religious Society of Friends), lays stress on the "inner light" as the core of religion. This is not unlike the religious instinct and intuition. But Fox also says that the inner light stems from the Divine Spirit which permeates the New Testament. Acceptance of the Holy Spirit requires a leap into the supernatural, a leap Liberal Religion is not prepared to make. To the extent that the Quakers consider the "inner light" as the seed of the divine in every person, Liberal Religion has little difficulty in identifying with them.

When L. B. Horner writes about Buddhism, he thinks that it does not deserve the name of religion because it is not related to a personal God, and it is not regarded as preparation for eternity.[19] Obviously, Horner speaks from the narrow viewpoint of Traditional Religion. He describes Buddhism as a "discipline for governing man's attitude to the here and now." For just that reason, the Liberal Church regards Buddhism as a religion, and it is generally so recognized. Küng, the Roman Catholic, calls Buddhism the strongest counterpart of Christianity.[20]

Robert Ellwood, a contemporary Californian, offers the following complicated definition: "A religion means a group centrally concerned with the means of ultimate transformation which has simultaneous expression in three areas: verbal (myth and doctrines), worship (ritual, cult, and other special behavior), and social (a structure of interpersonal action which enables a continuing group life)."[21] The phrase "ultimate transformation," Professor Ellwood explains, means the transformation from the preoccupation with the daily humdrum to the deeper spiritual values. It does not imply existence of a personal God.[22] The phrase "ultimate transformation" carries the same connotations as Tillich's "ultimate concern."

If this were a treatise on religion in general, one would have to devote space to magic and myth as the generators of religion. Max Weber's book on the *Sociology of Religion* is permeated with the suggestion that the practice of religion is a refined form of magic. The Greeks, whose influence persists in the Judeo-Christian tradition of the West, progressed from magic to myth. Myths are still with us, especially in Traditional Religion. In Liberal Religion myths have but poetic value. Liberal Religion has grown beyond magic and myth.[23]

Magic has not disappeared from Traditional Religion. This is most noticeable in the veneration of relics. These relics are often supposed to have magical power, especially healing power. They attract throngs of pilgrims. So does Lourdes in France, whose waters are believed to have magic power. Liberal Religion disdains such faith.

According to Harold Berman, anthropological studies confirm that, in all cultures, religion has four elements: ritual, tradition, authority, and universality.[24] Universality is an essential element of Liberal Religion, but not the other three elements.

William James (1842–1910) says in his *Varieties of Religious Experience,* "Religion, whatever it is, is a man's total reaction upon life, so why not say that a man's total reaction upon life is a religion?"[25] On that ground, James includes Liberal Emersonianism in the category of religion, as well as what he calls atheistic Buddhism. "The fervent opponents of Christian doctrine have often enough shown a temper which, psychologically considered, is undistinguishable from religious zeal."[26] It is appropriate, therefore, to regard Russian Communist Marxism as a religion, even though Karl Marx branded religion as the opiate of the people.

When Karl Marx defined religion in this way, he obviously thought of the Traditional Religion of his day: the rituals and ceremonies that tended to anesthetize people, and the dogmas that taught people to believe that the earth is a vale of tears, but that after death, they would experience paradise in heaven. Marx's definition has no application to Liberal Religion.

In the context of this book, Russian Marxism must be regarded as a Traditional Religion because, in spite of its hostility to other established religions, Russian Marxism is very dogmatic and no less convinced than the Church of Rome that it is the sole possessor of truth, to which its adherents must submit. Its authoritarian and hierarchical character is unexcelled. Its old-time religious character is illustrated by the fact that, according to Professor Berman, Soviet schoolchildren are taught to recite, "Lenin lived, Lenin lives, Lenin will live."[27] The French philosopher Auguste Comte (1798–1857) had the same narrow view of religions as Karl Marx, when he predicted that religion would disappear as man became less superstitious and more knowledgeable. He did not recognize religion as a permanent human response to the Creation.

The conclusion of this excursion into the realm of definitions is that religion is a monistic (unitary) phenomenon, which means that the divine power called "God" — or by some other name like "Life Force" or "Supreme

Spirit"—permeates the Universe. This unitary concept is in contradistinction to the concept of religion as a dualistic phenomenon, in which the divine power dwells outside the individual and the physical universe. The dualists who, in Bishop Robinson's words, seek God "out there," walk in two worlds: that of the physical environment and that which they perceive as the divine beyond. Liberal Religion tends toward the unitary approach, but some adherents still hold to the dualistic approach which is common in Traditional Religion. They believe, like Martin Luther, that there is a division between the heavenly kingdom and the earthly kingdom, and that man must choose one or the other.[28] Religion to these halfway Liberal Religionists is an undefinable mythical force, reminiscent of the God who, according to Old Testament stories, appeared in a pillar of clouds, and of Goethe's dunkler Drang (obscure groping) which moves mankind. People who hold these views may be called Halfway Liberal Religionists because they have foresworn supernaturalism and believe in rationality, but they still cling to some concepts which their progenitors have inculcated in them. More will be said about this in Chapter 6 on truth.

The great truth and the inspiration of Liberal Religion is that religion is immanent in the Universe, and a vital force if allowed to operate in unmasked glory. Persons can be called religious if they recognize themselves as part of the Life Force to which they are subordinated or, to put it differently, if they feel as part of the Universe.

The Sacred and the Secular

The phrases "secular religion" and "sacred religion" deserve some attention. The word "sacred" is unambiguous. It denotes matters which one considers holy and worthy of reverence. The word "secular" is not used with equal clarity. Its common meaning denotes the attributes of worldly or temporal affairs as distinguished from spiritual affairs. In the usage of others, "secular" means nonreligious, and that is the meaning in court decisions dealing with actual or alleged violations of religious liberty (see Chapter 17). If the law or the governmental action under review has a "secular purpose," it is upheld.

To many adherents of Traditional Religion, "secular" means "antireligious." Liberal Religion cannot accept the distinction between sacred and secular. Concern with the physical and material aspects of the world is a religious concern. To regard the physical world as a "merely secular" matter constitutes a disparagement of the Creation and of what Traditionalists call "the Creator." Reverence for all Life is one of the basic tenets of Liberal Religion (see Chapter 24). Even the Bible, in the apocalyptic and turgid writing of its last book, Revelation, obliterates the distinction between the sacred and the secular. The ideal Jerusalem of the future is depicted as a city without temples, because God (religion) permeates all (Rev. 21:22).

In the United States, it is fashionable to denounce liberal concerns as "secular," and to add a pejorative flavor to the word. This stupid fashion cannot conceal the fact that most civilizations mirror a development from superstition to sacred rites, and from rites to secular rationality. With his best selling book *The Secular City,* Harvard Professor Harvey Cox has put secularism on the religious map. Cox begins his book with a reference to the collapse of Traditional Religion. He holds that the citizen of the secular city experiences religious transcendence, although "in a radically different way than did his tribal and town forebearers."[29] In other words, Cox's secularism is religious. Howlett calls Cox a Christian secularist, which means that he wants "the Church to enter into the world. . . ."[30]

In his introduction, Cox quotes a Dutch theologian's definition of secularization as the deliverance of man from religious and then metaphysical control over his reason. The control to which this refers is the control over man's mind: the imposition of dogmas, myths, and sacred symbols. Liberal Religion seeks no such control, and therefore it affirms secularization without abandoning its character as a religion. Liberal Religion combines rational thought with a concern for worldly matters.

Secularization is the wave of the religious future. Henry Nelson Wieman, in his book *The Growth of Religion,* tells about what he calls radical secularism in both the United States and Eastern religions.[31]

To the distinguished subscribers of the *Secular Humanist Declaration,* the word "secular" appears to have a nonreligious meaning.[32] The only adjective which they allow to describe their ideal is the word "democratic." They speak of "democratic secular humanism." Professor Hook, in an article on Democratic Humanism, specifically rejects any connection with religious faith.[33] And yet, Liberal Religion, as set forth in this book, has hardly any quarrel with the contents of the *Secular Humanist Declaration.* Professor Hook and his co-signers of the Declaration probably have too narrow a view of the concept of religion, which is regrettable because such narrowness is also found among the foes of secularism in Liberal Religion. Paul Beatty, president of the Fellowship of Religious Humanists and also a signer of the Declaration, has pointed out that there is no significant difference between the secular humanists and the religious humanists.[34] Nevertheless, the secular humanists have disturbed some Liberal Religionists. Declared one: "It would be lamentable if Unitarian Universalists let the Moral Majority pin the name secular humanists on us. We are religious humanists."[35]

What the speaker was referring to is the crusade of the Moral Majority movement and its leader the Reverend Jerry Falwell who, early in 1980, issued a declaration of war against a list of perceived evils, which included secular humanism. More will be said about the Moral Majority in this chapter, and Humanism is discussed in Chapter 3.

When Dietrich Bonhoeffer demanded Christianity without religion, he obviously meant that a truly Christian society has no need for the sacred trappings of religion. Jesus clearly made the distinction between the secular and the sacred when he said, "Render unto Caesar what is Caesar's and unto God, what is God's" (Matthew 22:1; Mark 12:17). In the following centuries, the Church acquired so much worldly power that it used the government machinery to support and enforce what it considered to be its sacred mission. A religious nonconformist was regarded as a felon. Religious dissent was a crime punishable by the secular authorities. The popes assumed secular power; secular rulers became heads of the dominant church. Luther's Reformation was, in good part, based upon his antagonistic relationship with the secular power of the pope. This may have been the origin of Luther's conception of the Two Kingdoms of every Christian believer: the Kingdom of God under Christ, and the Kingdom of the World under civil authority. In construing these two Kingdoms, Luther of course perpetuated the distinction between the sacred and the secular. Secular matters were strictly barred from the Kingdom of God. This included reasoning power and thought. Luther proclaimed that reason was a despicable whore.[36] More about this in Chapter 4.

The Kingdom of God and the Kingdom of the World formed a mutual aid society. Luther, like Calvin, demanded that religious dissenters be dealt with as criminals. The theory on which this alliance of the secular and the sacred was based is that the prevailing religion, whatever it is, is the mainstay of the state, and every religious deviation therefore threatens the security of the state. Thus, religious deviation is branded as seditious.

The tradition of combining religion with matters of state was brought to the American colonies. Roger Williams rebelled against it. He demanded a separation between the sacred and the secular, although he does not seem to have employed these words. What is called secular today was to this Christian minister "the rotten natural world," as distinguished from the lofty realm of religion.[37] Roger Williams, not unlike Martin Luther, asserted that the state, as a secular institution, was fundamentally different from the Kingdom of Christ, which is solely concerned with matters of the spirit. The Church, according to Williams, is the antithesis of the state. The state is composed by all manner of men, each of whom is free to worship as he pleases. No one must be forced to worship against his conscience. On the other hand, the Church of Christ is composed of the religious elect who must not be interfered with by the government of the state. This theme will be further considered in Chapter 17 on religious liberty. In the present context, Roger Williams is merely noted as a classical American protagonist of the distinction between the secular and the sacred.

When Liberal Religion is called a secular religion, the appellation is often intended as a denunciation and a slur. Liberal Religionists should accept the appellation with pride. Unlike Roger Williams, they do not regard the natural world as rotten. Their religious concern is with this world rather than with the unknown world beyond. U Thant, the late Secretary General of the United Nations and a devout Buddhist, considered the distinction between the secular and the spiritual as an incomprehensible Western idea. He thought that this distinction in Western thinking was one of the principal causes of world tension.[38]

One reads much about America's secular religion. This is the name given to the tendency of Americans to exalt Americanism or the American way of life over any inherited, presumably sacred religion. The historian Henry Steele Commager wrote that Americans are apt to ignore the traditional teaching of any religion if it interferes with their way of life. "America naturalized God," he wrote, "and when they think of Heaven, they imagine it to operate under the U.S. Constitution."[39] It is true that, in vast segments of the American population, religion has become of social rather than spiritual importance. Berman suggests that this has led to a sanctification of the American way of life. The theme is elaborated in Professor Bellah's article on Civil Religion in America.[40] Whether called Secular Religion or Civil Religion (a phrase attributed to Rousseau), in the last analysis, it is, at least today, an extension of Traditional Religion. Bellah's article indicates that, under the influence of the Founding Fathers, the so-called Civil Religion was originally molded in a liberal cast; but today, the earmarks of Traditional Religion are stronger than ever before. What Americans love about their country is that it has a religious and a sacred quality. The polarization of the sacred and the secular remains a distinction without substance. As Emerson said, "there is no profane history, all history is sacred."[41]

The distinction between the secular and the sacred is particularly stressed by those religions which call for a separate priestly class whose members are charged with mediating between men and God. The best known religion of this kind is the Roman Catholic Church, where not only the priest but, on a higher level, the Virgin Mary and the Saints are called upon to intercede with God on behalf of the mortals. There are two principal reasons why Liberal Religion rejects this type of religion. The first was expressed by the British House of Lords, acting as the highest judicial authority of the realm. The Lords were called upon to determine whether a testamentary bequest to an order of nuns, which occupied itself with intercessional prayers, was exempt from death duty. The Lords ruled in the negative because they perceived no evidence that intercessional prayers were of any benefit to the public. The second and more basic reason is that, in Liberal Religion, God and man need no intermediary, because they are inextricably united. According to original Christian doctrine, the only intermediary between God and man is Jesus, the Christ. That, too, is rejected by Liberal Religion for the reasons stated.

A Universal Yearning

Marx said that religion is the opiate of the people—meaning that religion poisons the mind to the point of extinction, and that only mindless people are religious. It seems obvious that when Marx spoke of religion he merely thought of the Traditional Christian or Jewish rituals with which he was familiar. His contemporary followers have a similar narrow conception of religion.

This is demonstrable nonsense. Religion is the manifestation of a universal human yearning for a relationship between the individual and his environment which is sometimes expressed in abstract spiritual terms and sometimes in concrete terms of a living divinity. Marx himself has taken the place of such a divinity in the countries that accept his teachings as binding commands and where any violation is a punishable sacrilege. In whatever form religion manifests itself, it leads to introspection and reverence.

The universality of this phenomenon is exemplified by the Meditation Room of the United Nations in New York City, and Rule 62 of the General Assembly's Rules of Procedure. That rule reads, "Immediately after the opening of the first plenary meeting and immediately preceding the closing of the final plenary meeting of each session of the General Assembly, the President shall invite the representatives to observe one minute of silence dedicated to prayer or meditation."[42] This rule is being honored by all nations, regardless of their ideological or religious orientation, and it is not controversial. A Communist representative at the United Nations may meditate about Marx; others may meditate about Jesus, or Buddha, or Mohammed, or pray to whatever divinity they believe in. But there is no gainsaying that all of them are engaged in religious devotion.

This is true even if one does not share the view of Robert Mueller that the United Nations itself is the expression of a new form of religion, "a place of convergence for the dreams and prayers of all peoples for a better world."[43] The better world Mueller refers to, and the United Nations organization seeks to build, is on this earth. Traditional Religion, however, looks to a better world beyond the grave. When the Reverend Jim Jones arranged for the mass suicide and killing at the Guyana community of the People's Temple in 1978, he told the people it was time to leave and meet again in "some other place." While Liberal Religion must take cognizance of the universal human yearning, it does not agree that this yearning must be directed toward life after death.

Every human being yearns for love, belonging, and happiness. The yearning is strongest among disadvantaged people who feel lost and powerless. Their ranks are swelling with the many persons who are depressed by what they regard as overpowering inhumanity and materialism in the human society. Traditional Religion promises all these people redemption from unhappiness, and a better life in the hereafter, if they will only have faith in the religion which it presents. You must not feel unloved, says Traditional Religion, because God loves you, or Jesus loves you, or both. You must not feel lonely, because you belong to the great community of believers. Many grasp at these straws. Traditional Religion has been, and is, fabulously successful among the poor, the downtrodden, and the disadvantaged. That explains why slaves share the religion of the slavemasters and why the same religion prospers on both sides of the apartheid wall.

Coldly speaking, it must be said that Traditional Religion exploits this universal human yearning. It drugs the downtrodden and the despairing into a sense of being loved, happy, and part of a group. It is the task of the Liberal Church to wean these unfortunates and to convince them that life is worth living without the drugs.

A shrewd analyst of the Moslem world noted that the resurgence of the strict observance of the Islamic religion among its young people has occurred as a protest against corruption in government and against ostentatious materialism. Many feel that socialism and nationalism have failed, which makes people turn for solace to the old-time religion. Similar sentiments can be observed in the West. An effort must be made to channel these sentiments forward into the Liberal Church rather than backward into traditional conservatism.

Cosmology

The word "cosmology" denotes the theory of the origin and structure of the Universe. It is important in all religions.

The Bible cosmology states that God created the Universe out of nothing. The book of Genesis gives two accounts of the Creation. In the first account (Genesis 1), God created the world in six days. Night and day were created on the first day, but sun and moon were created only on the fourth day. Scientists would say that night and day cannot exist without the sun. In the first account, Adam and Eve were created together on the sixth day. In the second account (Genesis 2), Adam was created alone and God made Eve sometime later, out of Adam's rib. These inconsistencies do not trouble the true believers. The important matter to them is that God existed before the Universe and that He created it. This is Christian dogma.

To the Liberal Church, the Bible story is only one of the many different myths about the creation of the world. Some of them are told in Robert Graves' book, *Adam's Rib*. The progressive Roman Catholic theologian Hans Küng, in a book that bears the imprint of the ecclesiastical censor, says, "The six days of creation and the narrative of the creation of man are, as we are well aware today, images that do not describe the scientific course of the origin of the world; they proclaimed — and still proclaim to man even today—the splendor and uniqueness of the Creator and the greatness, simplicity, and goodness of His work."[44]

Modern Protestantism also perceives that the Creation story of the Bible is a symbol.[45] The fact remains, though, that Judeo-Christian religion holds onto the story that God created the Universe out of chaos. Theologians worry about such things as the purpose of Creation, but this is of no real concern to the Liberal Religionist. Creation is here!

Thomas Paine wrote that the Creation is the only word of God which he is able to recognize. Liberal Religion's cosmology generally is that the universe evolved gradually as is taught by the theory of evolution, which was first developed by Charles Darwin (1809–1882), an English Unitarian. Liberal Religion believes that the evolution is still in an ongoing process and it reveres creation as well as the process. "Creation's Lord, we give thee thanks, that this thy world is incomplete" is a favorite hymn which also contains the line, "As friends we share the Maker's plan."

While Traditional Religion in the West held fast to the Bible myth, the Jesuit scientist Father Teilhard de Chardin (1881–1955) was a great promoter of the theory of evolution, a position which cost him the right to publish during his lifetime. Teilhard de Chardin ascribed the Church's opposition to mere fright.[46]

Scientists are not agreed how the Universe was formed. Traditional Religion clings to the Bible cosmology in spite of the fact that the Bible authors could not have known what science has discovered since. When the Bible was written, its authors thought they knew the Universe. Scientists today teach us that much is knowable, but much is essentially unknown. We have learned that the earth is only a small part of the Universe, not its center. We read of the quasars (quasi-stellar sources of light) and of the black holes. It boggles the mind that quasars date back as far as fifteen million years, and that the starlight which we observe tonight was emitted millions of years ago. In the observation of the Universe, we appear to be always millions of years (a time span hard to conceive) behind the times. Astronomers study the Universe through differential equations and the tensor calculus, through radio waves and x-rays, through counting the many galaxies (of which the Milky Way seems to be the smallest), and through numerous other techniques which were formerly unknown and are incomprehensible to the ordinary person.

Today, these observations offer us three different theories about the origin of the Universe, none of which is in agreement with the Bible cosmology. The first is the Steady State theory, pursuant to which the Universe has not changed for at least one hundred billion years, except that the galaxies continuously recede from each other and ultimately disappear. The second is the theory of the Oscillating Universe in which the Universe expands and contracts steadily. The third is the Big Bang theory, according to which the creation is the result of a violent explosion.[47] The Big Bang is closest to the Bible story. A majority of the scientists favor it. The Russian physicist Jamow suggested in 1948 that the Universe was the result of a big explosion, or the Big Bang. Proof was lacking, but now it seems to have been found by two researchers, Drs. Arno Penzias and Robert Wilson, of the Bell Laboratories in Holmdel, New Jersey. They received the 1978 Nobel Prize in physics for their discovery. This may become superseded by future research. Whatever the truth turns out to be, the Liberal Church will accept it. It is not wedded to any myth or tradition. More will be said about cosmology in Chapter 6 on truth and in Chapter 7 on myths.

Chosen People

Since the Liberal Church will recognize only religious values which are of universal application to all members of the human race, it does not accept the idea of a chosen people. The Old Testament declares the Jews to be God's chosen people.[48] In his prayer dedicating the new temple, King Solomon said of the Israelites, "Thou didst separate them from the peoples of the earth to be thy heritage" (1 Kings 8:53). This of course does not explain why the Jews were chosen. The doggerel "How odd of God to choose the Jews" is not enlightening either. One explanation is that the Jews were slaves in Egypt and their liberation from that wretched condition indicates that God favored them above all other people.[49] Traditionalists still believe this to be true. As Herman Wouk, an orthodox Jew, says, "the idea is calculated to make any thinking modern person uneasy."[50] But then he explains it thus: "Their (the Jews') tradition teaches, and Western religion does, too, that they are the remnant of an old great house with an historic purpose that is from God. Of course, convinced rationalists find this impossible to swallow, and they are numerous today, and count many highly intelligent Jews among their ranks. They are left with the problem, how is it that the Jews have lasted so long and still last?"[51] The answer of the traditionalists is that Jews would not have survived the persecutions if they were not God's chosen people.

The idea of God's chosen people is also found in Luther and in Calvin's doctrine of the elect. Under that doctrine mankind is divided into two categories: the elect and the reprobate. The elect are those who, by the grace of God, believe in Christ as the Savior. They form the Church from which all others, including Papists, Unitarians, and Universalists, are excluded. The Mormon chapels and meeting places are open to all worshippers. But the Mormon temples (of which there are only a few) are reserved for the elite members of the church.

One probably should not judge harshly those who believe that their particular origin or brand of faith is superior to all others. It is a common human frailty. One finds it, for instance, among the Brahmins in Boston, the

First Families in Virginia, and the British aristocracy. Even egalitarian societies develop elite classes. Religious Liberals are not immune from the failing; some of them feel that Traditional Religion may be good for the masses, but they are different, a religious elite. One recalls the poster in George Orwell's satire, "All animals are equal, but some animals are more equal than others."[52] Elitism of course runs counter to the universal character of Liberal Religion. Donald S. Harrington, a contemporary leader in Liberal Religion, said that all men are chosen—chosen by God in a covenant which obligates God to let man be the bearer of evolution.[53] This approach, while intellectually difficult to grasp, makes the idea of the chosen people acceptable because no one is excluded.

The scion of a Brahmin family, a First Family of Virginia, or the British aristocracy may be held to be superior simply because of his ancestry. The concept of chosen people and religious elitism is very similar. Liberal Religion cannot accept either concept. It must follow Jesus' pronouncement, "Ye shall know them by their fruits." If the fruit is good, the root is unimportant. This is one of the reasons why tradition deserves far less consideration than is commonly accorded to it.

Scriptures

The Bible contains many lofty ideas that inspire Liberal Religion. Outstanding examples are the stories about the Hebrew prophets, the Sermon on the Mount, and many of Jesus' parables. Liberal Religion does not reject the Bible but recognizes that it is a collection of sixty-six books of richly different character which were written and edited by many authors over a period of a thousand years. The Bible contains histories, legends, sermons, poems, songs, political speeches, discussions, as well as religious tracts. To Liberal Religion, it is incomprehensible that all these should be regarded as sacred or the Word of God, as it is so widely believed in Traditional Religion. This belief is particularly curious because a number of books in the Bible, collectively known as the Apocrypha, are excluded by some churches and therefore are not regarded as the Word of God. Nobody seems to know the basis for excluding certain books and including others. The charming and harmless story of Tobit was excluded, but the love story called *The Song of Solomon* was included. The book of Esther, which makes no reference to God, and the cynical book of Ecclesiastes are thought to be part of the Word of God, but Ecclesiasticus, which is full of religious wisdom, is excluded. A large number of other books are also excluded.[54] The so-called fundamentalists believe that every word in the Bible is inspired by God and literally true. The most conservative of them insist on what they call the inerrancy of the Bible.

One would have no difficulty with the Old Testament in particular if, instead of regarding it as a holy book or a collection of holy books, it would be treated as what it really is: an historic and anthropological record of a primitive people and primitive personalities which was written, edited, and translated over a period of about one thousand years. Mrs. Church, in her book about the prophets, has aptly compared the Old Testament with the type of book the English Puritans might have written in 1645 if they had wanted to glorify their way of life and their tradition. They would have taken past records, which included legends and traditions of the Druids, Caesar's account of his visit to Britain, bits of Roman literature, the *Anglo-Saxon Chronicle,* Layamon's *Brut,* William I's *Doomesday Book,* Langland's *Piers Plowman,* a few Lollard sermons, part of Chaucer, some sermons from Hooker, and a selection of Elizabethan love lyrics, and combined them into one book. The heroes of the Old Testament are by no means paragons of religious virtue. To illustrate why Liberal Religion is not morally inspired by the Old Testament, mention should be made of the chronicles of Abraham, Isaac, and Jacob, the patriarchs who are revered by Jews, Christians, and Moslems, and of King David, the alleged ancestor of Jesus. Abraham is revered by traditional Jews, Christians, and Islamics as the holiest patriarch. His name is frequently invoked by Jesus and Paul. This religious status is based upon the Biblical report that Abraham made the original bargain with Jehovah. Jehovah promised that Abraham and "his seed" would prosper if, in return, they would bear sole allegiance to Him. Abraham was a clever nomad who became very rich in cattle, land, and slaves, even before he settled down in Canaan. During his migration, he spent some time in Egypt. In order to make himself popular, he allowed the male members of the Pharoah's court access to his beautiful wife Sarah, pretending that she was his sister (Gen. 12:13), which pretense he repeated when he met King Abimelech (Gen. 20:2). In order to curry favor with Jehovah, his benefactor, he was ready to murder his son Isaac, whom he took for this purpose to a deserted place under false pretenses (Gen. 22:5). Traditional Religion gives Abraham high marks for this as signifying absolute obedience to, and faith in, God. Kierkegaard's book *Fear and Trembling* is an ode to Abraham. Human sacrifices were not unusual in those times and the sacrificial killing of one's son was especially prized. The Bible reports this about King Moab.[55] As the prophet Micah wrote in a more enlightened age, some four hundred years later, such sacrifices are futile and do not please God (Micah 6:8). When Sarah became jealous of Abraham's concubine, Hagar and his first born Ishmael (the ancestor of all Arabs), Abraham sent both away into the desert.

Isaac is the second in the trinity of worshipped patriarchs. He seems to have been a rather undistinguished man, and it is difficult to perceive why anybody should be proud of him. His father Abraham's servant, found him a wife, Rebecca. The Bible reports that, like his father before him, he pretended that his wife was his sister in order to offer her sexual favors to strangers whom he wished to befriend (Gen. 26:6). When he was old and blind, his wife Rebecca conspired with his second son Jacob to deceive him (Gen. 27:10). Jacob, the third person in the revered patriarchial trinity, was a crafty and dishonest character. He wronged his brother Esau by extorting his birthright (Gen. 26:33) and with the aid of his scheming mother, by fraudulently obtaining Isaac's blessing (Gen. 27:19). Jacob then went to work for Laban, whose daughters Leah and Rachel he married. Before returning home, he devised a clever scheme to procure for himself most of Laban's livestock (Gen. 31:10), and then he stole the rest of Laban's personal possessions, including the household idols, hidden in a camel saddle, and fled with his wives and the loot (Gen. 31:18). Rachel, concealing the stolen idols in the camel saddle upon which she remained seated when her father came to search, excused her lack of courtesy with the pretense that the ailment common to women was on her (Gen. 11:35). Jacob was much revered and given the name of Israel. All this happened, according to the Bible, under the guidance of Jehovah.

Next to Abraham, David is the most extolled character in the Old Testament. The status of Jesus is sought to be enhanced by the statement that he (or rather his father Joseph) is of the seed of Abraham and David. David was lustful and treacherous. The favorite story about him is how he, as a youngster, killed the great Goliath. People enjoy this story of violence as they enjoy the burning of the bad witch in the fairy tale of Hansel and Gretel. When David had become king he fell in love with Uriah's wife. In order to procure her for himself, he sent Uriah to his death by deceptive means (2 Sam. 11:15). He had himself annointed king while his predecessor Saul was still on the throne. These and other stories about David make him a less than admirable character, even though he may have been a good general and a fine poet. His great political achievement was that he made Israel a nation.

The Mosaic rules for building a camp for the nomadic tribe (Deut. 23:12), and the detailed directions for building a sanctuary (Exod. 25:8) carry no religious message. The Bible record about the conquest of Canaan by the Israelites is not religiously inspiring. It is full of wars, murder, and treachery. The following story illustrates the unedifying character of the Bible: The great competitor of Jehovah was always Baal, the god who was worshipped by the original inhabitants of Canaan. One day, the Prophet Elijah decided to have a contest between the gods, and the Baal worshippers accepted the challenge. A bullock was killed and placed on the altar. Both sets of priests called upon their God to send fire from heaven and to consume the bullock. There was no response to the prayer of the Baal priests. Elijah and his colleagues were successful, however. And then Elijah ordered the Israelites to kill all followers of Baal (1 Kings 18:40). This is only one of the bloodthirsty stories fit for the anthropological records of a primitive society, but which have no place in a religious book, as Liberal Religion conceives it.

The geneological recitals and the "begats" of the Bible may have historical significance, but they are not of sacred character. The frequently heard trumpet call to a "return to biblical morality" is entirely inappropriate. The claim that the Bible is the inerrant word of God offends the sensibilities and the intelligence of the Liberal Religionists.

Thomas Paine, in his still very readable book *The Age of Reason,* has demonstrated the absurdities in the Bible to the point of ridicule, and he accuses its authors of denigrating religion and God. While Paine's arguments are sound, the ridicule is inappropriate because the Bible had, and still has, a tremendous influence.

The Bible is the Judeo-Christian canon. Like most canonical sacred writings, it was officially closed in order to avoid the intrusion of new and especially undesirable additions and interpretations.[56] The Liberal Church will not recognize any such closure. Revelation, according to Liberal Religion, is not sealed. Religious thoughts play a significant part in Homer's epics (often referred to as the Greek Bible) and in Dantes' *Divine Comedy.* But no one claims that these narratives are in any way sacred, inerrantly true, or divine revelations. Homer and Dante are not lesser authors than the many persons who wrote and edited the books of the Old and the New Testaments.

The scriptures of the Liberal Church include not only the Bible, but also the Moslem Koran, the Hindu Gita, the Buddhist writings, and all other religious writings. The scriptures also include the works of such authors as Shakespeare, Emerson, Jefferson, Thomas Paine, Kahlil Gibran, Walt Whitman, Martin Luther King, Jr., and numerous others, some as yet unborn.

The finest parts of all the classical scriptures are the words of the prophets. James Luther Adams has pointed out that the prophets of the Old Testament were often forthtellers, not foretellers.[57] But we fall far short of understanding the full nature of prophecy if we think of the prophets merely as critics dealing with religious and ethical generalities. In the great ages of prophecy, the prophets, whether inside or outside the churches, have been foretellers as well as forthtellers.[58]

If the word "scripture" is reserved for the Word of God, the Liberal Church must say with Thomas Paine that the only Word of God is the creation which we behold. Traditional Religion considers the Bible as the Word of God which must not be subordinated to reason, experience, creedal interpretation, or even literary criticism.

Mohammed claimed that the existence of only one holy book (the Koran, in his case) is a mark of prestige for a religion. If this is true, then Liberal Religion lacks that particular mark of prestige.

Revealed Religion

As the Liberal Church does not acknowledge a supernatural power, so its religion is not supernaturally revealed. Revealed religion in the traditional sense is a religious system imposed by a supernatural power.

According to Tillich, "the word, 'revelation,' has been used traditionally to mean the manifestation of something hidden which cannot be approached through ordinary ways of gaining knowledge," and "revelation is the manifestation of the mystery of being for the cognitive function of the human reason."[59] Revelation is not all that complicated. Paul wrote (Gal. 1:12): "the good news that I preached is not a human affair. I did not receive it from any man, and I was not taught it, but it came to me through the revelation of Jesus Christ." What Paul is really saying is that the thought of Jesus Christ inspired him. Inspiration means that the spirit moves one, and if one speaks of the Holy Spirit, it means the same thing. Inspiration is a simple word and it adequately, as well as clearly, explains what occurs when somebody claims that a truth has been revealed to him or her. Those who proclaim the Will of God claim that God has spoken to them through voices or visions.

Voices and visions are also a form of inspiration. John Haynes Holmes wrote the hymn: "The voice of God is calling . . . whom shall I send to succor my people in their need? . . . We answer send us upon thine errand." This, in common parlance, means that we are inspired to render social service. Joan of Arc was inspired to lead France in a war of liberation against the invading English forces. She was an unsophisticated country girl, and she did not understand simple inspiration. Therefore, she claimed that the voices of God and of the Virgin Mary told her to act. However, as Bernard Shaw points out in the preface to his play *Saint Joan*: "If Newton's imagination had been of the same vividly dramatic kind, he might have seen the ghost of Pythagoras walk into the orchard and explain why the apples were falling. Such an illusion would have invalidated neither the theory of gravitation nor Newton's general sanity. What is more, the visionary method of making the discovery would not be a whit more miraculous than the normal method. The test of sanity is not normality of the method, but the reasonableness of the discovery. If Newton had been informed by Pythagoras that the moon was made of green cheese, then Newton would have been locked up." What Shaw says about reasonableness anticipates an aspect of Liberal Religion which is discussed below in Chapter 4.

Many biblical figures claim to have heard voices or seen visions. The Prophet Amos did so ("The Lord showed me") when he admonished his people to desist from their evil ways as otherwise dire consequences would befall them. Another example is the Prophet Ezekiel who introduced all his statements with "The voice of the Lord came to me."

One of the earliest reported incidents occurred in the desert when Moses saw a bush apparently burning but not consumed, out of which came the voice of God telling him to lead the Israelites out of Egypt (Exod. 3:2). The story of the bush can be dismissed as poetic embroidery, but the inspiration was obviously real. This kind of vision may be more easily understood if one recalls the famous "I have a dream" speech of Martin Luther King, Jr., in Washington, D.C., in 1963. In the Old Testament (Num. 12:16) God is quoted as saying, "If there be a prophet among you, I the Lord will make myself known unto him in a vision and will speak unto him in a dream."

A modern illustration of revealed religion is found in the Mormon Church whose full name is the Church of Jesus Christ of the Latter Day Saints, a brand of Traditional Christian Religion. Until recently, no person of African descent could be a Mormon priest. In 1970, when the Mormons became increasingly embarrassed by this discrimination, they issued a public statement in defense of their religious position, the substance of which was as follows: "We love the Negroes and agree that they are entitled to the same civil rights as white persons. Our theology denies no person his constitutional privileges. Our religion, however, owes its origin and existence to divine revelation. God revealed to our founder and first prophet Joseph Smith that Negroes are 'not yet to receive the priesthood for reasons which we believe are known to God, but which he has not made fully known to man.' Our living prophet President McKay has received no message from God on that subject and we, therefore, are bound to what God revealed to Joseph Smith. Let us trust in God and Jesus Christ."[60] Then, in June 1978, Spencer Kimball, the eighty-three-year-old president of the church, announced that God had revealed to him that black males could be priests in the Mormon Church. The president of the church, and he alone, is regarded as God's prophet, seer, and revelator. Mr. Kimball followed in the footsteps of Joseph Smith, the founder of the Mormon Church, who relied upon more than one hundred and thirty revelations. That black females are still excluded from the priesthood is not particularly discriminatory because white females are likewise excluded. Equality of man and woman in the Mormon Church must await another revelation.

In 1979, Sonia Johnson was excommunicated from the Mormon Church for promoting the Equal Rights Amendment to the U.S. Constitution. She protested and called Mormon culture a "savage misogyny," but she did not question the validity of revelation and affirmed her faith in the tenets of Mormon religion.

Apparently, members of the Mormon Church were not particularly impressed by the recent revelation, as many of them claim to be in frequent communication with God. These alleged revelations deal not only with matters of religious faith, but sometimes they refer to the location of a well, or the purchase of stocks. People of the Traditional Religion sometimes claim that God told them to do certain things, and they claim this to be a revelation from the supernatural power.

Most humans experience sudden inspirations from time to time. Only those steeped in Traditional Religion call it divine revelation. A young professor at a denominational college in Florida received an attractive employment offer in the North. He therefore desired to terminate his employment contract with the college in Florida. When he spoke in these terms to the college president the latter was incensed. The young professor then told the president that God had called him to the North. "That," responded the president, "is another matter," and he withdrew his objection.

Some consider Christianity a mystery religion, wherein God is known only through his revealed word, which only priests can, or may, interpret. This is the opposite of Liberal Religion which knows God through its experience of his creation.

The Jews also believe that the Bible is the revealed Word of God. However, the Reconstructionist Movement, founded by Rabbi Mordecai Kaplan, a professor at the Jewish Theological Seminary, scoffs at the concept of divine revelation. This group defines Judaism as a "civilization" rather than a religion.

In his address on accepting the Templeton Prize for Progress in Religion, Ralph Burhoe invested the ancient concept of revelation with a new meaning which is persuasive and in tune with Liberal Religion. He said, "I see modern science as a new gift of revelation about the not readily discernible total reality. . . ."[61]

Ethics and Morals

Liberal Religion demands of its adherents strict moral and ethical conduct. It is often thought that morality and ethics are inherent in all religions. This is not so. Henry Nelson Wieman devotes a subchapter of the book *The Growth of Religion* to "The Religious Way Distinguished from Morality."[62] In an earlier book, Wieman explained, "morality is not religious when it ignores the more remote and presumably vaster possibilities of good and evil . . . Religion is not moral when it becomes so absorbed in the remote and cosmic possibilities of good and evil," and does not care for the practicalities of life.[63] It will be noted that Wieman makes no distinction between morality and ethics. Indeed, most people use these words interchangeably and consider them as synonyms. Even Felix Adler, the founder of the Ethical Culture Movement, uses the word "moral" in explaining what Ethical Culture means.[64] Actually, there is a distinction, even though it may be irrelevant in the present context. Morality denotes conduct and action. Ethics refers to the principles which guide one's conduct and actions; it results from an intellectual process. Liberal Religion requires conduct and action to be guided by principles. James Luther Adams says that neither moralism nor the observance of ethical principles supply the dimension of depth which are essential to Religion.[65] Wieman states the position of Liberal Religion by concluding: "No religion is fully normal and wholesome which is not moral, and no morality is satisfactory which is not religious. The two must merge if either is to fulfill its function as human living requires."[66]

Primitive religion arose to propitiate the seemingly hostile forces of nature and consisted of religious exercises, rituals, and prayers which had no ethical and moral content. To this day, some adherents of Traditional Religion seem to feel that mere diligence and exercises make them ethical, moral, or religious. In other words, the Jew who eats kosher food and observes the ritual laws, as well as the sabbath laws, is considered to be very religious. A Christian who attends religious services regularly and prays often is esteemed as a very religious person. And, so it is with Moslems and others in the realm of Traditional Religion.

The Greek, Roman, and the ancient Germanic gods were rather immoral or, at least, amoral deities. On the other hand, the Babylonian King Hammurabi decreed the famous moral code of laws without even pretending that the local gods had anything to do with the code. The Jews introduced ethics into religion, and Judaism is probably the earliest of the so-called ethical religions. According to the Bible, the Ten Commandments of Moses came from God and ever since, morality and ethics are supposed to have fused with religion. However, religious teaching has been unable to keep up with the increasing moral tensions and economic complications of life. By recognizing the inability, if not the impotence, of Traditional Religion, one does not denigrate its valiant attempt to achieve ethical standards. However, thundering prophets and pious incantations have been in vain.

Moral Majority is the name of a contemporary conservative movement founded by a fundamentalist radio preacher the Reverend Jerry Falwell. Falwell and his people call for a return to what they call the Bible morality. They are very serious about this and do not recognize that the morality in biblical times was on an exceedingly low level. This caused the exhortations of the Hebrew prophets and of Jesus which, unfortunately, were never heeded. Moral Majority is a political action group of fundamentalist religionists. As will be discussed in Chapter 18 on politics, Liberal Religion does not share the widespread condemnation of efforts to obtain religious ends through political activities. The Moral Majority was very successful in 1980. They succeeded in eliminating political leaders who were on their hit list and they have vowed to enlarge the hit list in the future. The tactics used indicate that the Moral Majority does not love its neighbors, nor do its followers display any of the Traditional Religious virtues. Moral Majority is a catchy name for a decidedly irreligious effort. It is a prime illustration of what is called ethical relativism, a phenomenon which merits mention in the present context.

Often, people violate moral and ethical norms deliberately. This is thought to be justified by the particular circumstances of a given situation, for instance, alleged racial bias, unfair government action, personal injustice, or, as in the case of Moral Majority, alleged liberal excesses. To protest or combat the alleged evil, conduct which otherwise would be immoral and unethical is regarded as moral and ethical. This is "ethical relativism." Curiously enough, such ethical relativism is condoned by Traditional Religion. Traditional Religion and ethical relativism co-exist. Living examples thereof are Father Berrigan in the U.S., Reverend Paisley in Northern Ireland, Prime Minister Begin in Israel, and the Imam Khomeini in Iran. Liberal Religion does not countenance such co-existence. It demands that ethical and moral norms, once recognized as such, must be adhered to.

The teachings of Jesus, especially the Sermon on the Mount, are largely lost on the Christians. They like to hear about it in their church schools and from their pulpits, but they pay no further attention to it. The so-called ethical religions, which developed after the primitive religions, decree that thou shalt not kill or murder, but to this day, history is full of murderous activities which are condoned by Traditional Religion. The guerillas in Rhodesia and the militant protestants in Northern Ireland are, or were, led by clergymen. In Iran, the holy men who inspired the so-called Islamic revolution ordered midnight executions. These are only a few examples. Traditional Religion has lost its credibility as a source of ethics and morality.

It must also be noted that when Traditional Religion denounces contemporary morality, it refers primarily, if not solely, to sexual morality. This is a rather narrow view of morality.

The foregoing is not a repudiation of the ethical principles and moral pronouncements which are found as precious morsels in Traditional Religion. The primitive precepts of the Ten Commandments, the passionate postulates of the Hebrew prophets and the sophisticated ethics of Jesus are part and parcel of the Western culture which we affirm. The contemporary trend toward doing one's own thing, regardless of who gets hurt, violates fundamental ethical principles and offends Liberal Religion. The difference between right and wrong, virtue and vice, truth and falsehood, is part of all religions. However, Liberal Religion is not as certain as Traditional Religion that ethics and morality cannot stand on their own feet, that they are inextricably bound up with religion. It is noteworthy that in the Christian religion, neither the Nicean creed nor the creed of Athanasius contain any ethical precept.

The founding of the Ethical Culture Movement in 1876 was an early effort of Liberal Religion to emphasize the ethical aspect of religion and to demonstrate that ethics can be cultivated and inculcated through a religious organization and by a free pulpit which is not fettered by Traditional Religion. Traditional Religion has no answer for the difficult ethical questions of our times which grow out of nuclear development, the arms race, the population explosion, and the conflict between technology and the environment. The Institute of Society, Ethics, and the Life Sciences in Hastings-on-Hudson, New York, a leader in the field of bioethics, is headed by a philosopher and a psychiatrist with legal training.[67] There is no noticeable input from religion. This is a challenge to Liberal Religion.

Religion and the Law

Hardly a week goes by that Religion is not in some court of law. Judges are frequently called upon to decide whether and to what extent a religious organization, some religious belief, or some religious practice must yield to the commands of the law. The special problems involving religious liberty are dealt with below in Chapter 17. The position of God in the law is dealt with in the next chapter. At the present juncture, some general observations concerning the relationship between religion and law are appropriate.

When the Bible refers to the law, it means the body of laws ascribed to Moses. This is the law which Jesus said he came to fulfill and not to abolish (Matt. 5:17). Actually, Jesus desired to reform that law or, at least, the administration thereof. In the Judeo-Christian tradition, that law no longer has any binding force except for devout Jews. The religious factions in the state of Israel have held the balance of political power and were thus able to impose many of the ancient rules on the law of Israel. In 1950 this religious group was able to defeat a constitution on the ground that "Israel's Torah is its constitution."

In the world of Islam, the Koran, the alleged revealed Word of God, is the core of the legal system.[68] Saudi Arabia, the place of Mohammed's birth and where Mecca is located, is a foremost example of such theocracy. The hereditary king is both the head of state and the Imam or religious leader. He is the final arbiter of legal disputes, a kind of one-man Supreme Court. Most cases are decided by religious courts. The law of Islam is compiled in the Sheria which not only contains the applicable parts of the Koran but also the traditional rules of interpretation. Public morality committees, officially recognized by the government, act as religious police and attempt to supervise personal behavior as prescribed by the Koran, such as five daily prayers, fasting at prescribed times, and the seclusion of women. They also crack down on such prohibited behavior as the public use of musical instruments, public smoking, and dancing. At the present time Iran, although a republic, seeks to enforce the same religious laws.

The countries of the Judeo-Christian tradition in Europe have separated religious laws from worldly laws, but this has not resulted in a complete separation of church and state. The kings of the Scandinavian countries are still the heads of the state church. The British monarch is still the head of the Anglican Church, and the Anglican bishops in Britain are still chosen by the British prime minister, even if the prime minister is not a member of the Anglican Church. The United States, through its constitution and Jefferson's efforts, achieved a complete separation of church and state. And yet, many concepts of Traditional Religion were absorbed by the law, for instance, the law on family relations. A typical example of the obstinate perpetuation of Bible concepts is contained in Section 107 of the Internal Revenue Code of the United States, which deals with the tax exemptions of the rental allowance granted to "ministers of the gospel." The official regulations include in this term, rabbis and Jewish cantors who clearly do not believe in the Gospel. Apparently, when Congress intended to confer a tax benefit on all clergymen it could not think of any descriptive term other than "ministers of the Gospel." Another section of the Tax Code exempts from Social Security Tax of the self-employed, any member of a religious sect which considers support of an insurance scheme sinful (Sec. 1402g). This exemption from Social Security Tax on religious grounds has been extended to all employees. The Amish religion has asserted this privilege.[69]

The Civil Rights Act created a new definition of religion, which will be discussed in Chapter 17 on religious liberty.

American law holds religion in particular awe, which, at times, leads to bizarre results. If any group proclaims itself a church or religious society, it thereby automatically creates an invisible shield which law enforcement and taxing authorities hesitate to penetrate. A man who dons a clerical collar thereby often succeeds in fending off legitimate inquiries as to his religious affiliation. A female in a nun's garb, who sits at a public place with a tincup in front of her, is presumed to collect money for religious purposes. If contending factions of a religious organization appear in a court of law, the judge will refuse to entertain any action which may touch on the truth or falsity of alleged religious beliefs because that would be an interference which the First Amendment of the United States Constitution forbids. To illustrate, in 1979 the Unification Church brought a libel action against the publisher of a book that compared the Unification Church to occult sects and to Nazism. The action was dismissed because the court refused to make an inquiry into the religious beliefs of the Unification Church.[70] In another case, the late Justice Robert Jackson of the United States Supreme Court wrote in a dissent which represents contemporary legal thinking and certainly the view of Liberal Religion, that it is improper to submit the truth or falsity of religious belief to a jury, because religious sincerity cannot be severed from religious verity. Justice Jackson's view was based on the American principle of religious liberty, a topic to be discussed in Chapter 17. Justice Jackson wanted to withdraw a religious belief from consideration by the courts and jury although he considered it "nothing but humbug."[71] A similar attitude seems to have prevailed in the Roman Empire. According to the book of Acts, Roman proconsul Gallio refused to adjudicate a case involving the observance of religious laws (Acts 18:15). Gibbon tells us that in Rome, all modes of worship were considered equally true by the people, equally false by the philosophers, and equally useful by the magistrates.[72]

An Internal Revenue Service spokesman was recently quoted as saying, "If you are sincere in your belief, we will recognize you as a church, even if you worship trees." But, he added, such recognition does not mean that members or ministers of such a church could use their religious affiliation

as a tax shield.[73] This energetic stance of the Internal Revenue Service occurred recently because of the increased mail order business in ministerial
degrees. It is a refreshing departure from the American subservience of the
law to religion, which stems from the time when religious organizations
could be easily identified because they were few in numbers. Also, in these
earlier times, the religious institutions performed functions such as the care
of the sick and the poor, which are regarded today as governmental functions. Traditional Religion claims that it serves the state and the community
by fostering spiritual values which, in the opinion of Traditional Religion,
justify and even demand tax exemption for religious institutions. Sometimes the law rebels. Thus, over the objection of the Roman Catholic
Church, it was held that a gift for the celebration of masses for the soul of a
deceased person is a private donation and not a tax exempt gift. Liberal
Religion goes much further. It can concede religion a special legal status
only in cases where the burdens of government have been reduced. The
operation of a hospital is an obvious example. In all other instances, a religious society or church does not merit any preferential legal status. This is a
complex problem of which more will be said later (see Chapter 17).

Religion, and especially Liberal Religion, can only prosper in an orderly
society that protects both minorities and the free expression of opinion. It is
therefore a mistake to disdain the phrase "law and order." The fact that
some objectionable politicians may have invoked the phrase for objectionable purposes is not a reasonable cause for denouncing law and order.

Grace and Mercy

Grace is one of the loveliest words in the theological dictionary. It is also
a word of many meanings, none of which is relevant to Liberal Religion.

The basic meaning in Traditional Religion is that grace is a free gift of
God. It cannot be obtained by human effort. Faith is such a gift. Tillich
goes so far as to denounce the Protestant doctrine of justification by faith
(as distinguished from the Roman Catholic doctrine of justification by good
works). Tillich teaches that the proper doctrine is justification by grace
through faith.[74] Divine love is also regarded as a gift of grace. According to
Traditional Religion, the estrangement of modern man from the world can
only be overcome and healed by divine grace.[75]

The reason why the concept of grace is unacceptable to Liberal Religion
is that it does not allow for any human effort in the attainment of the moral
and ethical goals of life.

"Here by the grace of God go I" is a phrase uttered by a person who
beholds another who is afflicted with a misfortune. The speaker is pleased
that he or she is not the victim of the same misfortune. The implication is
that the speaker could not have avoided the same misfortune, except for the

gratuitous gift of God's grace. Liberal Religion does not accept this. It agrees with the Bible saying (Exod. 23:8), "thou shalt take no gift, for the gift blindeth the wise and perverteth the words of the righteous."

In other contexts, God's grace is praised because he is a merciful judge. Mercy is undeserved leniency; it is, in Shakespeare's words, "an attribute to God himself." Nobody is so strong or so good that he or she disdains mercy. However, it is one thing to accept mercy on occasion, and another to elevate it to a rule of social intercourse. If one does, one abolishes self-responsibility and self-reliance. Paul himself said if you have to work for it, it is not grace (Rom. 4:4). In the Gospels, John distinguished grace and truth from the law. He said (John 1:17), "for the law was given by Moses, but grace and truth came by Jesus Christ."

To rely on God's free gift in social intercourse without any human effort or responsibility amounts to spiritual freeloading, which is not acceptable to Liberal Religion.

At funeral services of Traditional Religion the clergy often requests God to have mercy on the soul of the departed. This assumes that, without such mercy, the soul of the departed is doomed and will suffer eternal damnation. Liberal Religion finds this inappropriate. In the first place, Liberal Religion doubts the immortality of the soul. (This is more fully discussed in Chapter 11). In the second place, if the soul is immortal, its fate in any afterlife should depend upon what was done before death and not upon undeserved mercy. And lastly, such mercy cannot be granted by an unknown supernatural deity.

God's mercy is also invoked in other Traditional rituals. A common attitude assumes that all human beings are depraved by nature and constantly in need of God's mercy because mankind is inherently evil. It is an attitude which Liberal Religion does not accept; it denies that life is worth the reverence which Albert Schweitzer and other great prophets teach. The constant prayers for God's mercy are not compatible with the affirmation of life, which is of the essence in Liberal Religion.

Liberal Religion has the same difficulty with the traditional concept that man must be "reconciled" with God. For instance, reconciliation is at the core of the confession adopted in 1967 by the United Presbyterian Church in the U.S. The Liberal Religionist feels like Thoreau when he was on his death bed and was asked by a pious aunt whether he had made his peace with his maker. Thoreau replied, "I do not recall having quarreled with him." Liberal Religion sees no need for reconciliation in the traditional sense. There is, however, another meaning to this word which will be discussed later in Chapter 7.

Ecumenical Religion

Liberal Religion must not be caught up in the so-called ecumenical movement. Ecumenical religion is an outgrowth of the abandon to good feeling. The ecumenical movement seeks unity on the lowest common denominator: the fact of having a belief. The content of the belief is unimportant. Good taste demands that any belief must be respected, but good taste is opposed to moral passion. Ecumenism is much ado about nothing. It tries to bridge the differences of doctrine between contending Judeo-Christian bodies. If Lutherans pray with Roman Catholics, they hail it as a monumental religious event. If Methodists join Presbyterians in a communion service, both regard it as a religious achievement. When Jews and Christians meet to tell each other what they believe, they regard this as religious progress. It is true that happenings of this type are novel and progressive, but only in the narrow world of Traditional Religion. During the reign of Pope John XXIII, Cardinal Bea came to Harvard and delivered a series of lectures on Christian unity which sent many people into a state of euphoria but had no effect on reality.

A Lutheran layman, some time ago, described the ecumenical movement in economic terms. He called it "price fixing among similar religious packagers competing for a shrinking market."[76]

Liberal Religion must not be mixed with Traditional Religion. The late Dr. Preston Bradley, Unitarian Minister of one of Chicago's largest churches, declared in 1956 that he had also joined the Congregational Church in the spirit of ecumenical unity.[77] Similarly, Adlai Stevenson, member of a Unitarian Church, joined the Presbyterian Church during his second presidential campaign, and thenceforth alternated on Sundays between Unitarian and Presbyterian services. Dr. Bradley and Mr. Stevenson thus worshipped on trinitarian as well as anti-trinitarian altars. There were, and are, others who favor multiple church membership.

A pulpit exchange between clergymen of different denominations is very desirable because it fosters mutual understanding and respect. This is different from blurring the distinctions, especially the distinction between Liberal Religion and Traditional Religion. Upon reading Dr. Bradley's article, one gains the impression that this Unitarian preacher would also have joined the Baptist Church and the Roman Catholic Church if they would have accepted him. He would have liked to join all religions which, as he wrote, are based on the teachings of Christ. Therefore, what was called the ecunemical spirit did not embrace many of the other great religions.

Liberal Religion would betray its fundamental principles if it joined in a broad religious enterprise that professed beliefs contrary to the truth as Religious Liberals see it, if they joined in the mouthing of prayers alien to their faith, and if they supported an ecumenical movement that excluded all those who do not consider Jesus as the Savior. Businessmen have been known to make contributions to competing political parties. Politicians often find it advisable to join simultaneously, the Elks, the Lions, the Rotary Club, and other organizations. Religion should not be regarded on the same level.

The problem is even deeper. We live in an era of business mergers. Religion has been infected by its spirit. There is a cry for bigger and better denominations. It is more efficient to operate a big enterprise. The zeal to build such enterprises is greater than the care for individual conscience, intellectual integrity, and religious individuality. One observes the same trend in religious mass meetings, especially those of the fringe religions, of which more will be said presently. The ecumenical spirit is often an excuse for the assembly line dispensations by tycoon religionists and ecclesiastical publicists. All this has little to do with true religion.

The so-called interfaith efforts diminish Liberal Religion. They stress togetherness and aim to blur the lines between religious individuality. They advocate mutual toleration. We more than tolerate Traditional Religion, we respect it. But, we should not want any part of it.

Fringe Religions

One of the forces with which Liberal Religion must deal are the fringe religions. The term "fringe religion" is here used as a collective name for the plethora of sects, cults, and organizations that have sprung up in large numbers and exert an awesome, often terrifying influence. This influence is frequently spread over the American television networks, for which reason these fringe groups are often collectively referred to as the "electronic church," though television is not their only medium of communication.

Some established religions—Christianity among them—began as cults or sects. They are no longer on the fringe and, therefore, are not considered in this section. Nor will much space be devoted to the so-called "evangelicals." Their emotional emphasis on Traditional Bible religion is anathema to Liberal Religion. The movement is reminiscent of the Great Awakening in America of the eighteenth century which was repudiated by most theologians as a vulgar travesty of religion.[78] The Great Awakening faded away after a few decades, but it left behind a deepened interest in religion. A similar impact of the evangelicals is not noticeable. They have not decreased the crime rate nor the drug traffic. However, in recent years, the powerful television preacher Jerry Falwell has endeavored to arouse the evangelicals to political action. This will be discussed in Chapter 18 on politics.

Some of the electronic churches seem to respond to a desire for entertainment, although it is religious entertainment that is offered. Billy Graham and Oral Roberts, who occupy a special niche as evangelists, are show producers as much as preachers of religion.

The fringe religions are mostly offshoots of Traditional Religion. They flourish because many adherents of Traditional Religion are tired of the old humdrum; but instead of turning to Liberal Religion, they crave a jazzed-up and more showy version of Traditional Religion. Conventional congregations sometimes invite pastors who are trained in sorcery to preach and perform. What they do is called gospel magic. For instance, the announced Bible text is "Thy word is a lamp unto my feet" (Psalm 119). As the preacher mounts the pulpit, the Bible bursts into flames. This is one way to keep people from joining a fringe religion.

Most fringe religions are of the evangelical kind and outward directed, but some are inward directed, such as the Transcendental Meditation movement. Some fringe religions are a mixture of Christianity and Oriental religion, as is the Hare Krishna sect. Some are a mixture of Christianity and Marxism, like the People's Temple which galvanized the attention of the world in 1978 because of the mass killing in Guyana. Besides these cults, the best known seems to be the Unification Church, which is known for its wealth, its aggressive methods, and for its followers who are known as "Moonies" because the head of the church is Reverend Moon, a Korean. Asbury Theological Seminary in Kentucky is the center of the Good News Evangelical Movement which appears to be a group of conservative Methodists who exalt scriptural Christianity, and who will not allow what they angrily call re-interpretation of the Scriptures. Then there is the Church of Armageddon, on the American west coast, under the leadership of a man who calls himself Love Israel. There is a group called the Way International, which is based in Ohio. Similarly named is a fundamentalist Bible cult named The Way The Truth And The Life, under the leadership of a hairdresser, Ben Sepio. The Pennsylvania Forever Family, founded by a vacuum salesman named Traill, moved to New York and now calls itself the Church of Bible Understanding. The Theocratic Commune Natural Health Service is a cult in Detroit; and there is the Glory Barn Faith Assembly in Indiana. The Church of Scientology deserves special mention because, ever since it was founded in 1954 by a science fiction writer, it has been embroiled in aggressive law suits, both as a plaintiff as well as a defendant. It claims over five million members. The Universal Life Church in California sells doctor of divinity degrees for $10.00 apiece. The number of mail order pastors is on the increase. The Basic Bible Church in Houston, Texas consists mainly of airline pilots who have purchased their ordination certificates from a disbarred lawyer in Fort Worth, in order to escape taxation. More will be said about this in Chapter 17 on religious liberty and its abuse. Mercantile exploitation in Christianity is referred to at the end of Chapter 8. One of the mail order graduates of the Universal Life Church is Clifford Jones who, as Reverend Hekeem Abdul Rasheed, formed the Church of Hekeem in California where, for $500, anybody can become a minister. The Worldwide Church of God in Pasadena is a fundamentalist sect which has been rocked by a financial scandal. California seems to be a breeding ground of fringe religions. The state is trying to stem the growth, yet there are many other cults springing up in the market place to capture the attention of a willing, and often desperate audience.

What they seem to have in common is that they instill in their members a sense of comfort, security, and discipline which the followers do not find elsewhere. It is probable that the contemporary loosening of family ties is one of the reasons for the increased flowering of the cults; these groups satisfy an emotional need for belonging. Another reason may be an unfilled need for authoritative discipline which was at one time supplied by the family.

Most cults have a charismatic leader who very frequently exercises authoritative power. If it is not a deified deceased personage like Jesus or Lord Krishna, it is a living guru or a man like the Reverend Moon of the Unification Church or the Reverend Jim Jones of the People's Temple. In the 1930s, a black preacher calling himself Father Divine, attracted a great many black people in the metropolitan area of New York. Some charismatic preachers have disdained separate cults and have built their personal religious empires within the framework of Traditional Religion. Reverend Billy Graham and Reverend Oral Roberts are the two most obvious examples. What these men and the cult leaders have in common is a wide popular appeal owing to their mesmerizing personalities and their promise of redemption from the miseries of life on earth. Like many other cult leaders, they have also accumulated great wealth.

The wealth and the big real estate transactions of Reverend Moon's Unification Church are notorious. After the mass suicide and killing of the members of the People's Temple in Guyana in 1978, it was found that their leader Reverend Jim Jones kept substantial bank accounts in Switzerland. Reverend Jones also had sexual relations with many of his female followers. If one leaps several centuries back, one recalls the peculiarities of John of Leyden, the Anabaptist leader who reigned in the besieged city of Munster. Amidst austerity he lived in splendor, amassed a fortune, associated with many females, and proclaimed himself the Messiah of the New Jerusalem. John of Leyden is immortalized in Meyerbeer's opera *Le Prophète*. It would be interesting to investigate why and how certain personages can simultaneously satisfy their enormous appetite for money and women and, at the same time, attract the deep religious devotion of their followers. Such an investigation might shed light on the nature or the practice of Traditional Religion.

The Hare Krishnas, known for their bald heads, saffron robes, and their requests for donations in transportation terminals, built a palace of gold in the hills of West Virginia. *Time* magazine describes it thus: "The fussily-decorated palace consumed 63 tons of imported marble, 10 tons of wrought iron, 3 tons of carved teakwood from India, onyx for inlaying thousands of square feet of gold and copper leaf, 42 crystal chandeliers as well as enough stained glass for 80 windows."[79] In West Germany, some Hare Krishnas were convicted of criminal fraud because their castle on the Rhine was maintained with funds which had been collected for aid to children.

Mention should be made of an offbeat cult which seeks to gain good fortune by animal sacrifices. The American Society for the Prevention of

Cruelty to Animals (ASPCA) recently caused the New York police to raid a garage and confiscate sixty-two animals that were held for such sacrifices. According to an ASPCA official, the sect involved belonged to the Santaria cult which was derived from a Nigerian religion called *Yoruba* that was brought to Cuba by slaves in the nineteenth century. The Santaria sect is reported to be widespread, but it clearly does not have the same impact as the other fringe religions.

The so-called Charismatic Renewal Movement includes Roman Catholics and members of established Protestant denominations. It may spread beyond the United States and beyond Christianity. Charismatics stress ecstatic communion prayers and have proposed that Pentecostal Sunday (when the Holy Spirit allegedly descended) be celebrated as an ecumenical day of worship. The movement seems to be an answer to the unsatisfied hunger of many Christians for more ecstasy and less traditional liturgy. If the movement should spread, the established churches may be expected to put up a fight because it threatens the established order of Traditional Religion.

There is no denying that Jesus was a charismatic religious leader and that his original followers constituted a cult. However, the contemporary cultists cannot invoke the example of Jesus and his followers. Unlike today's cult leaders, Jesus was not a headquarters executive. He was a poor itinerant preacher without power or control position, nor did he aspire to such a position.

The word "cult" seems to have an undesired connotation. Some time ago, Reverend Moon angrily declared that his Unification Church was not a cult. On May 30, 1979 a religious group called Eckankar published an advertisement in *The New York Times* in which it was stated: "Eckankar is only a direct path to God. It is not a cult, nor do its members follow special diets or communal lifestyles." Nevertheless, the advertisement makes it clear that Eckankar is another fringe religion in the traditional mold. The Eck teachings, it says, "have existed for millions of years, for they show how man as Soul can return to his home in the heavenly worlds." Sri Darwin Gross is presented as the present 972nd living Eck Master and spiritual leader. The Greek philosopher Pythagoras is claimed to have been an early Eck Master.

The religious attitude of most cult members is irrational and, for that reason alone, incompatible with Liberal Religion. Traditional Religion senses a competition for followers. The sharpest encounters with the cults are with evangelically oriented Protestants and with Jews. There is less friction with the Roman Catholic Church because it is so strongly structured that it does not feel threatened by the cults, even though some Roman Catholics seem to drift towards charismatic religion. The fact that a substantial number of young Jews are reported to have joined the Unification Church tends to show that the Traditional Jewish religion has not fulfilled the religious yearnings of some young Jews, as is apparently true in the case of the Jews For Jesus cult. In short, the established conventional religions see in the cults a most unwelcome competition. One distinction between Traditional Religion and the cults is that the latter are less all inclusive; slaves and slavemasters will not unite with the same cult.

The gravest charges against the cults are that they gain members by brainwashing and coercive methods. The charge of brainwashing is of dubious merit. One recalls that former governor Romney was so discredited by the statement that he had been brainwashed into supporting the Vietnam War that he had to give up his bid for the presidency. If the term "brainwashing" means that a person's brain has been inundated with illusory notions, a member of the Liberal Church might well assert that children who are brought up in Traditional Religion are being brainwashed. The charge ill behooves the Traditional churches, especially as most cults are mere extentions of Traditional Religion.

The charge of coercion is a different matter. Children are often coerced by their parents to join a Traditional church. However, the charge against the cults goes further. Violation of criminal law is asserted. In a number of cases, the charge of coercive conduct is tried by a court. Some of the cults are charged with claiming tax exemption under false pretenses. The Unification Church has been investigated by a subcommittee of the American House of Representatives. There can be no objection to submitting the cults to due process of law.

The so-called deprogramming efforts of disappointed parents and relatives cannot be countenanced. As believers in religious liberty, Liberal Religionists cannot condone efforts of concerned relatives that are directed towards the forcible removal of converts from a cult. The only legitimate weapon against the success and attraction of the cults is a demonstration of the vitality of Liberal Religion, which offers intellectual as well as emotional fulfillment.

For obvious reasons, the drug related religions have clashed with the criminal law. Best known is Dr. Timothy Leary's LSD religion which involved the use of marijuana. He was dismissed from the Harvard University faculty in 1963 and tried in 1966. LSD is not only the chemical abbreviation of a drug compound, but also stands for League of Spiritual Discovery. Adherents of the Native American Churches are inspired by the chewing of peyote and the smoking of prayer cigarettes. These drug religions are more akin to incense burning in Traditional Religion than to the austerity and rationality of Liberal Religion.

3

God

The Traditional View

Frederick May Elliot had been the president of the American Unitarian Association for twelve years when he died in 1958. He dreamed of an American Liberal Church which would unite Unitarians, Universalists, Hicksite Quakers, Ethical Culturists, and Reformed Jews. He discussed this project with his friend Joshua Liebman, the renowned liberal Rabbi of Boston. Rabbi Liebman told him that Reformed Jews could never join such a broad-based organization because the worship of God is central even to Reformed Jews. Although Dr. Elliot personally shared this worshipful attitude, he knew that many religious liberals would not accept it. This was the end of Fred Elliot's dream.

God is not essential to Liberal Religion. The traditional view of God is that of a supernatural, elderly male with a flowing white beard, as depicted in the Sistine Chapel by Michelangelo. It is the anthropomorphic view of God, i.e. God conceived as a being with the attributes of a human who speaks, hears, feels, and acts like a human. Thus, the head of the Southern Baptist Church of America—the largest American denomination—pronounced in 1980 that God does not listen to the prayers of Jews, because they do not believe in Christ. By the same reasoning, God does not listen to the prayers of the Moslems and other non-Christians who make up the majority of the human community. The best response to this pronouncement is the joke which Bob Hope once made on a television show: God does not laugh at the jokes of Myron Cohen.

65

Liberal Religion disdains this traditional view. Thousands of words have been written about God and the concept of God. This is not the place to trace the development of the God concept in any detail. Different cultures and different communities have developed different concepts. Gods were not always represented in human form. Fire was once regarded as a god. Frequently the gods "constituted an unordered miscellany of accidental entities."[1] Later a regular system of divinities developed in which each god had special jurisdiction: Mars, the Roman god of war; Demeter, the Greek goddess of agriculture; and Loki, the Germanic god of fire will suffice as examples. The Judeo-Christian tradition is based upon the concept of a monotheistic God who is pervasive in our Western culture. The Bible supports an anthropomorphic concept of God. For example, in Gen. 1:26, God says, "Let us make man in our image." Bible believers will be embarrassed if living beings who look like bug-eyed monsters or gelatinous blobs should be found on other planets. In the last book of the New Testament, God is likewise depicted as a man with white hair, fiery eyes, and a deep voice (Rev. 1:14) as Michelangelo depicted him in the Sistine Chapel of the Vatican. This is the popular superman image of God, the traditional stereotype. This is the God whom Nietzsche and some theologians in the 1950s pronounced to be dead.

The second commandment forbids the devout to make any image of God. And yet, the reader of the Old Testament—which tells of the anger, the exhortations, and the covenants of God—is hard put to conceive God other than in anthropomorphic terms. In the cool of the evening, he took a walk in the Garden of Eden (Gen. 3:8). He sat down to have dinner with Abraham (Gen. 18:18). He conversed with Moses (Num. 12:8). This concept does not change in the New Testament. God remains determined to punish all humanity for the original sin of Adam and Eve, but he allows himself to be appeased by the bloody crucifixion of Jesus. Calvin said, "Christ, in his death, was offered to the Father as a propitiatory victim . . . the body of Christ was given up as the price for redemption."[2] Reverend Moon, leader of the Unification Church, called Mr. Fraser's defeat in the campaign for a seat in the United States Senate an act of God,[3] indicating that in Traditional Religion God will even intervene in local American elections.

One of the least attractive features of the Biblical God is that he so frequently indulges in bargain-making. The bargains are called covenants. The earliest covenant occurred when God proposed to Abraham that if Abraham would follow His commandments, God would make Abraham's descendants His chosen people and place them under His protection. According to the Jewish tradition, God made one condition which Abraham accepted: All males must be circumcised.[4] This is what Paul said was unnecessary for a follower of Jesus Christ, even though Paul and Jesus had been reared in the Jewish tradition. The idea of the original covenant between Jehovah and the Jews is still alive in the synagogue.[5] The most important bargain resulted from the service that God rendered his people when he liberated them from the Egyptian slavery. In return God demanded a service which is expressed in the following admonition found repeatedly in the Old Testament and in the Jewish liturgy (Deut. 5:6 and Exod. 20:2): "I am the Lord thy God who brought you up out of the land of Egypt and out of the house of bondage and, therefore, you must not worship any other god." Max Weber says that this idea of a covenant is uniquely Jewish and that the proposition of a contractual relationship between God and man cannot be found elsewhere.[6] This is not so. A minister of Liberal Religion, Donald Harrington, has said that God still has a covenant with man, which limits God. "Man," Harrington said, "is God's chosen vehicle for evolution. He and God are bound together in an everlasting covenant which binds them both."[7] When these words were spoken at the Annual Assembly of the Unitarian Universalist Association in Denver in 1972, most listeners were astonished. It was not a statement typical of Liberal Religion.

The Hebrew tribal God (or portable God, as Dimot calls him)[8] evolved into a universal God, for which reason Judaism is held to be the originator of monotheistic religion. As such, it is a logical point of departure for Liberal Religion, which reveres the unitary force of the Universe. Max Weber points out that Judaism and Islam are the only strictly monotheistic religions. Christian trinitarianism and the veneration of the saints are deviations from the monotheistic approach. According to Weber, only Judaism and Islam are truly monotheistic.

In Islam, Allah is all-powerful—just like the God of the Judeo-Christian tradition—and he bestows favors or inflicts punishment according to his whim.[9] The worship of Allah was spread by killing those who would not accept him.

The Biblical God and Allah are considered omnipotent. Indeed, all Traditional God concepts imply omnipotence. Gods of limited jurisdiction—such as Mars, Demeter, and Loki—are held to be omnipotent within their jurisdictions.

The idea of omnipotence is hard to reconcile with the imperfections and injustices of the world. Liberal Religion, therefore, does not subscribe to the idea of divine omnipotence. Liberal Religion's reverence for life and its respect for the Universe includes all imperfections. It challenges adherents to remedy these imperfections and to participate in the ongoing evolutionary process. Man, not God, is responsible for the elimination of imperfections and injustice. In this sense, Liberal Religion is a salvation religion.

Liberal Religion will accept a nonpersonal, nonsupernatural God concept. Max Weber writes that the masses find it difficult to accept an abstract concept of God.[10] However, to conceive of God as the creative force in the Universe is not altogether abstract, no more abstract than electricity. Liberal Religion will use the word "God" (although sparingly) to describe the life force pulsating throughout the Universe. This recalls Thomas Paine's statement that the Creation which he beholds is the only "Word of God" that he recognizes. Therefore the question, "Does God Exist?"—the title of one of Father Küng's tomes and a source of worry for many thoughtful believers— does not arise in Liberal Religion. It can only arise if one doubts the existence of a personal God. In Liberal Religion, the question is the same as "Does the Creation exist?" or "Does the Earth exist?" Of course it does; nobody can even raise the question.

Dietrich Bonhoeffer, a devout Christian, called this abstract concept of God a working hypothesis, and on July 14, 1944 he wrote in one of his last letters from prison: "There is no longer any need for God as a working hypothesis whether in morals, politics, or science. . . . In the name of intellectual honesty, these working hypotheses should be dropped."[11] This did not mean that Bonhoeffer abandoned the God concept altogether. He concluded that: "God is teaching us that we must live as men who can get along very well without Him. The God who makes us in this world without using Him as a working hypothesis is the God before whom we are ever standing. Before God and with Him, we live without God."[12] This is not the place to discuss Bonhoeffer's theology and its deep influence on contemporary theological thinking. Bonhoeffer is quoted here mainly because he characterized the modern use of the God concept as a working hypothesis. The idea has been suggested before and since.[13] Liberal Religionists often use this working hypothesis. The hypothesis is workable. As Harvey Cox states at the end of his book *The Secular City,* "rather than clinging stubbornly to antiquated appellations or anxiously synthesizing new ones, perhaps, like Moses, we must simply take up the work of liberating the captives, confident that we will be granted a new name by events in the future."[14]

Thomas Paine, who regarded most of the Bible's content as mythical, wrote that Psalm 19 conveyed an acceptable idea of God.[15] He quotes the following version of the Psalm which is the one that was put into verse by Addison (1672–1719):

> The spacious firmament on high
> With all their blue etherial sky
> And spangled heavens, a shining frame
> Their great original proclaim . . .

The General Human Assumption

The reason why all civilizations seem to have a concept of God is that few people can comprehend the operations and manifestations of the Universe without assuming a superhuman directing force. Primitive man almost naturally conceived this directing force as a bearded superman in heaven. How else could primitive man explain the terrible forces of nature, the eruption of volcanos, the destructive power of a hurricane, the unrelenting pounding of the sea, or an electrical storm. This image of the white bearded superman still persists in contemporary religious language. It is difficult to imagine that Congress had anything else in mind when it enacted the Universal Military Training and Service Act of 1948, requiring conscientious objectors to prove their belief in a Supreme Being. The same image is reflected in the frequent appellation, "Our Heavenly Father." This is galling to feminists, even those who adhere to Traditional Religion.[16] Weber says that Christianity's success is due to its masculinity and its exclusion of women.[17] In the age of science, the primitive concept has waned.

Human beings still muse about such phenomena as the wondrous manifestations of heredity, the annual reappearance of certain plants, the unaltered change of seasons, and the regularity of migratory bird flights. In the words of Goethe, "the lofty works uncomprehended are bright as on the earliest day,"[18] and man seeks an explanation. Two explanations offer themselves: One is that it all happens by chance, coincidence, or accident. Or secondly, that all is caused by an overriding intelligence and immanent order. The first explanation appeals to few people. Albert Einstein rejected it in his famous remark, "God does not play dice with the world." For most people, the explanation of an overriding intelligence and immanent order seems more likely. Such an assumption may (but need not) be based upon belief in a heavenly father or mother or an anthropomorphic god. Liberal Religion, which disdains belief in an anthropomorphic god, generally agrees with the assumption that there is the presence of an overriding intelligence and immanent order.

The concept of God as the linchpin of the Universe is common to all religions. Liberal Religion does not need the Bible, dogma, or myth to support its reverence for the life force commonly called God. The word "God" is not always liked, but it is so ingrained in our linguistic habits that it would be a waste of time and effort to avoid it. For similar reasons, it does not seem worthwhile to explore the proofs of God's existence which have occupied learned theologians and philosophers since ancient times. No rational argument can convince a thoughtful nonbeliever of a religious truth or of the existence of what is called God. The Religious Liberal simply relies on the conclusions he has reached on the basis of observation and experience.

Theism

Persons who believe in an anthropomorphic God (a deity in human form) are called *theists*. The God of the Bible is, and can only be understood as, an anthropomorphic God who praises and curses, smiles and rages, makes promises and threats, bargains and, in short, has all the attributes of a powerful human. Those who proclaim or have proclaimed the death of God are likewise theists, because they think of God in supernatural anthropomorphic terms. If a person is asked whether he or she believes in God and the answer is in the affirmative, the general assumption is that the question and the answer refer to the personal God of the theists.

Most religionists in the West think of God as a personal deity with whom they have intimate contact. The following story will serve as an illustration. Jesuit Father de Brevery, a friend of Teilhard de Chardin, was employed in the United Nations headquarters in New York. He was offered a field position in Asia, which he wanted to accept if a certain person of his choice would be chosen as his successor. To this end, he went to see the Secretary General, Mr. Hammarskjöld. As he related to his friend, Robert Mueller: "Before entering Hammarskjöld's office, I crossed myself and reminded God that it was essentially his affair."[19] This kind of person-to-person relationship to God is characteristic of the theist.

The traditional Lord's Prayer is addressed to "Our Father who art in Heaven," which assumes, as a matter of course, that God is a fatherly gentleman. It will be recalled that Sigmund Freud thought of God as a powerful father figure who is indispensable to humans. Freud had a narrow view of God, which Liberal Religion does not share.

Some members of the Liberal Church are theists. They may not believe in a supernatural anthropomorphic God, but they cherish a God concept which is equivalent thereto. James Luther Adams, a theist himself, offers the following definition: "God is the inescapable commanding reality that sustains and transforms all meaningful existence."[20] This reality is conceived as something outside of human existence, not a projection of human thought. It is, in short, the Creation itself. God is revered as the creative principle. Some liberal theists utter beseeching prayers to God while insisting that their God is not a supernatural person but the evolutionary process. They pray to the process. It may be a bit puzzling and ambiguous but it is comforting that the liberal theist does not insist that the Liberal Church embrace his or her God concept. Says Professor Adams, "The word of God is so heavily laden with unacceptable connotations that it is for many people scarcely usable without confusion."[21]

Many modern ecclesiastics—inside and outside of the Liberal churches—who use the word "God" and pray to God, assure us that the word is merely a symbol, a poetic expression. The trouble here is that poetry in a foreign language is difficult to understand. To translate or interpret the word "God," requires a reasoning process that many people dislike, especially when they attend a worship service and are in a religious, as distinguished from a purely intellectual, mood. Most of those who use God-language think of God as an entity in human form.

The Alternatives to Theism

The alternatives to theism are: deism, agnosticism, atheism, and humanism. *Deism* is a derivative form of theism. We will now turn to an investigation of these various positions.

Deism: In the screenplay *Oh! God,* the actor George Burns portrays God in a business suit. When someone criticizes him for all the evil in the world, God (Burns) becomes very indignant. "I did not create the evil," he says, "I gave you humans a perfectly good world, but you messed it up." This, in a nutshell, is the theological doctrine in which the founders of the American republic and men like Thomas Paine are reported to have believed. If that is so, the reference to the Almighty and to the Creator in the Declaration of Independence is compatible with modern thinking. It frees the God concept from the responsibility for the evil in the world; it also eliminates the assumption of Traditional Religion that God is omnipotent and omniscient. If God were omnipotent and omniscient, he would hardly be worthy of the admiration accorded to him by Traditional Churches, because such attributes would make him responsible for the unadorned evils in the world. This is what learned theologians call the problem of theodicy, namely, how to justify calling God good in the face of evil.

The difference between the theist and the deist is that the former assigns operational responsibility to God, whereas the God of the deist has retired from operational responsibility. This is, to be sure, an oversimplified statement of deistic religious beliefs. Jefferson, Franklin, Paine and most of the Founding Fathers of the American republic are recognized as deists,[22] and in England the religion is centuries old. It is significant that the most important authors writing on the subject of deism are not professional theologians. It is also significant that deism stresses rationality and rejects all unreasonable elements of Traditional Religion. Charles Blount (1654–1693) wrote the first treatise on deism, called *Oracle of Reason.* In the book, he denounced as absurd the doctrine of Original Sin.[23] The English deists of the seventeenth century blamed the corruption of religion on its extraneous supernaturalism of impostering apostles, self-interested priests, Jews, and heathens.[24] The outstanding French deists were Voltaire and Rousseau. Among the Germans, Gotthold Ephraim Lessing and Kant can be classified as deists. All deists, except Voltaire, professed adherence to Christianity and merely rejected what they held to be a violation of rationality. It has therefore been said that the deists rejected historical Christianity but accepted pure and original Christianity. Thomas Paine in his *Age of Reason,* has summarized the position as follows: "The true Deist has but one Deity; and his religion consists in contemplating the power, wisdom, and benignity of the Deity in his works, and in endeavoring to imitate him in everything moral, scientific, and mechanical."[25]

The deist doctrine of God is not the same as the "Death of God" theory which stirred up so much ecclesiastical dust in the 1960s. Only those who believed in a supernatural, personal God had to grapple with the question as to whether God was still operative or dead. For the deists and the humanists—the two major elements of the Liberal Church—the question did not arise. They simply revere the creative force of the Universe.

The philosophical theory of *agnosticism* states that it is impossible for man to attain knowledge of God. In contemporary practice, agnosticism is a religious cop-out, a refusal to commit oneself. Agnostics are neither theists, deists, atheists, or humanists. They do not know what to believe. Agnostics who attend the Liberal Church are not doing so in order to "play it safe," as Pascal advised. They do it because they share the reverence for life which they find in the Liberal Church.

The religious agnostics do not seem to have progressed much since the year 400 B.C., when the book of Job was written. It will be recalled that in that ancient poem Job, a good person, suffered grieviously and he questioned why he must suffer while evil persons prosper. The author of the story cannot answer that question; he does not know. The only possible explanation is that (the anthropomorphic) God knows best—an explanation which the Liberal Church cannot accept.

The scientist Carl Sagan writes that his research has not proven that God exists, nor has he found compelling evidence of the nonexistence of God.[26] This is another way to describe an agnostic. Agnostics say they do not know; they suspend judgment.

Agnostics are welcome in the Liberal Church—agnostics who still search for answers. Indeed, the search for truth is one of the tenets of the Liberal Religion, a topic that will be discussed in Chapter 6.

Atheism: Atheists are also welcomed in the Liberal Church. They are popularly perceived as enemies of God, and, for that reason, Traditional Religion distrusts them. Actually, an atheist is a person who says that he lives without a God concept. The fact that Liberal Religion embraces atheists makes it highly suspicious to Traditional Religion. The Romans called Jews and Christians atheists because they did not participate in the emperor worship. Plato called atheists people who believed that sacrifices or flattery could influence the gods. Ancient rabbis denounced the atheists as Epicureans because the Greek philosopher Epicurus (342–270 B.C.) did not believe that the gods interfered in human affairs. They called Adam an atheist since, by hiding from God, he denied God's omnipresence.

Atheism is the collective name for an attitude towards religion without a belief in God. The Bible labels as fools those who reject belief in Jehovah. The Church persecuted them and burned them at the stake. After the Second Vatican Council in 1965, the Roman Catholic Church endeavored to be more understanding and regarded atheism, which was still rejected, as a mental illness. The Church, one document said, must strive to detect in the atheist's mind the hidden causes for his denial of God.[27] The common image of an atheist is a person who does not believe in a supernatural God. In a more sophisticated sense, an atheist is a nontheist. Thus, Erich Fromm calls himself a "nontheistic mystic."[28] Buddhists are atheists.[29]

Past efforts of true believers to convince an atheist of the existence of God generally failed because the efforts were too contrived. A charming exception is told of Diderot (1715-1784) who paid a visit to the Russian Court and made a big speech about atheism there. He was then invited to a debate with the mathematician Euler, a theist. At the debate, Euler hurled a meaningless but complicated algebraic formula at Diderot, asserting that the formula proved the existence of God and inviting Diderot to disprove it. Diderot did not understand algebra, was embarrassed, and forthwith returned to France.

More typical was the argument of Saint Anselm (1033-1100), Archbishop of Canterbury, whose proof of the existence of God is summarized by the Cornell astronomer Carl Sagan as follows: "Since we can imagine a perfect being, he must exist because he would not be perfect without the added perfection of existence." This so-called ontological argument was promptly attacked on two grounds: (1) *Can* we imagine a completely perfect being, and (2) Is it obvious that perfection is augmented by existence? Professor Sagan does not accept this argument for the existence of God on the grounds that it assumes what it intends to prove.[30] To the modern ear, such pious arguments seem to be about words and definitions, rather than about external reality.[31]

Thomas Paine (1737-1809), whom the late President Theodore Roosevelt called a dirty little atheist, wrote, "What more does man want to know than that the hand or power that made these things is divine, is omnipotent." He continues:

> I know I did not make myself, and yet I have existence, and by searching into the nature of things, I find out that no other thing could make itself; and yet millions of other things exist, therefore, it is that I know by positive conclusions resulting from the search, that there is a power superior to all these things, and that power is God.[32]

As the utterance of Theodore Roosevelt exemplifies, atheism is a swear word in American politics. In his 1960 presidential campaign, Richard Nixon said that everybody is qualified for the presidency except atheists. This aroused the late Bishop James Pike into stating that, in his experience, atheists generally cared more about ultimate questions than Christians.[33]

Generally, atheists shun the word "God." And yet, people who call themselves atheists will be heard to say, "I got rid of my cold, thank God" or, thanking God for some other good fortune. When confronted, the atheist will say he or she did not mean it, and one can be certain that he or she did not wish to thank that old whitebearded, anthropomorphic God. But, is the atheist grateful to some other God? Paul Tillich denies that there are atheists in the world, because, as he says, everybody reveres some power or some principle. Madalyn Murray O'Hair, the leader of atheism in America, who, a few years ago in Texas, established the Center for Atheism, is as fervently dedicated to her cause as a Savonarola. The phrases "Godless Communism" and "Atheist Marxism" refer to the fact that the followers of Marx and Lenin do not revere the God of Traditional Western Religion. They worship at different altars. Words like "Godless Communism" raise one's intellectual hackles. That expression disregards any God concept other than the belief in a supernatural God. The speaker seems to be unable to denounce Communism without dragging in religion.

The phrase "there are no atheists in foxholes" has a different connotation. The idea here is that soldiers in foxholes are naturally afraid and, in their fear, they are driven to pray to a supernatural, personal God. When the writer once visited a hospital ward, a very old woman, obviously in great pain and not quite conscious, cried, "Mama, Mama!" It is possible that people in distress seek relief and comfort from some remote quarter. This can hardly be regarded as a religious impulse. It does not prove the atheist wrong.

The Anglican Bishop Robinson, in his book *Honest to God,* says he has "a great deal of sympathy with those who call themselves atheists. For the God they are tilting against, the God they honestly feel they cannot believe in, is so often an image of God instead of God."[34]

Erich Fromm characterizes atheism as a declaration of independence from the principle of a supreme ruler, rather than an answer to the spiritual problem of man.[35] This means that atheism is not more than anti-theism; and that, like theism, it regards a personal God as essential to religion.

In Liberal Religion the idea of atheism is irrelevant. While the name of God is sometimes invoked as a convenient word (and for lack of a better word), God is not essential to Liberal Religion. If a person denies God, in so doing, he does not necessarily deny religion. The venom with which many Traditionalists speak of atheism signals hysteria rather than reason. A typical example occurred during the war between Iran and Iraq. An Iranian mullah denounced an Iraqi bomb as an atheist missile.

Humanism: Humanism represents a radical departure from theism. In theism God is the centerpiece of religion; in humanism man is the centerpiece. In the words of Protagoras (481–411 B.C.), "man is the measure of all things." All religious values are human values. Every pronouncement of the divine reflects human thought. Humanism does not recognize any revelation from without—no supernatural divinity.

Voltaire said that if God did not exist, he would have to be invented. The word "invention" implies a conscious human effort, such as the construction of the golden calf by the Israelites in the desert. This is not the humanists' way. What Voltaire should have said is that God, like electricity, is a discovery of the human mind. That is why humanism places man rather than God at the center of things.

A fine, nontheological description of humanism is found in the 1970 prospectus for the new magazine *Smithsonian*:

> Man has reached peaks of development when his honesty of purpose, his sense of responsibility, and his love of beauty combined to create what we call civilization. Man, who he is, how he got there, where he is going, how he lives and dies, what he does and what is done to him; man in his present state, untidy, often demoralized, ever hopeful, solving problems and creating new ones, crowding this planet but reaching beyond the moon, both violently destructive and endlessly creative, he is the most interesting subject in the world.

The difference between religious humanists and theists is primarily one of emphasis. Both are reverent in face of the Creation. As Professor Adams sees it, "they differ in defining the context in which human existence and human good are to be understood."[36] Religious humanists do not wish to be called atheists, because they have a reverence for a nonpersonal, nonanthropomorphic divinity concept. Erich Fromm describes his essentially humanistic position as "nontheistic mysticism."[37] When reverent, the theist bends his/her knees, the humanist stands erect.

Because the word "God" carries so much traditional and, to many humanists, unacceptable religious ballast, humanists generally have an aversion to the word—except, perhaps, when they listen to one of Johann Sebastian Bach's passions. Religious humanism, while worshipping the immanent power and the unity of the Universe, has not yet found a substitute word for "God."

While humanists will at times use the word "God," they definitely do not accept or think of the anthropomorphic God of the theists. Humanists, like Emerson, believe God to be entirely impersonal. Like Emerson, they think of God as the common nature—the nature which is common to all—the energy which moves the Universe itself.

William James describes modern transcendentalism and Emerson's religion in terms that may appeal to humanists, even though Emerson might not have accepted the classification: "No deity in concreto, not a superhuman person, but the immanent divinity of things, the essentially spiritual structure of the universe is the object of the transcendentalist's cult." James then cites Emerson's Divinity School address which advocated the worship of abstract notions. "Emersonianism seems to let God evaporate in abstract Ideality."[38] The word "evaporate" here denotes spirituality. The immanent divinity of things and the essentially spiritual structure of the Universe are incompatible with the Traditional theistic God who made covenants in a manner which restricts his own freedom, as well as that of humankind.

It would be presumptious to classify Emerson as a humanist. The term did not exist during his time. But the following passage in his divinity address comes close to the position of today's religious humanist: "He [Jesus] saw that God incarnates himself in man, and evermore goes forth anew to take possession of his world. He said in his jubilee of sublime emotion: 'I am divine. Through me God acts; through me he speaks. Would you see God, see me; or see thee when thou also thinketh as I now think.'"

In 1980 a group of distinguished scholars issued a document in which they denounced the spreading influence of fundamentalist thinking and extolled what they called "secular humanism."[39] In calling humanism secular, they perpetuated the habit of drawing a distinction between what is worldly and what is sacred, a distinction which is terminological rather than real.[40]

It is nevertheless a fact that "secular humanism" is the name which the evangelicals and the Moral Majority Movement bestow on what they consider an evil ideology. In the lawsuit by which two fundamentalist organizations sought to prevent the Smithsonian Institution in Washington, D.C., from spending public funds for an exhibit on evolution, the plaintiffs asserted that the exhibit supported the religion of secular humanism, which they sought to smear by stating that secular humanism was a religion which also favored the right to divorce, universal education, birth control, and a world community.[41] Secular humanism is, as stated above, one of the targets of the Moral Majority Movement. At a recent national meeting of Christian evangelicals, attendants were urged to fight "secular humanism," which was described as the established religion of America and the enemy of Christianity.[42] Reverend Falwell, the leader of Moral Majority, declared at the same meeting, that it would take a long time to repair the damage caused by "secular humanism."[43] The secular humanists, or all humanists, are not as powerful and influential as the fundamentalists seem to believe. What emerges, however, is that the term "secular humanism" is here to stay.

Some Liberal Religionists, by virtue of their stress on individual freedom of belief, are apt to over-emphasize their particular brand of Liberal Religion when they theorize about religion. Happily, in real life Liberal Religionists are not so analytical. Humanists (of whatever hue) join with theists, deists, agnostics, and atheists in their common Religious Liberalism. It is well to close this survey by recalling the life of Charles Darwin, one of our spiritual ancestors. In his autobiography, Darwin expresses disdain for Christianity,[44] calls himself a theist,[45] then an agnostic,[46] and confesses to rationalism.[47] His children were baptized and confirmed in the local Anglican Church, but educated as Unitarians.

The "God is Love" Concept

Everybody loves love. Love has many facets. It is no denigration of love to say that the sweeping statement "God is love" is an empty phrase. It is an invention of Paul and his contemporaries. However, it is not an empty phrase to the true believer in Paul's Christian religion, which is based upon the wretchedness of man. The wretched person is naturally comforted by the assurance that God loves him/her. It seems that, figuratively speaking, Traditional Religion first knocks the believer to the ground and then administers first aid with the statement that God loves him or her. The creative force in the Universe can wright terrible mischief, as in the case of earthquakes, hurricanes, and similar disasters which the law calls Acts of God. The phrase "God is love," therefore, is not appropriate in Liberal Religion's theology.

One of the great catastrophies of prehistorical days—one which is told in a variety of traditions—is what the Bible calls the Great Flood. According to biblical tradition, God became displeased with his own creation and decided to drown it, destroying every living thing and being, except Noah the alcoholic, and the beasts Noah could round up. God thereby certainly did not demonstrate any love for the world.

Isaiah exclaims Jehovah's love for His people (Isa. 54:5), but he also says that this love is based upon pity. Love based upon pity is not true love. At best it is compassion, which is a different matter entirely. In fairness to the Old Testament, it should be added that the Prophet Hosea extols pure divine love and, for that reason, is regarded as having profoundly influenced the leaders of Judeo-Christian religion who came after him. In the fourth gospel, which is permeated with romantic and mysterious notions, John says that "God so loved the world that He gave up His only begotten son" (1 John 2:16). In other words, God demonstrated his love by having his son killed, which is reminiscent of Abraham's willingness to kill his son. Such bloody sacrifices are not unusual in primitive societies. The Liberal Church today cannot see anything religious in such a repulsive practice; and it certainly is not proof of God's love, as contemporary Traditional Religion asserts.

In Verdi's opera, Don Carlo the king asks the Grand Inquisitor whether it would be compatible with his (the king's) Christian religion to have his son assassinated. The Grand Inquisitor replies that such killing would be quite proper, and he cites as his authority the gospel story according to which God has his own son killed for the greater good of the world. This operatic anecdote illustrates Traditional Religion's perverted notion of divine love.

Liberal Religion does not abjure love. It exalts love and values it highly. But it does not pretend that the world is all love, and it does not demand that each person must love all others.

The love of God is a concept that permeates biblical religion. In the book of Isaiah, as translated in the Jerusalem Bible, we read:

I did foresake you for a brief moment
But with great love will I take you back

In excess of anger, for a moment
I hid my face from you
But with everlasting love I have taken pity on you
Says Yaweh, your redeemer. (Isa. 54:7)

These poetic words signify the indulgent love of a temperamental father for his errant child. This is one side of Traditional Religion. The other side is that the love of God demands that God's creatures must love God and each other. The Apostle John said bluntly, "He that loves not knoweth not God, for God is love" (1 John 4:8). And what is the proof of God's love? "God has sent his son into the world that we might live through him" (1 John 4:9). John also said: "Love not the world, neither the things that are in the world. If any man loves the world, the love of the Father is not in him" (1 John 2:15). This means that God loves his children, but not the world in which they live and which presumably he has created. God, according to this teaching, is an anti-secularist.

It is all a bit confusing. In Traditional Religion, there does not seem to be a clear distinction between the love of God, the love to God, and the love among God's creatures. The confusion is compounded by a linguistic problem. Paul's famous paean, "Though I speak with the tongues of angels" (1 Cor. 13:14), uses the word "love" in the Jerusalem Bible, but in the St. James version it reads "charity."

Liberal Religion need not concern itself with such theological gymnastics. Religious Liberals love the Universe and consider themselves parts of its creative forces. But they do not expect love in return. James Luther Adams calls this selfless love the love of God—the word "God" denoting the power that holds the world together.[48] Adams believes in reciprocity. He says men cannot feel the love of God unless they have first received it.[49] He speaks, of course, from the viewpoint of the Liberal Christian. Tillich, on the other hand, does not seem to hold to such reciprocity. He says that, according to Lutheran theology, God created the world for the purpose of having an object which he could love. The implication is, as Tillich says, that God needs something that he could not have unless he created it. Reciprocal love from the creation to God does not appear to be expected.[50]

The ancient Jewish command "Love thy neighbor as thyself," which Paul called the quintessence of the law, sounds fine, but it is an inadequate ethical standard for the modern world. Many people today do not love or even like themselves. That is why they flock to psychiatrists, psychologists, ecclesiastical counselors, and confessionals. What the Liberal Church requires is compassion for one's fellow man and one's neighbors, regardless of whether or not one loves oneself. Christianity claims to be the religion of love. Most followers of Christianity evidence very little love. The late scientist Father Teilhard de Chardin wrote, "Christian love is incomprehensible to those who have not experienced it."[51] The world has not experienced it since Francis of Assisi. Father Teilhard de Chardin does not tell whether he himself has experienced it. One knows, however, that his ecclesiastical superiors forbade him to publish the results of his scientific research to which he had devoted a lifetime. Chapter 8 has more to say on the subject of Christian love.

Because the word "love" is equivocal, theologians frequently prefer to substitute the New Testament word "agape" to distinguish the spiritual aspect of love from the sexual and erotic. In the *Festschrift* for James Luther Adams, Tillich wrote, "Christian love is not dependent upon trinitarian or antitrinitarian or other dogmatic tradition, but upon the divine spirit which grasps men of all creeds through the power which is manifest in Jesus as the Christ."[52]

Here again, God and Divine Love seem to be limited by the perimeter of Christianity, which is unacceptable and unbelievable to the universality of Liberal Religion.

The Will of God

It should also be said that the traditional reference to the "Will of God" is inappropriate and even repugnant to Liberal Religion. The "Will of God" is a fiction. That this phrase in reality reflects the will of those who assert it is demonstrated by biblical history. The earliest parts of the Bible deal with a very primitive people. They engaged in bloodshed and cruelty to their enemies, which their leaders said was the "Will of God." When, centuries later, the Prophet Amos came on the scene, God's Will had softened. Amos merely threatened that God would cause famine and smite the places of worship.

A person may assert that vaccination is against the "Will of God." He may be convinced that this is so. However, the strength of a person's conviction does not prove its truth.

When the evangelist Oral Roberts was engaged in a fund raising campaign, he announced that God told him to build a new medical school building for Oral Roberts University. Many other humans claim to have been so addressed by God. Joan of Arc had her voices. The priests of ancient Greece who issued decrees made obedience thereto easier by announcing that they were merely transmitting messages from their divine masters. The Spartan lawmaker Lycurgus did the same and as Durant wittily added, "this was not the first time that a state had laid its foundation in the sky."[53] The ancient Athenians, being very rational people, would not be so deceived. When Solon developed the constitution and a body of law revolutionizing the economy and the administration of justice, he made no claim that he was transmitting divine commands. The empire which was established by

Charlemagne and lasted until Napoleon, was called the "Holy Roman Empire" signifying the claim to divine sanction. It is understandable that the old Hebrew prophets claimed to carry a message from the Lord, otherwise the primitive crowds would not have given credence to the message. The fact is, of course, that these prophets merely communicated their own thoughts. The "Will of God" has always been, and is today, an expression of the wishes of the person who proclaims it. In thus proclaiming messages from God, these religious spokesmen treat God as a veritable ventriloquist.

While such proclamations have at least some inspirational grandeur if uttered by an Amos or Hosea, they sound downright petty and arrogant in the humdrum incantations of Traditional Religion. And yet, most Traditional Religionists pretend to know the "Will of God." The perversity of this attitude is epitomized by the prayers of warring factions, for example, those in Dublin and Ulster, Ireland. Each side asserts that God wants to destroy the other. To cite another example, the missionary who is bent on conversion knows that his/her work is God's Will even if the victim of his/her efforts leads a virtuous life and adheres to a respectable religion. Characteristic also is the experience of a grandmother who repeatedly refused the strong demand of a four-year-old child, the daughter of a Baptist minister. Finally, the exasperated child cried, "but God wants you to do this." The child had learned the magic words of Traditional Religion.

The Fear of God

Jehovah wanted to be feared by the Israelites. If they strayed from the path, if they disobeyed the commands, he terrified them in order to instill the fear of God. That is how the fear of God came to play an important part. To live in the fear of God is supposed to be a virtue. Liberal Religion must reject this idea altogether. If God is good, why fear him? The answer which suggests itself is that the Israelites constantly violated the commandments of their religion, as did their religious heirs in Judaism and Christianity. Only an intimidating threat of God outlining the dire consequences of misconduct could keep people in line. Good behavior could only be induced by fear. The fear of God became a synonym for the upright conduct which the fear instilled. The fear became a virtue. In a passage of the delightful book of wisdom called Ecclesiasticus (25:11)—not to be confused with Ecclesiastes—which is not included in the King James Bible, we read: "No one excels the man who fears the Lord, the fear of the Lord surpasses everything. What can compare with a man who has masterd that?"

A more conventional example is found in King Solomon's prayer at the dedication of the temple, in which he implores God to let the people fear him (1 Kings 8:40). It is interesting to note that this same passage is differently phrased in the more modern Jerusalem Bible. There Solomon is quoted as asking God to let the people revere him. Fear becomes reverence. This may be a difference in translation; it may be a difference in accent; or it may be a difference in substance. This is a problem for learned Bible scholars. It is conceivable that the fear of God should be understood as "awe" or "dread," which would give the entire concept a different connotation and, as such, might become reconcilable with the concepts of Liberal Religion.

Traditional Religion does not mean this. When it refers to fear, it means the psychological condition of the terror-stricken person who is terrified of God Almighty. In Psalm 2, we read, "Serve the Lord with fear, and rejoice with trembling." And in Psalm 34, "I will teach you the fear of the Lord." Paul admonished the Philippians to work out their own salvation with "fear and trembling" (Phil. 2:12). In Acts, speaking about the earlier missionary efforts of Paul (then still Saul), it is reported that the churches in Judea, Galilee, and Samaria were content and "walking in the fear" of the Lord (Acts 9:31). In the Book of Revelation (14:7), an angel from heaven is envisioned saying with a loud voice, "Fear God and give glory to him."

And lastly, *Fear and Trembling* is the title of a book by the Danish theologian Søren Kierkegaard (1813–1855), who was moved by what he regarded as the precariousness of human existence, and who is considered the father of modern existentialism.

All this is alien to Liberal Religion. It cannot glorify what it fears. It has no fear of God, or of the Universe, or the life force which it affirms and reveres.

God and the Law

God plays an important role in the law. If lightning strikes a barn and the barn burns down, the event is called an "act of God"—and so is an earthquake or any other damaging incident for which no person can be held responsible. Acts of God, as the law uses that term, are always disasters. And yet, in all New York courtrooms, and possibly in other courtrooms, there is an inscription on the wall over the bench and facing the public, reading, "In God We Trust." The implication is that the justice which one seeks from the judge on the bench is not adequate, trust in God if you seek justice.

The attorney general of California recently ruled that the phrase, "In God We Trust" on United States coins has no religious significance. For the same reason he saw no religious significance in the Biblical quotation on the cover of a telephone book, "And God said, Let there be light, and there was light." The attorney general seemed to tell us that the word "God" is just a meaningless expression. It is not so understood, and the people who ordered it painted above the judicial benches in New York did not so understand it.

Rather, they hark back to the idea that God is the supreme lawgiver, as was Jehovah who handed down the Ten Commandments to Moses.

The Biblical concept of God as the source of the law is reflected in the philosophical theory of natural law. That theory assumes the existence of law which is higher than the manmade law which evolves through the legislatures and judicial decisions. A New York judge recently ruled that the fifth commandment supersedes a statute which was enacted by "mere mortals." The doctrine of natural law and its incompatibility with Liberal Religion are discussed in Chapter 14.

When in our civil or criminal proceedings a witness is sworn in, he is asked "to tell the truth, and nothing but the truth, so help me God." Most witnesses swear this oath and, one suspects, without giving much thought to God. Devout Jews and most atheists object, though. Devout Jews object to swearing as they feel that the oath would require them to take the name of the Lord in vain. Atheists are just allergic to the use of the word "God." Liberal Religion will not object to the use of the word "God" by a person to whom the word is meaningful. It will object if the word is parroted mindlessly. The law does not really require the words, "so help me God." It is enough to solemnly affirm that one's testimony will be truthful. The irony of the situation is that the false oath of convicted perjurers has generally been wrapped in the incantation, "so help me God."

The God of History

There is still another cloak in which God is presented in Liberal as well as Traditional pulpits. Theologians speak of the God of history or the Lord of history. Victor Murray points out that Psalms 95–100 represent God as the controller of history.[54] According to the Bible, God is very history conscious. He reminds Moses that He is the God of Abraham, Isaac, and Jacob (Exod. 3:6), a reference which is frequently repeated in the New Testament. God often reminds the Israelites that it was he who freed their ancestors from Egyptian bondage. By the same token, God would be responsible for the liberation of the American colonies and the bombing of Hiroshima.

This is a rather insupportable way of looking at history. In the introduction to the *Systematic Theology,* Tillich denounces the use of the term "Lord of history,"[55] but then he writes that the reality of God is a "directing authority,"[56] which seems to mean that God directs the Creation and what is going on in it. That theme appears again in Tillich's third volume.[57] In the introduction to volume II, Tillich speaks of the "riddle of history" which he sees as part of life. He also teaches that, in Christianity, Jesus, as the Christ, is the center of history; but in volume III, under the heading "History and the Christ," he tells us that, after an atomic explosion of the world, Christ may become an irrelevancy. It is not intended here to wrestle with the teachings of Tillich. The references are made to show why it happened that God was linked with history at all. According to Traditional Religion, history will end when the world comes to an end. Tillich's final chapter is devoted to the "End of History." He points out that the word "end" has two meanings: (a) termination, and (b) aim.[58] The aim, theologically speaking, is eternal life. Either way, it is understandable that, in Traditional Religion, God is considered the Governor and the Lord of history. When the end is reached, he will transform himself from the Lord of history to the Lord of justice who sits in judgment over the resurrected bodies, as depicted by Michelangelo in the Sistine Chapel.

All this is unacceptable to a thoughtful Religious Liberal. That God governs history is an idea plagued by several flaws. For one thing, history is accident prone. For instance, if Napoleon had not suffered a blackout on the battlefield of Waterloo, history might have taken a different turn. Of course, it is always possible to believe that God, in the manner of Jehovah in the Old Testament, cursed Napoleon and inflicted the blackout upon him, but Religious Liberals cannot believe this. Secondly, world history has just begun. Until recently world history was a conglomeration of national histories. There is no real history of humankind. Again, it is possible to believe that each national history was governed and guided by a national God or by the universal God, but Liberal Religion does not accept this either.

Lastly, Liberal Religion rejects the idea of the end of history in either of the two senses of the word which Tillich puts forth. The end of time has been predicted many times. Jesus and his followers expected it momentarily. Bishop Usher calculated the exact date of the end of the world and that date has passed. Others had to revise their predictions several times because the expected event did not occur. The scientific discoveries of the present age have made us aware that a blowup may occur any day. And yet, we expect to live, and history will continue. As Berman says, this is a rebuttable presumption,[59] but nobody so far has attempted the rebuttal. Science tells us to be pessimists; and yet, human vitality is such that we live with the conviction of on-going existence. This conviction can be explained only by a divine spark in us and, in this narrow sense, even Liberal Religion can accept the concept of God in history.

According to Erich Fromm, human history began against the plan of God. To Fromm, the rebellion in the Garden of Eden and the consequent expulsion from the garden marks the beginning of human history "because it is the beginning of human freedom."[60]

It is better to make history than to suffer it. If history is understood as an active force causing events to happen, Liberal Religion, as an activist religion, must align itself with history. It could then, and in that sense, accept the term "God of history."

The Holy Spirit

If one conceives God as the spiritual aspect of human endeavor or human existence, Liberal Religion has no difficulty with the concept of the spirit of God or the divine spirit. Its habitat is the soul, (see Chapter 11). Neither does one have a problem with the Bible passage "My spirit shall not always strive with man" (Gen. 6:3), which merely signifies that man is not always infused with spirituality. It is far more difficult to conceive the spirit of God as an independent part of God. This trinitarian view of God offends rationality and is incompatible with Liberal Religion's reverence for the unity and integration of life.

The difficulty of explaining the Holy Spirit as some purely spiritual force is also demonstrated by the Bible story of Mary's conception. The Holy Spirit is supposed to have cast its shadow upon her without physical contact. A shadow presupposes the existence of a substance. Traditional Religion cannot explain the Holy Spirit except in corporeal terms. In medieval paintings, the event of Pentecost is depicted as an outpouring of a liquid substance.

While modern Bible translations and liturgies speak of the Holy Spirit, the King James version refers to the Holy Ghost, possibly because that phrase conveys the idea of the spirit in a more anthropomorphic, human image. The triple divinity of the Father, the Son, and the Holy Spirit is a concept found in ancient Rome, Greece, India, and China, and is, therefore, not unique to Christianity.[61] St. Augustine had already said that the trinity is an image which is very remote.[62] It has no Biblical roots. Nevertheless, it is the source of much theological strife. For instance, there is the argument known by the Latin phrase "filioque" which concerns the question of whether the Holy Spirit proceeds from the Father to the Son and then to man or directly from Father to man.[63] To Liberal Religion this is just more evidence of the irrationality of the Trinity concept. To Liberal Religion the Holy Spirit can only be understood as the divine spirit permeating the entire Universe and is identical with the power revered by Liberal Religion and sometimes called by the name "God."

Liberal Religion accepts the statement of the Roman Catholic theologian Küng that the Holy Spirit is at work not only on Catholics or Christians, but in the whole world.[64] The logical extension of this thought is that Traditional Religion has no monopoly on holiness.

The concept of holiness is not alien to Liberal Religion. An example one may cite is Edwin Wilson's hymn: "Where is our holy Church? Where race and class unite, As equal persons in the search for beauty, truth, and right." It then speaks about the holy writ, the holy person, and the holy land. The hymn defies the traditional view about holiness. The Lutheran theologian Rudolf Otto wrote an extremely lucid and readable book about the idea of the holy. To him, holy is the extra dimension in life which is nonrational and otherworldly. He calls it "numinous," a word derived from the Latin word "numen." Numen is very common in theological parlance, and it means "divine power." According to Otto, the numinous holy element in religion is outside of the self,[65] and for that reason, distinct from Liberal Religion. Otto prefaces one of his chapters with the quotation, "A God comprehended is no God."[66] This indicates that his concepts are alien to Liberal Religion, which insists that it desires to comprehend what it reveres as holy. Otto concludes that the essence of the numinous holy must be understood as a mystical apprehension of spiritual as distinct from profane values. What Otto refers to as mysterious apprehension is a mood everybody experiences at times, for instance, when he or she comes upon the vistas of a snowcapped mountain or rides through the night, as in the earlier illustration. If one yields to one's mood and retreats from rationality, it is not an indication that one is unable to reason. Liberal Religion knows that there are limits to one's reasoning power but, as will be discussed later (see Chapter 6), the truth is marching on: The holy and the Holy Spirit are not by definition beyond comprehension.

Conclusion

The God concept so permeates our civilization that one cannot ignore it, whether one believes or not. As was said at the beginning of this chapter, God is not essential to Liberal Religion. One can be religious without using or thinking of the word. Some adherents of Liberal Religion associate "God" with Old Whitebeard, the supernatural, personal God of the Bible, as depicted in the Sistine Chapel. Liberal Religion has no reverence for that personal God. But reverence does exist for the life force pulsating through the Universe, the creative and ever recreating life which we experience. Many in Liberal Religion think of this when the word "God" is used.

Professor Hans Küng recently published a learned tome entitled *Does God Exist?* As was said above, in Liberal Religion this question makes as little sense as the question whether the solar system exists. Father Küng's book is a veritable storehouse of almost overwhelming learning. Professor Küng obviously has absorbed the world literature on the subject of God. While he seems to treat all facets of the topic with detached objectivity, this Roman Catholic theologian naturally affirms the existence of a personal God, although in a sophisticated manner. He concedes that the Old Whitebeard image, which is common in Traditional Religion, is preposterous. However, he clings to the personal God concept which, he says, may also be called transpersonal or superpersonal.[67] This new terminology does not alter substance, and Liberal Religion rejects it.

Küng draws a distinction between the Biblical God, which has a name, and what he calls the philosophical God, which is nameless:

> The philosophers' concept of God is abstract and indeterminate
> The God of the philosophers remains nameless
> He does not reveal himself.
>
> The biblical faith in God is concrete and determinate
> The God of Israel [in Küng's book, this is also the Christian God]
>   bears a name and demands a decision
> He reveals himself in history as he who is, as he who will be,
>   guiding, helping, strengthening.[68]

Clearly, the God of Liberal Religion does not belong in the second category. The God of Liberal Religion is nameless, not a person. It is an abstract concept. To some in Liberal Religion, it may even be a philosophical concept. To most, it is more. It is the concept of the immanent creative power in the Universe which induces an instinctive and intuitive reverence. Father Küng does not recognize this reverence as religious because he does not recognize a religion with a "nameless" (nonpersonal) God. Although Professor Küng knows that different religions have different Gods, these Gods to him are always personal Gods. He writes:

> The understanding of God on the part of the [nonbiblical] religions
>   as a whole is definite but not coherent
> The gods of the religions display may contrast in names and natures,
> They contradict and refute one another, it is impossible to believe
>   all of them at the same time.
> A rationally justifiable decision is required.
>
> The biblical faith in God is in itself coherent, it is also rationally justifiable and has proved itself historically over many thousands of years.
>
> The God of Israel is for believers, the one, sole God who has no other gods besides him.
>
> He bears unmistakable the one named Yaweh, man is to believe in him alone.[69]

Liberal Religion must admit that the biblical faith in God is coherent. That it has proved itself over thousands of years is correct in the sense that most people in the West, and those who were converted, have professed adherence to it and still do. Liberal Religion discerns, however, that these professions are hollow and do not reflect the convictions nor the deeds of the proclaimers. Liberal Religion observes a waning of biblical faith because,

Father Küng to the contrary, it is not rationally justifiable. Martin Luther, who had the same faith as Father Küng, recognized this.[70]

Unlike our Halfway Liberal Religionists,[71] Father Küng does not believe that science and religion belong to different realms. Küng discusses the problem of science and religion at length and asserts that the biblical God controls science. Unlike the Moral Majority and other American conservatives, he affirms the theory of evolution, as did Teilhard de Chardin, the famed Jesuit. Küng writes:

> God does not operate on the world from above or from outside as unmoved mover, but from within as the dynamic, most real reality in the process of evolution of the world, which he makes possible, directs and completes. He does not operate above the world process but in the world process in, with, and among human beings and things. He is himself source, center, and god of the world process.[72]

According to Küng, science has a place in religion because God controls it. He is critical of Albert Einstein, even of his famous saying that God plays no dice. In rebuttal, Küng quotes another scientist:

> Does God play dice then? Certainly. But he also follows his rules for the game. And only the gap between the two provides both meaning and freedom.[73]

But then Küng advances scientific arguments against the proposition that God makes rules for the game.[74]

Einstein, a representative of Liberal Religion, would not tolerate vague notions. Küng, a representative of Traditional Religion, prefers a scientist who sees in the unexplored part of the universe "something more profound playing a role . . . in the field of natural sciences."[75]

Professor Küng, in proclaiming faith in the personal God, admits unequivocally "There is no proof of God."[76] In an earlier book, he stated that the Church "is primarily there not to be admired nor to be criticized but to be believed."[77]

By using Professor Küng as a foil against which to summarize Liberal Religion's view of God, full justice has not been done to this very learned theologian. On the other hand, it is helpful to the aim of this book to take the measure of Liberal Religion against this modern and sophisticated representative of Traditional Religion.

4

Reason and Faith

Rationality

Rationality is the keynote to the Liberal Religious faith. Any faith that cannot withstand the test of rationality is rejected. How does one apply the test? What is to count as rational? Conformity with the principles of reason is usually known by instinct or experience. Instinct, however, is not scientifically acceptable. Experience is a more respectable test; it is the basis of so-called empiricism. Thus, empiricism (even without knowledge of astronomy) teaches us that the sun cannot be made to stand still in the manner the Bible tells us Joshua commanded it. Empiricism is a branch of what learned people call epistemology, the science of the origin, structure, methods, and validity of knowledge. The Germans, who seem to have originated this branch of learning, call this the *Erkenntnis* Theory (Knowledge Theory). Epistemology is more difficult to grasp than logic, with which even those of us who cannot master algebraic formulae are more familiar. Logic is a more convenient means for determining rationality.

It is not clear why William James calls privacy "unwholesome," but otherwise one must agree with him that reason's task is "to redeem religion from unwholesome privacy, and to give public status and universal right of way to its deliverance."[1] James, while disdaining caprice and sentimentality, distinguishes rationality from intellectualism, a distinction rarely understood by the foes of rationality. A rationalist does not deny that religion is a matter of the heart.

Unlike the fundamentalists, Liberal Religion's insistence on rationality will not allow it to accept the Bible as literal truth. This does not imply that the believers of Traditional Religion have no reasoning power or are less intelligent than the Liberal Religionists. The difference is that Traditional Religion does not apply the test of rationality to its faith, at least not with the same unrelenting and uncompromising vigor as Liberal Religion. As Max Weber points out, the dominant interest in modern Lutheranism (and he obviously speaks of German Lutherans who are more progressive than American Lutherans) is to combat the rationalism of the intellectuals.[2]

Martin Luther had no use for reason and reasoning power. He knew and admitted freely that the Bible and reason cannot be reconciled, but he nevertheless believed in the absolute truth and inerrancy of the Bible, and postulated such a belief as indispensable. Durant has prepared a summary of Luther's writings in which Luther, with his inimitable coarseness, denounces reason:

> All the articles of our Christian faith which God has revealed to us in His Word are in presence of reason sheerly impossible, absurd, and false. What (thinks that cunning little fool) can be more absurd and impossible that Christ should give us in the Last Supper, His body and blood to eat and drink? . . . or that the dead should rise again at the last day . . . or that Christ the Son of God should be conceived, borne in the womb of the Virgin Mary, become man, suffer, and die a shameful death on the cross? . . . Reason is the greatest enemy that faith has . . . She is the Devil's greatest whore . . . a whore eaten by scab and leprosy who ought to be trodden underfoot and destroyed, she and her wisdom . . . Throw dung in her face . . . drown her in baptism."[3]

These passages show how an otherwise rational person—and there can be no doubt that Luther was a rational person—can throw rationality overboard when it comes to religious beliefs.

Rationality is sometimes denounced as cold and unfeeling rationalism. It is equated with materialism, sometimes with communism, and in any event as "godless atheism." Without discussing materialism and communism, it must be said that this characterization of rationality is profoundly false. As to the association with godless atheism, it is strange that the exaltation of the reasoning power which distinguishes humans from other members of the animal kingdom should be regarded as godless. The contrary is true. A denigration of rationality is an offense to nature, to the creator or to God who endowed humans with that reasoning power. Even Mohammed, a representative of Traditional Religion, said: "God has not created anything better than reason, or more beautiful than reason. The benefits which God giveth are on its account, and understanding is by it, and God's wrath is caused by disregard of it."[4] Mohammed also said, "The ink of the scholar is more holy than the blood of the martyr."[5]

The anti-intellectual attitude of Traditional Religion has persisted to this day. Intellectuals, i.e., persons who place a high value on the pursuit of knowledge, are branded as enemies of religion. Typically, the Ayatolla Khomeini, who extolls the value of traditional Islam religion, has denounced the universities of Iran. The purveyors of Traditional Religion in America have frequently attacked learning and research. They, like the Ayatolla Khomeini, obviously feel or know that what they preach cannot survive in the searching light of reason.

No less a person than the famed psychiatrist Carl Jung has criticized rationalism in his posthumous work *Man and His Symbols.* Jung wrote: "Modern man does not understand how much his rationalism (which has destroyed his capacity to respond to numinous symbols and ideas) has put him at the mercy of the psychic underworld. He has freed himself of superstition (or so he believes), but in the process, has lost his spiritual values to a positively dangerous degree. His moral and spiritual tradition has disintegrated, and he is now paying the price for this breakup, in worldwide disorientation."[6] Jung also wrote, "Our present lives are dominated by the goddess reason which is our greatest and most tragic illusion."[7]

A reply to these provocative statements will shed further light on the concept of rationality as a keystone to Liberal Religion. (1) Dr. Jung obviously is ignorant of the deep spiritual quality of rationality. (2) It is preposterous to say that rational thought has inhibited the response to divine matters (numinous symbols and ideas). This can be said only if one conceives divine matters in an extremely narrow sense. Were it otherwise, this book could not have been written. (3) It is true that some old traditions have disintegrated. This happens to all living things, and it is no cause for alarm or mourning. (4) If the worldwide disorientation, of which Jung writes, consists only of the ascent of rationality, mankind is fortunate that the pre-rational breakup occurred.

Liberal religion does not deify reason; it is aware that, like all human faculties, reasoning power has its limitations. There are regions beyond the frontiers of both knowledge and rational power. More will be said about this in Chapter 6 on truth. One smiles with some contempt and an ever so slight bow to Dr. Jung at the request of Faust's disciple, Wagner, who exclaims, "Much do I know, but to know all is my ambition."[8]

Wanting to know "all" is, of course, a vain if not silly ambition. Wanting to know more is praiseworthy. Unlike Traditional Religion, Liberal Religion is not a closed system and so always seeks to know more. Traditional Religion does not admit its lack of rationality. On the contrary, it claims strict rationality. The systemization of Traditional Religion is, of course, rational. So are its ethical and moral codes. However, this form of rationality, is based upon an assumption which is derived not from reason, but from faith. That assumption is the existence of a supernatural God. Paul complains in his letter to the Romans that the pagans have refused to see that it is rational to acknowledge God, for which reason Paul denounces these pagans as irrational (Rom. 1:20). One is entitled to wonder if Paul was aware of the less than rational contradictions in Genesis 1 and 2 concerning the creation of the world. Or, how Paul would explain the two different versions of the Ten Commandments which cannot both have been written by God or Moses.[9] That God created the world and punished Adam and Eve for disobeying him can be regarded as rational only if one accepts the existence of an all-powerful, supernatural God as an implicit assumption. The rationality of Traditional Religion is thus founded on an irrational faith.

Faith

Faith is the nonintellectual side of religion. It represents a religious instinct existing before the thought process begins and persisting when that process ends at the frontiers of knowledge. The religious instinct is what the prophet appeals to when he summons people to listen to his call.

Most people live by faith. The child is born with faith in his father and mother. The youngster lives by faith unless and until that faith is destroyed by life experiences. Most people marry on faith. Commercial credit trans-actions—the lifeblood of our economy—are based to a small extent upon audited figures and largely upon faith. The scientist who patiently repeats an experiment until success is achieved, is driven and sustained by faith. The religious nature of the scientist's faith was expressed by Teilhard de Chardin, the Jesuit Father, when he wrote that there is less difference than people think between research and adoration. It is also faith which distinguishes the optimist from the pessimist.

Such faith is inborn. But it may be shaken by events and adverse experiences. A person may then say, "I do not know what to believe." Here is where Traditional Religion overpowers the individual. It teaches faith and says, "You must believe this and that." Thus it comes about that faith, instead of being a natural instinct, becomes an object of training, something requiring assent. Faith becomes institutionalized. The adherent readily accepts what the institution teaches; he or she is what is called "faithful." Faith thus degenerates into credulity. The Religious Liberal has faith, but he is not credulous.

The theologians of Traditional Religion have built up systems of faith which vary in detail. Some of the systems are more flexible than others, but all are built on the rock which is regarded as sacred truth and which does not allow further rational exploration. The person who says "I know that my redeemer liveth" does not really know it but proclaims as knowledge what he/she has been taught to believe. Traditional Religion may tolerate doubt, but to reject any tenet of the faith it teaches is regarded as heresy.

The faith of the Religious Liberal is controlled by reason because the Religious Liberal is convinced, and instinctively believes, that rationality is the keystone to religion. The faith of the Traditional Religionist is a matter of obedience to command, and there is no room for rational speculation. An orthodox Jew, when challenged about a particularly outmoded dietary rule of the Bible, replied, "All is commanded by God and my obedience to God is such that I cannot pick and choose as to which of his commands I will obey and which not." The Roman Catholic Church, claiming to be the sole possessor of religious truth, demands absolute obedience. Protestantism is very strict because of the doctrine of justification by faith.

The unquestioning trust in God characterizing Traditional Religion naturally produces an anti-rational attitude. The extreme anti-intellectualism of this type of faith is expressed in the famous saying of the Church Father Tertullian (145–220): *"Credo quia absurdum"* ("I believe it because it makes no sense"). This is not quite as foolish as it sounds, because Traditional Religion believes that man cannot fathom God's reason, and what makes no sense to man may very well make sense to God.

The concept of religious faith is often looked upon with distrust by liberals because they associate it with the Traditional Religion they have come to reject — a religion based upon what Channing called "inherited or passive faith." There is also the suspicion that faith means blind and deaf faith — the faith of the so-called true believer. The true believer has been defined as a person whom no amount of evidence or experience could dissuade from his cherished views and principles.

It is clear that the faith of a closed mind or a faith which is merely inherited cannot be acceptable to rational religion. However, religious faith need not be of that nature.

In their monumental work entitled *The Story of Civilization,* the Durants seem to assume that faith and reason are at opposite poles and irreconcilable. The fourth volume of their work is entitled *The Age of Faith*. It covers the period from 325 A.D. to approximately 1300, in other words, the Middle Ages. This, through the Renaissance and Reformation, led to the "Age of Reason." The seventh volume of the work deals with that period. The authors do not characterize our own age, but they suggest that it can only be one or the other. Will Durant says that the Age of Faith may return if "the Age of Reason achieves catastrophe."[10]

Our apparent inability to cope with the technological development of our time, the helplessness in the face of political upheavals and murderous activities in many parts of the world, might lend support to the conclusion that mankind's collective brainpower is bankrupt, that the Age of Reason has indeed achieved catastrophe.

That is not true. However, if pressed to prove the point, logic alone would not suffice. One would have to resort to an expression of faith in order to buttress the argument that the Age of Reason has not ended.

The Age of Faith, as Durant describes it, is the age whose spiritual roots are in the One God concept of Judaism, Christianity, and Islam. The rationalists removed the traditional God from his central position. They set up new and rival gods who commanded and demanded faith. For instance, Hegel and Marx have deified history, as they conceived it. They taught that the course of history is as inevitable as the ancient law of God. Russian Marxism, while denouncing religion as opium for the people, has become a new faith in the present age. The dogmatism and the discipline of Russian Marxism might even be cited as proof that reason and faith cannot be reconciled, that reason stops where faith begins.

Marxists, of course, have no monopoly on faith in the political field. Most political extremists are "true believers" who are deaf to cold reason. When a political candidate appeals to your heart, he does not address your reasoning power or your mind. He wants to win your feelings and your faith. One remembers the famous saying "The heart has its reasons which reason knows nothing of."

Blaise Pascal (1623–1662) said this, and it is true. It means that our feelings are prompted by many impulses which are not actuated by rational consideration. It does not follow that religion must be based upon such nonrational impulses. This, however, was apparently the opinion of Mr. Pascal, which is remarkable because he was a child of the Age of Reason. He was a mathematician, a scientist, and has come to be regarded as the father of the modern computer. Yet he wrote at some length that it would be unwise to rest religion on reason because the mystery of life cannot be explained by reason.[11] If we would trust reason alone, we should have to despair, because we would have to conclude that life and the Universe have no meaning. According to Pascal, God and the meaning of life must be felt by the heart, rather than by reason. He admonishes us to listen to our hearts and to place our faith in feeling.[12] Religious faith can give meaning to life and nobility to man. He means of course the religious faith of the Roman Catholic Church.

Pascal makes one argument in defense of religious faith which does not seem to come from the heart but rather from a computer. This is his famous argument that "belief is a wise wager." What harm will come if one gambles on the truth of religious belief, and it proves false? If you gain, you gain all; if you lose, you lose nothing. Wager, then, without hesitation that God exists. If you find that very difficult, then just fall into the groove of the rituals of the church and pretend that you believe. Bless yourself with holy water, have masses said, and so on. By a simple and natural process this will make you believe and will dull your wit. "It will quiet your proudly critical intellect. Go to confession and communion. You will find it a release and a strengthening power."[13]

Here we note a kind of religion which is coldly calculating in its approach, but not rational in the sense in which we understand the term today. Pascal advocates a conscious effort to silence the intellect in order to gain religious happiness and faith. One must suppress reason in order to gain faith.

Perhaps this is good psychiatry, but, surely, it is bad religion. It is a doctrine furnishing grist to the mill of modern anti-religionists who conceive religion to be just a body of doctrine, liturgy, and ritual which has built up over the years and has obscured the substance of religious faith.

How much more appealing than Pascal's is Emerson's approach to the same problem. In the essay on *Self-Reliance,* Emerson relates how, in his youth, an advisor admonished him to adhere to traditional church doctrine rather than follow such impulses as might drive him. Such personal impulses, said the advisor, might originate from the devil. Emerson replied that he did not think that his impulses came from below, "but if I am the devil's child I will live then from the devil."

Traditional faith is based upon supernatural revelation. It is Mr. Pascal's kind of faith which still permeates Judeo-Christian religion. The Old Testament is full of stories that the Israelites had to combat superior enemies whom Jehovah had sent against them. The Israelites are then admonished that they could win the battle if they would only affirm their faith in Jehovah. Similarly, in the Sermon on the Mount, Jesus tells the people not to worry about bread and clothing or other material things. Look at the lillies of the field and the wild flowers, they do not toil or spin, and yet they are beautifully dressed. Trust in God for material things; don't be a person of "little faith." In the letter to the Hebrews, Paul recites a long honor roll of biblical characters, starting with Abel, Noah, and Abraham, who succeeded in whatever they were doing simply by having a faith in God. In the letter to the Galatians, he disparaged the law and wrote that one can only be made upright through faith in Christ, by which he meant faith in the bodily resurrection of Christ, which nobody had witnessed but in which he believed (Gal. 4:25). The Pharisees among the Jews believed him; the Sadducees thought him a liar and traitor.

The Protestant reformers, under the leadership of Luther and Calvin, taught that man can be saved only by faith in God and in the redeemership of Jesus — not by good works. According to the Bible, James, the brother of Jesus, opposed this Pauline view. He wrote: "What does it profit my brethren, though a man says he has faith and have no works? Can faith save him?" (James 2:26).

Liberal Religion agrees with James and disagrees with Paul. Good works are absolutely essential in the ethical and religious scheme of things. A good deed is more important and more eloquent than any pious profession of faith. The heavy accent on faith in Protestantism still persists, but it does not reflect a true situation. As Alan Watts's research has shown, fear sways all Christians far more than faith.[14]

A good deed will ordinarily be prompted by faith beyond the immediate practicality. The good deed is often an act of faith. Those who ridicule the "do-gooder" are mostly people without faith.

It has been said that the maxim "honesty is the best policy" is unethical because it advocates honesty on purely utilitarian or practical grounds, instead of demanding honesty as a virtue for its own sake. This is like criticizing a young man for marrying a rich girl. The fact that she is rich in no way reflects a flaw of character or a lack of loveliness. The fact that honesty is practical does not detract from its ethical or religious merit.

A practical and rational outlook on life may be the result of utter selfishness. On the other hand, it may also stem from an abiding faith in the evolutionary process and forces of creation, as we find it, as well as a respect for the power of reason which is man's outstanding gift.

In Liberal Religion, religion and faith cannot be on separate levels. The original or radical rationalists had no use for religion at all; it was so much eyewash or opium for the people. Being disenchanted with Traditional Religion, they considered all religious thought to be irrational. To borrow a phrase from Jean-Paul Sartre, they confused disenchantment with truth.

Some think that Liberal Religionists must be neurotic because they do not enjoy the comfortable certitude of Traditional Religion. This concern is unfounded. Adherence to rationality gives Liberal Religionists an enormous self confidence and a faith which they consider unassailable. They think that rationality is the safest protection against spurious religiosity.

As the rationalists gained more insight and humility they began to accept the concept of religious involvement with the world. The Ethical Culture Societies of America and their counterparts abroad called themselves religious societies. Humanists became comfortable in the Unitarian Universalist Church, side by side with theists and deists.

Most Americans have faith in freedom, in self government, and in democracy. The truth of this faith cannot be found in history. It is a faith based upon abstract concepts of right, morality, and justice. This faith has been called an American secular religion, apparently to distinguish it from sacred religion.

Whether secular or sacred, the faith in freedom and democracy has a religious quality because it stems from a concern beyond personal survival and it expresses a yearning for a better world order. While history furnishes no evidence that a society which operates in accordance with these ideals is viable, sound reasoning supports the proposition that a state of freedom, self government, and democracy can be achieved. Therefore, the faith in these ideals is a rational faith.

But faith it is. If one is called upon to defend the virtues of democracy against its detractors who proclaim the greater efficiency or practicality of a nondemocratic (or undemocratic) civilization, one almost invariably is thrown back to one's faith in freedom and faith in the dignity of the individual, which is regarded as more important than the advantages of efficiency in a nondemocratic society.

If the great mass of our people cease to have this faith, our country is likely to be taken over by the radical right or the radical left, both enemies of democracy. The Russian Revolution undoubtedly was a sustained success, not because the great masses of the people had studied the works of Marx or Lenin, but because they had faith in the gospel of these men.

Sheer faith sustained the people of Britain in the darkest days of World War II. The American war correspondent Edward R. Murrow, in the book *This I Believe,* described it thus: "But at bottom this calm confidence stemmed from the belief that what they were defending was good; the Englishmen had devised a system of regulating the relationship between the individual and the state which was superior to all others and which would survive even though cold military calculations concluded that the state was doomed."[15]

As Max Lerner, the astute contemporary historian and columnist, once wrote, "It is an axiom that belief can always beat nonbelief." Or, in the words of a poet, "Faith moves mountains."

The Civil Rights Movement in the United States illustrates this point. Faith in freedom, and not mere rational argument, has caused most Religious Liberals to join the movement. White liberals are in this movement because it is demanded by their sense of decency, their urge for brotherhood, and their faith in man. They find themselves shoulder to shoulder with believers in Traditional churches. It is likely that Traditional churchmen are inspired primarily by what they conceive to be faith in God, whereas Religious Liberals will generally be motivated by what they conceive to be faith in man. These are different kinds of faith; and while their voices blend in the Civil Rights chorus, one would not want to eliminate or even blur the difference.

However, in both cases the motivation—not merely a rational force but the reason of the heart—is a faith grounded on ultimate concern. It is the ultimate concern which Paul Tillich taught us is the essence of religion, and, indeed, a synonym for the word "God."

We recognize, of course, that the matter of religious faith is not primarily important in the context of political and social issues. The real impact of religious faith comes in ordinary, daily living, for example, when one encounters a business failure or some personal tragedy.

Pascal told us that if one turns to reason for an answer, one is likely to despair because reason cannot explain the meaning of life. Only faith in the God of Judeo-Christian tradition can help us. Pascal advocates a blind faith, faith without skepticism, almost a superstition. One recalls the biblical poem of Job, whose anger, anguish, and despair about his misfortunes were finally lifted by reconciliation with God and faith in God's goodness.

It is interesting to note that modern existentialism, which permeates so much of our contemporary thinking, seems to proclaim a similar turning away from reason. According to Sartre, one of its foremost spokesman, man is utterly alone in the world, abandoned to the forces around him, dependent upon his own willpower to alleviate the anguish and despair which he can never quite overcome. There is, in the words of one of Sartre's plays, "no exit."

Religious people believe that they will overcome adversity. Traditional Religion believes that the aid of a supernatural God will achieve this. Liberal

Religion, on the other hand, believes that human beings will be able to cope without supernatural help. If Sartre is right, existentialism must lead to suicide. This view is rejected by the existentialist Albert Camus, a Nobel Prize Laureate, who devoted an entire book to the proposition that suicide is not legitimate, that faith in life will overcome all despair.[16]

Traditional Religion demands faith on the authority of Scripture. Says Küng, "For the Christian, the Church is primarily there, not to be admired nor to be criticized, but to be believed."[17] But, as Emerson says, "the faith that stands on authority is no faith," and then he criticizes the Christian Church for its erroneous efforts to give Jesus a position of authority.[18]

Can faith cure sickness? The answer to that question has many facets. The Gospels report episodes of faith healing by Jesus; and, significantly, Jesus was not successful as a faith healer among people who had no faith in him (Matt. 13:58). Paul was a faith healer and gained in authority by so-called miraculous cures (Acts 19:11-17). To this day faith healers abound. Some of their cures may be drug related; others are in the fields of psychosomatic medicine, psychiatry, or psychology. Faith healers sometimes sound like the proverbial snake oil salesman, and the comparison is often apt. The "Christian Healing Crusade" was part of the thriving business of a Mr. Parker and his Foundation for Divine Meditation which resulted in a conflict with the Internal Revenue Service.[19] And yet, there are rational explanations for some of the faith healers' doings, even if they are accompanied by some hocus pocus. Liberal Religion insists on rationality. Faith or prayer is no substitute for medical help. The dogmatic rejection of medical assistance by the Christian Science faith, which is part of Traditional Religion, cannot be countenanced.

Some persons will say despairingly, "I am unhappy; I wish I could believe in a supernatural God and be happy, but I cannot believe and so I am not happy." To such a person Liberal Religion answers: "Do not despair, you need not pine for an irrational faith. You know from experience that the sun rises in the morning and sets in the evening. You know that one season follows the other with regularity. You know that the birds which have left their summer nesting place to migrate south will return to the same place next summer. You know, in short, that there is order in the Universe. And you have experienced the beauty of the stars, the mountains, and the sea. If you realize that you have this knowledge and experience, you must also be aware that the natural events around you justify happiness with, and faith in, nature without the need to search for an elusive supernatural cause."

Propagation of the Faith

The faith of Liberal Religion is largely unknown because little effort has been made to disseminate it. One day after his election in 1978, the late

Pope John Paul I announced that he regarded evangelism as the foremost task of the Church. The congregation for the propagation of the faith has always been an important segment of the Roman Curia. Why, one must ask, has the Liberal Church shown so little zeal for the propagation of its faith?

Several answers suggest themselves; one or all may be correct, and each of them deserves some introspective pondering by Liberal Religionists.

(1) Unlike the Roman Church, the Liberal Church is not convinced that its faith is the only true one. This insight, however, is a characteristic strength of Liberal Religion and deserves to be broadcast.

(2) The Liberal Church considers propagation undignified and incompatible with its high ethical standards. It therefore tends to look with contempt upon those whom it regards as peddlers of religion. Such highbrow attitudes are inappropriate because ideas can only be spread by communication. An idea which is not communicated is bound to be sterile. Liberal Religion would have no right to exist if it had not many communicable ideas. It has a moral duty to fructify our contemporary civilization with these ideas. Propagation of the faith is imperative.

(3) Since they are less certain about the truth than the pope's Church, Religious Liberals are somewhat shy. They tend to regard their lack of certainty as a weakness, of which they are ashamed. The result of this attitude is that many potential adherents of Liberal Religion, most particularly our own young people, are turned away.

(4) A contrary attitude may also at times be responsible for the failure to propagate the Liberal faith. That attitude is one of conceit, elitism, or hubris. Traditional Religion is good only for the masses, or so the argument runs. Liberal Religion is something special for which we, but not other people, are suited. This is an insidious frame of mind which bespeaks the opposite of religion.

The reticence of the Liberal Church may be explained by these or other causes. The only reason for exploring the causes is the need to overcome this reticence. The peoples of the earth, especially the uncommitted and the young, are hungry for evangelistic efforts. If the Liberal Church does not participate in the general competition for the souls of men, it betrays its reason for existence.

The public articulation of the tenets of Liberal Religion need not necessarily be directed at conversion. There are many persons with ties to Traditional Religion who have not the foggiest notion as to what Liberal Religion stands for. They have no opinion (or at best a low opinion) of the Liberal Church. The propagation of the Liberal faith may not gain converts but at least it will command more respect than exists at present. This, in turn, will make for a better and more salubrious spirit in the community.

5

Emotion and Mysticism

The emphasis on rationality in religion tends to belittle or even reject emotion. When Frances Trollop wrote in 1832 about the domestic manners of the Americans she remarked on the "cold, comfortless stillness of Unitarianism."[1] Unitarians have never been able to shake this image. One suspects that the reputation for unemotionalism stems from an exaggerated sense of religious reticence, which must be overcome. The fact that they do not share the frenzy of a revival meeting and that they do not allow incense to dull their senses is no proof that Liberal Religionists are bereft of human emotion. They merely insist that religious emotions must not infringe upon the realm of reason.

Emerson wrote, "A certain tendency to insanity has always attended the opening of the religious sense in men."[2] Among the examples he cites are the trances of Socrates, the conversion of Paul, the convulsions of George Fox and his Quakers, and the illumination of Swedenborg. "What was in the case of these remarkable persons a ravishment has, in innumerable instances in common life, been exhibited in less striking manner. Everywhere the history of religion betrays a tendency to enthusiasm."[3] Plato also observed this emotional aspect of religion. He wrote that "he who is not being inspired and having no touch of madness, will not be admitted to the temple."[4]

William James began his famous lectures on the *Varieties of Religious Experience* by pointing out that many religious people are neurotic and even psychopathic, moved by emotional deviation from the standard of normalcy and placidity.[5] Neurotic emotions, according to James, are valuable only if coupled with a superior intellect.[6] That is why many leaders of the contemporary cults and fringe religions, although neurotic, do not command the respect of Liberal Religion. James's statement also supports the tenet of Liberal Religion that emotion must be controlled by reason. This does not deprecate emotion as a creative force in one's life. Being neurotic does not mean that a person is mentally ill. Says James: "There are moments of sentimental and mystical experience that carry an enormous sense of inner authority and illumination with them when they come. But, they come seldom and they do not come to everyone."[7] The call for moral passion in the preface to this book is a frank appeal to emotional involvement.

According to the liturgies of Traditional Religion, God's desire for praise and glorification is almost insatiable. That type of liturgy alone alienates many Religious Liberals. It may be doubted that these repeated ejaculations come from the heart. However, if Religious Liberals use the word "God" to describe their reverence for life and their love for the Universe, or if they express these sentiments without using the word "God," their emotion comes from the heart. It is not diluted by vain repetition.

Emotion is a biological fact and must be recognized as such. All humans have emotions and Religious Liberals are no exception. The emotions of Religious Liberals are directed towards the natural rather than the supernatural, towards happiness in this life rather than the life after death. The Liberal Church knows that human reason has its limitations and that there are unexplored areas beyond the frontiers of learning. Also, the human brain has a limited capacity. Socrates said, *"Scio me nescire"* ("I know I am really ignorant "). Many facets of life cannot and need not be comprehended by reason. Like others, Religious Liberals fall in love and know not why. If a Religious Liberal is overawed by the sight of a snowcapped mountain, he need not have studied geology or meteorology in order to be so moved.

Hymn singing in the Liberal Church is an emotional outlet for religious commitment and devotion. Some Unitarian Universalist Fellowships shy away from hymn singing just because they are afraid of, or do not wish to admit, emotionalism.

Listening to great music is an emotional experience for all but the deaf and those who are doggedly determined not to be moved. When listening to a Mozart symphony or concerto, one may be moved to reflect on the harmony of the Universe. When listening to Mahler's music, that may be a little harder; but Mahler, too, evokes a feeling of the depth and breadth of creation, its stresses and their resolution. In rock and roll music, the tunes may be overwhelmed by the rhythmic elements, but many listeners will also sense harmony and be transported. Whether Mozart, Mahler, or rock and roll, one senses what Emerson called the oversoul, and if this is mystic emotionalism, so be it. Religious Liberals need not be ashamed of it.

Mysticism appears in every age, every land, and in all religions. In Liberal Religion mysticism, like emotion, is under the discipline of rationality. Emotion and mysticism are barred if they violate rationality. However, there are many human experiences that can not be rationally verified. Science has not yet been able to explain many aspects of what happens in the Universe. We observe or experience it but we cannot explain it. That is the mystery of life. Thus understood, mystery and mysticism are not irrational. It is, therefore, quite appropriate for Liberal Religion to speak of the mystery of life.

Albert Einstein said that the sense of the mysterious stands at the cradle of true art and true science.[8] Father Teilhard de Chardin, the Jesuit scientist, explained the interdependence of science and religion thus: "Neither in its impetus nor its achievements can science go to its limits without becoming tinged with mysticism and charged with faith."[9] And, at the other side of the religious spectrum, the psychologist Erich Fromm calls his position a nontheistic mysticism.[10] Pope John Paul II wrote in his encyclical entitled "Redeemer of Man" that Christ is the Lord of history because of the mystery of redemption.

A mystery must be distinguished from a miracle. Miracles are sometimes imagined and are often contrived. In prehistoric times, long before Jesus, the Greek god Asclepius was reported to have raised men from the dead. Pilgrims to his temple in Epidaurus experienced miraculous cures.[11] It seems obvious that the tendency to believe in such miracles is ingrained in human nature. Contemporary pilgrimages to Lourdes, and the crutches which pilgrims leave behind at the shrine of St. Joseph in Montreal, bear witness to this. To the pilgrims, such miracles are a religious experience and are possible because of their religious faith. Liberal Religion does not share this faith, but it cannot scoff at the mystical devotion of the pilgrims.

The deists of the seventeenth century branded biblical miracles as forgeries, fabrications, and the products of miraclemongers.[12] Such harshness is not necessary to uphold the banner of rationality.

A phenomenon which is difficult to explain is sometimes called a miracle. The person who experiences it is deeply astonished and, with a sense of awe, labels as "miraculous" what he finds hard to explain. Thus, in Unitarian Universalist church schools, children often use a book called *How Miracles Abound,* by Bertha Stevens. The book tells the story of a star, a magnet, a dew drop, a goldfish, and other natural phenomena which impress the receptive mind as wonderful and miraculous; and these things are then explained as science has learned to explain them. The first impression is mystical and the sense of awe is not destroyed by scientific explanation. "All the subjects illustrate the orderliness of the Universe. All illustrate natural force of some sort, whether gravitation, magnetism, crystallization, chemical attraction, or the vague but transcendent thing called life force."[13] How does one describe the concept of eternity, especially to children? The late Sophia Fahs asked a Unitarian Sunday school class to cut an apple and look at the seeds. These seeds, she explained, show how the apple tree reproduces itself continuously, and thus she showed the children the meaning of eternity and the mystery of life. This is the kind of mysticism which the Liberal

Church likes. Where sentiments are aroused by intoxication and mystic transport, religion becomes artificial rather than genuine.

However, ecstasy is not alien to the Liberal Religions. Howlett, in his book on the *Fourth Faith,* which is about Liberal Religion, says, "In immersing yourself in that kind of faith, you may know religion's ecstasy, not of the trance or the stigma, but the ecstasy of experiencing the discovery of truth, the exultation of perception of beauty you did not suppose existed, the sensation of love that calls from you deeds of generosity and self-sacrifice you had not supposed lay within your power."[14]

While we reject irrational mysticism, there is no gainsaying that it has sustained many persons, individuals who otherwise would be in deep despair from which Liberal Religion could not have rescued them, because they shudder at its rationality. A prime example of this attitude is the religious stance of the former American slaves and many of their descendants. They have readily accepted the religion of the slavemasters. Why? A surprising answer is suggested by the scientist Carl Sagan. He says that birth is the common experience of the oppressed and the oppressor. Blurred perception and vague premonitions are the best that the newborn infant can manage. "I think," Sagan writes, "that the mystical core of the religious experience is neither literally true nor perniciously wrong-minded. It is rather a courageous if flawed attempt to make contact with the earliest and most profound experience of our lives."[15]

Obviously, mysticism has psychiatric and psychological implications. In the context of this book, not more than a hint thereof is appropriate.

The Spanish painter, Miro (1893–), once disclaimed responsibility for his paintings because they were always born in a "state of hallucination induced by some kind of shock." This may point to another explanation of religious mysticism.

The historian Morrison, speaking of the liberation of New England from the yoke of Calvinism by such Religious Liberals as Emerson, Hawthorne and Whitman, observes that, in spite of these efforts, Unitarianism failed to gain strong support because it did not supply the note of mysticism which so many people crave.[16] Some contemporary Religious Liberals therefore seek to reintroduce mystery into Liberal Religion.[17] When this is done without regard for scientific truth and irrationality, it is, in the above quoted words of Sagan, a flawed attempt. It is flawed because it jeopardizes the integrity of Liberal Religion.

6

Truth

Four men gaze at the sunset on a mountain. The lower part of the mountain is a green forest. The upper part is a rocky cliff shrouded in clouds. The sun plays on the clouds. "The mountain is pink," exclaims one man who is a painter. The second, also a painter, says, "No, it is purple." The third man is a devout religionist. He says, "God lives on the mountain behind the clouds; the mountain is white." It has been revealed to him that God lives on that white mountain. The fourth man is a geologist. "I have been up there," he says, "it is grey slate."

All four men tell the truth as they see it. None of the four tells a deliberate falsehood. If one would apply a lie detector test, all four would pass. When A has fatally shot B there is only one truth about the cause of death. When human recollection and human observation intrude, the truth of even simple events is hard to discover. Individual recollections and observations may, and often do, differ. There is a well-known experiment staged by a criminology professor in his classroom. He had a number of students break into the classroom during a lecture; the intruders overturned furniture and caused a tumult. Thereafter, he asked for written reports of the event from all those who had witnessed it. The reports differed widely. How much stronger are the variations where religious feelings and predispositions are involved?

If we acknowledge subjective truth, what then is to be said regarding objective truth or absolute truth? There is none! This is hard to accept, especially in religion. Religion, like love, demands total and undivided devotion.

Most people like strawberries. Some delight in them. But some people avoid them because they experience allergic reactions. Similarly, Liberal Religion cannot stomach such stories as the Risen Christ; the bodily ascension of Elijah, Jesus, and Mary to heaven; and various other religious stories that defy reason and science. Liberal Religion, while respecting the subjective truth of Traditionalists, does not believe the truth of claims that run counter to scientific knowledge. Thus, in the above example of the four mountain gazers, Liberal Religion will reject the observation of the devout one who says that God lives on the mountain. It will concede that the construction of the eye and the play of the sun's rays may support the two painters perception that the mountain is pink or purple. But, in the last analysis, Liberal Religion, as religion, will accept the scientist's view that the mountain is grey slate, provided there is no scientific evidence to the contrary. The mental reservation which is implied in the last proviso, exposes Liberal Religion to some ridicule from Traditional Religion, which admits of no such uncertainty.

All religions proclaim adherence to a continuing search for truth. In this respect Liberal Religion cannot claim uniqueness. However, it makes a difference *where* one searches for truth. In Verdi's opera *Un Ballo de Mascera,* the fortune teller Ulrica says she must talk to Satan to research the truth. Liberal Religion searches in science and in all avenues open to the human mind. Traditional Religion does not allow such an open-minded search. It limits the search to the bounds of Scripture. When Father Küng stepped over these bounds, the Vatican said that he no longer qualified as a Roman Catholic theologian. Earlier, Father Pierre Teilhard de Chardin was forbidden to publish his scientific findings, because these findings did not conform to the truth which is recognized by the Vatican. Any such limitation is anathema to Liberal Religion.

Traditional Religion is based on permanent devotion to *one truth.* It is a closed system. It spreads like permafrost over the spiritual life of the believers. It may be amended within the confines of the system. Examples of such emendation are the papal pronouncements in 1950 that the Virgin Mary had physically ascended to heaven, and the announcement in 1978 by the president of the Mormon Church that, henceforth, black males may be priests. Liberal Religion rejects any closed system; it does not accept the permanency of any truth, teaching, or belief. Liberal Religion does not accept that which is contrary to ever-evolving scientific knowledge.

Because they are rationalists, the Halfway Religious Liberals will not repudiate scientific knowledge. They nevertheless maintain that naked truth is a contradiction in terms.[1] They also insist that science and religion are poles apart.[2] Many of us do not comprehend science, and therefore shy away from it. It is hard to grasp the stupendous magnitude of the cosmos, the existence of billions of planets of which the earth (which Bernard Shaw called the insane asylum of the solar system) is only one. The problems of the microcosmos (for instance, genetic science) are equally complicated for the nonscientist. An uncomplicated faith in the unknown beyond, therefore, represents to many an attractive and true religion. That is a shelter in which a one-planet deity may be worshipped without regard to the larger solar system. A few decades ago, somebody wrote a book called *Philosophers Lead Sheltered Lives*. This may also be said of some religious people. True Liberal Religion looks beyond the shelter. It encompasses all planets and all life, known and unknown. It trusts science.

As Chapter 4 indicated, the trust in science is based on experience, which is the basis of Liberal Religion. Traditional Religion rests on a world view which reflects the knowledge available to the authors of the Bible and which is centered on the planet Earth. The personal God of Traditional Religion is a one-planet deity. Science has now demonstrated that the planet Earth is only a small part of the Universe. Periscopes, radio signals, and numerous other devices have shown that the cosmology of Traditional Religion is incorrect. There is tangible, verifiable proof of scientific truth. We are therefore justified in trusting science, and to let it lead us to new discoveries. The laws of physics, chemistry, and biology have proven to be reliable and have aided humanity in understanding the macrocosmos of the Universe, as well as the microcosmos of the individual. The insights we have gained as a result of scientific discoveries are insights into the realities of life. Religion is a dimension of life. Therefore, Liberal Religion is intertwined with science and relies on it.

Science is not readily discernible by common sense, as Ralph Burhoe pointed out in his address on accepting the Templeton Prize for Progress in Religion. That does not place science outside the realm of religion. Burhoe suggests that it may be regarded as a new gift of revelation.[3]

One of the most recent revelations stems from the ongoing research in the field of recombinant DNA technology. Scientists have learned to splice genes and, without peril, to produce a new organism. This discovery has profound effects on immunology and other fields of medicine. However, it runs counter to the biblical prohibition of the mixing of genes (Lev. 19:19). The authors of the Bible forbade it, or rather they laid the prohibition in the mouth of God. It was thought that gene mixing was an impermissible and unhealthy attempt at magic. One cannot criticize the Bible authors, because they did not know any better. Liberal Religion, however, is critical of those who consider the Bible as unerring or who believe that an omniscient God banned forever what modern genetics has achieved.

Traditional Religion is not based on scientific truth and will not even allow perceived truth. It relies solely on revealed truth. This is a type of "truth" which lies outside the bounds of verification. As Professor Küng says, "The Church is here not to be admired or criticized but to be believed."[4] Traditional Religionists hold to be true what their authorities and their traditions teach. In the Liberal Church, neither authority nor tradition is sacrosanct. Liberal Religion will discard any tradition and any authority that is shown to be in error. This attitude is what theologians call empirical naturalism.

In the Scopes Trial (The Monkey Trial) in 1925, William Jennings Bryan appeared as the attorney for the state of Tennessee in order to uphold the statute which forbade the teaching of evolution in the public schools. Clarence Darrow, for the defense, attacked the statute as foolish and unscientific. The following colloquy characterizes the conflict:

> DARROW: The Bible says Joshua commanded the sun to stand still for the purpose of lengthening the day, doesn't it, and you believe this?
>
> BRYANT: I do.

Darrow later asked Bryant what he thought about the age of the earth and Bryant made a reply which seems to characterize Traditional Religion: "I do not think about things I don't think about." Bryant was no fool. He had served as Secretary of State in the Wilson administration and, before that, he was a three-time candidate for the presidency on the Democratic ticket. It can be assumed that he was well acquainted with the basic teachings of astronomy. But obviously for him, as for most adherents of Traditional Religion today, religious belief was a thing apart from knowledge and experience. Science could not shake his faith in the supernatural.

This view persists today. Indeed, it seems that opposition to the teaching of evolution is more vocal than ever. The opponents are called creationists because they believe that the world and all living things were created spontaneously by a divine entity, as related in the Bible. They proclaim that the conflict between evolutionists and creationists is a conflict between Christ and Antichrist, between the Judeo-Christian ethic and atheism.

In 1978 the National Museum of Science of the Smithsonian Institution in Washington, D.C., arranged for an exhibit which demonstrated the developmental stages of man as taught by the theory of evolution. The National Bible Knowledge Association and the National Association for Fairness in Education commenced a lawsuit demanding that the Smithsonian should also display an exhibit which would demonstrate the scientifically discredited cosmology of the Bible.[5]

In fairness to Traditional Religion, it must be said that not all of its adherents support creationism. Liberal Religion stands squarely on the teaching of evolution. It relies for its truth upon science and therefore is subject to the hazards of science. The greatest hazard is that what is true today may be found untrue tomorrow. This is a challenge which Liberal Religion not only acknowledges, but accepts with enthusiasm. When the Bible was written, it was universally held that the sun moved around the earth. The story that Joshua prolonged the day of battle by making the sun stand still, therefore, did not run counter to science, assuming that Joshua had supernatural power (Josh. 10:13). In the sixteenth century, Copernicus discovered that the sun was a fixed star, and that the earth was in motion around it. That converted the Joshua story from a possible truth to an absolute untruth. When Galileo confirmed the discovery by Copernicus, the Vatican silenced him because it would not allow the authority of the Bible to be questioned. Learned contemporaries of Galileo refused to look through his periscope because it showed sunspots which were not supposed to exist. Traditional Religion has always resisted, and still resists, the search for new truths. In its closed system there simply are no further questions. It was not only the pope, but also Calvin and Luther who were irritated by Copernicus and Galileo.

The impermanent nature of a given truth is only one side of the hazard of religious devotion to science. The other side is that science and technology have an autonomy of their own and may lead to results that are so unforeseen and upsetting that humans will find it difficult to cope. That is why Traditional Religion clings to the closed system and why the adherent of Traditional Religion enjoys a sense of security and certainty which is absent in Liberal Religion. The Liberal Religionist is more venturesome, though no less confident.

Not long ago *The New York Times* carried an article about a student at Princeton Theological Seminary who refused to read a certain textbook because "it might harm his faith."[6] Liberal Religion condemns all efforts to inhibit the search for truth. Thus, it is in irreconcilable conflict with Traditional Religion. The Genesis story of the Bible teaches that it is a sin to eat from the tree of knowledge. Spinoza was excommunicated from the Jewish community because his research and philosophy did not conform to traditional teaching. Andrew Dickson White, the founder of Cornell University, wrote a book, *The Warfare of Science with Theology in Christendom,* after publication of which many American ministers advised high school graduates that it was better to receive no further education than to attend Cornell.[7] Galileo was threatened with torture because he wrote that the earth moved. Father Teilhard de Chardin, whose research results did not conform with the traditional teaching of his church, was forbidden by his ecclesiastical superiors to teach in his native France and to publish any of his major works. He was also forbidden to write on any philosophical subject and to accept a professorship at the College de France.[8] Another example of how Traditional Religion inhibits the search for truth is the research on the external fertilization of the human egg which, in 1978, led to the birth in England of the so-called test-tube baby. That research was begun in Italy by a scientist named Daniel Petrucci. He discontinued his research when the Vatican forbade it. Fellow scientists in the United States and other parts of the Western world were similarly intimidated by the pressure of Traditional Religious forces.[9] Centuries earlier, the Roman Catholic Church had stopped the study of anatomy because it required the dissection of human bodies. Such dissection was believed to interfere with the resurrection of the bodies as taught by

Traditional Religion. Therefore, Michelangelo and Da Vinci had to dissect bodies in secret, which enabled these great artists to make the magnificent drawings and paintings of the human body which we still enjoy and admire. Rabelais, a physician, defied the Church and taught anatomy by demonstration from the human body.

Medicine has learned a great deal since that time and it has utilized much experience. But, it still is not an exact science. The head of one of America's most prestigious teaching and research hospitals wrote, "the only solid piece of scientific truth about which I feel totally confident in is that we are profoundly ignorant about nature."[10] And about medicine he wrote, "what it needs is a lot of time and patience, waiting for science to come in, as it has in the past, with the solid facts."[11]

Truth cannot hide if knowledge is allowed to flourish. We live in an age of knowledge explosion. In the past three decades scientists have made tremendous progress in opening up new vistas in the fields of astronomy, biology, and engineering to name but a few obvious areas. This has naturally enlarged knowlege in the social sciences. The new knowledge increasingly tends to discredit many old religious stories. That is one of the reasons why knowledge is not always welcome, why intellectuals are scorned, and why, in some quarters, knowledge is branded as the enemy of God. There are those who do not want to learn, those who keep their ears stopped, their eyes averted and their minds closed. This is anybody's privilege and it should be respected. A woman is entitled to say, "I do not want to hear about my husband's picadillos; I believe in him and I want to continue to believe in him." So it is with religion. It is, to say the least, unkind to force knowledge on somebody who prefers ignorance; and to terrorize somebody with the truth, who likes to dwell in the realm of myth and fiction.

Liberal Religion, however, prefers knowledge to ignorance and it is not terrorized by the truth. It not only prefers knowledge and truth, it demands them. According to the standards of Liberal Religion, a person who is uncomfortable with both knowledge and truth is uncomfortable with religion, and is not religious.

The need for research to disclose the truth is therefore obvious. We must not allow theologians, whether organized or not, to interfere with that search. The opposition by closed system theologians to the search for truth may be based on good faith (no pun intended), but it may also have ulterior motives. The astronomer Carl Sagan seems to suggest the latter when he writes, "As we learn more and more about the universe, there seems to be less and less for God to do.[12] Religions that are unwilling to conform to scientific changes are, in Sagan's opinion, doomed.

Liberal Religion is guided by empirical naturalism, which means verifiable natural experience as distinguished from nonverifiable mystical or revelatory intuition. However, revelation in the sense of inspiration (or as scientific revelation) and mysticism are not alien to Liberal Religion.

There remain many phenomena on or beyond the frontiers of knowledge that will allow for religious speculation. For instance, the wonder of bird migration has not yet been scientifically explained. Some scientists guess that the birds may be guided by magnetism or the stars. Others think that the birds are guided by infrasound waves which humans cannot sense.[13] While Liberal Religion believes that science will ultimately find a natural explanation, it is merely a belief and Liberal Religion is in no position to deny the truth of those who believe that the birds are guided by a supernatural power. Another example of uncertainty is astrology, which is the ancient theory and practice of foretelling from stellar observations not only astronomical, meteorological, and other natural events, but also the course of individual human affairs. Science has not yet altogether explained what astrology teaches. The phenomenon of extrasensory perception is also in the twilight between scientific and unscientific belief.

Empirical naturalism in religion does not necessarily tell the whole truth. This insight strengthens Liberal Religion's stance that it is not the sole possessor of truth. In this, it is distinct from all Traditional Religions.

The Roman Catholic Church has never allowed any doubt that it is the exclusive owner of the truth. In his 1979 encyclical "Redeemer of Man," Pope John Paul II cites Jesus' statement, "You shall know the truth and the truth shall make you free." The pope couples this citation with an exaltation of "authentic freedom" as distinguished from "unilateral freedom" and a warning that the relationship to truth must be honest. Obviously, he refers to the monolithic concepts of the Roman Catholic Church. Actually, the cited words of Jesus occur only in the fourth gospel (John 8:32) and they refer to the freedom which a person experiences if he or she frees himself or herself from the enslavement of sinful habits and thoughts. Liberal Religion could cite this Bible passage as a warning against slavish adherence to traditional beliefs.

Traditional Religion was humiliated when the astronauts found no divine beings in outer space, and no dwelling space for deceased humans. Now some scientists believe, and seek to prove, that there is life and intelligence on other planets, and that this has been the case for some time. If their research is successful, Traditional Theology may face new dilemmas, as in the case of the discovery of the Dead Sea Scrolls.

Liberal Religion cannot be embarrassed by the discovery of new truth, because it expects it. The scientist Bronowski wrote in *The Ascent of Man*: "There is no absolute knowledge. And those who claim it, whether they are scientists or dogmatists, open the door to tragedy. All information is imperfect. We have to treat it with humility. That is the human condition and that is what quantum physics says."[14] It is also what Liberal Religion says.

The insight that Liberal Religion is not the only possessor of truth leads to respect for other religions. However, it does not require us to adhere to a bland ecumenism in which our free faith is submerged.

James Luther Adams warns that the openness, tolerance, and freedom of Liberal Religion is risky in that it "can produce the mind that is simply open at both ends. These wonderful attributes can spell the loss of character and serve as an invitation to confusion, sheer variety . . . and diffused identity."[15]

The awareness of this limitation of knowledge does not discourage Liberal Religionists. On the contrary, it encourages them in their effort to extend the frontiers of knowledge. The quest for truth is unending. Some hold that the quest for truth is the essence of Liberal Religion. At least one Unitarian Universalist congregation proclaims that the quest for truth is a sacrament, the most sacred element of its religion.[16]

Bronowski's *The Ascent of Man* almost summarizes the theology of Liberal Religion. The theory of evolution, put to the fore by Charles Darwin, a Unitarian himself, is to this day the scientific foundation of our knowledge of life and, therefore, of Liberal Religion. While the theory of evolution has been bitterly opposed by Traditional Religion because it cannot be reconciled with the biblical cosmology, Liberal Religion will always defer to new scientific insights. Science and religion are not enemies. Figuratively speaking, they are siblings who spring from the same author.

A religious discourse on truth must not omit the concept of heresy. The word "heresy" denotes an opinion which is at variance with accepted doctrine. Formerly, the church burned heretics at the stake. Today, dissenters from Traditional Religion are merely tried in a heresy trial and, if found guilty, excommunicated or barred from the religious community. Professor Küng was not excommunicated; he was merely forbidden to teach Roman Catholic doctrine. Mrs. Johnson was excommunicated from the Mormon church. Liberal Religionists have always challenged the traditional doctrine and, therefore, are almost always heretics. When, in 1964, Dana McLean Greeley, then president of the Unitarian Universalist Association, eulogized John Haynes Holmes of the Community Church in New York, he said that Holmes was "born and reared in the finest heretical tradition of liberal religion."

In the heresy trial against Joan of Arc, as re-enacted in Bernard Shaw's play, the Church representatives beg Joan to recant so that they may spare her the death at the stake. The crucial charge in all heresy proceedings to this day is that the accused persists in religious error. Dissent from established doctrine is a deviation from the truth, which Traditional Religion considers as sinful error.

Liberal Religion does not countenance this attitude. Error, far from being sinful, is an instrument of progress. As Lewis Thomas puts it: "We learn, as we say, by trial and error. Why do we always say that? Why not 'trial and rightness,' or 'trial and triumph'? The old phrase puts it that way because that is, in real life, the way it is done."[17] Thomas also points out that the truth can only be explored if several alternatives are presented, one of which will emerge as truth and the other as error.

In 1531 the Spanish physician Servetus, a founding father of Unitarianism, exploded the errors of the trinity. This led to a joint manhunt by the forces of Calvin and the Roman Catholic Church, and the burning of Servetus at Calvin's stake in 1553. The errors of the biblical cosmology were discussed earlier in Chapter 2. And yet, the biblical record of the creation of the world persists, as does the story of Adam and Eve in paradise, the scientific doctrine of evolution notwithstanding.

Science teaches that there is a mathematical order in the physical phenomena of life. For Liberal Religion, that scientific truth cannot be ignored and must override contrary religious beliefs. However, science has not yet demonstrated how these phenomena hang together, whether by chance or with the aid of some supreme intelligence. We do not know; and there is, therefore, room for speculation, for religious faith, and for further search. The pragmatist will say that traditional belief in the governance of a supernatural God is the truth, because the pragmatist truth is what works. Since Traditional Religion has sustained so many people, it works and, therefore, it must be true. Not so. Pragmatic truth is not scientific truth. E. F. Schumacher, the British economist who became famous as the author of *Small is Beautiful,* wrote a *Guide for the Perplexed* in which he avers that there can never be any scientific proof of the ultimate cause of life. For which reason, E. F. Schumacher advocates a faith beyond logic[18] which seems to be another form of Traditional Religion. Schumacher recognizes evolution as a valid scientific discovery but says that whatever Darwin discovered does not exclude a supernatural design. He considers the Doctrine of Evolution a disastrous mistake, even as science fiction.[19] He criticizes an English school which dismissed a teacher who, contrary to a prescribed syllabus, taught children the biblical view of Creation instead of the Darwinian view.[20] This is not the place to argue with this late eminent author, but it is worthy of note that a man like him, while not wedded to Traditional Religion, still does not defer to scientific truth as Liberal Religion demands.

When Albert Schweitzer offended many Christian traditionalists and pietists with his rational explanation of the life of Jesus, he found solace in Paul's letter to the Corinthians, which concludes that man has no power to resist the truth. Liberal Religion agrees, even though Paul was alluding to the absolute truth which he preached, whereas Liberal Religion holds that no truth is absolute or eternal.

The elusive nature of truth makes skeptics of many Liberal Religionists. Old time religionists are often critical of Liberal Religion because it leads to skepticism. In response, it should be said that skepticism is not the same as cynicism. Liberal Religion is not cynical. It does not question its own or other people's motives and decency.

In conclusion, Liberal Religion does not claim to be the sole possessor of all truth. Truth evolves through the ages, and there are many areas of uncertainty. For that reason, Liberal Religion admits that there may be differing religious truths. But, it does not concede the truth of any religious thought which is in conflict with what science has definitively revealed.

7

Myths and Symbols

Myths

The nature and importance of myths has provoked considerable controversy. Alan Watts,in his book *Myth and Ritual in Christianity,* says it is impossible to be scientifically objective about the subject because "if one attempts to be objective, one is automatically pigeon-holed with the liberal."[1] For that very reason, the present approach is objective, which means, without subjective sentiments. According to Carl Jung's posthumous work *Man and His Symbols,* myths are important to psychiatrists for the interpretation of dreams. This is not the place to deal with the psychiatric aspects of myths, and so this particular aspect of the subject is disregarded. Also disregarded are the myths of poetry. The make believe found in poetry is often quite lovely, and we would not want to miss its flights of fancy. However, poetry's imagination often excels its knowledge. Truth is best told in prose.

Myths are by definition fictional rather than representations of the truth. In his book *On Being a Christian,* which does not bear the ecclesiastical imprimatur, Father Küng concedes that myths are not the truth and may not be taken literally.[2] Much of religion grows, or has grown, out of myths and magic. Some primitive societies are still enveloped by myths. For example, the religion of the aboriginal Australians is expressed in ceremonies in which mythical scenes are re-enacted. When this writer attempted to purchase a book on the religion of the aborigines in an Australian bookshop he was told: "The aborigines have no religion, they have only dreams. The best-known dream is the dream of the creation of the world."

115

Dreams are true as dreams, just as stories and legends are true as fiction. Neither dreams nor fictions are historical or scientific truth. It is widely believed that mythology is essential to religion, and that religion cannot be understood or experienced without the medium of mythology. Mythology has been defined as "the use of imagery to express the other-worldly in terms of the world and the divine in terms of human life, the other side in terms of this side."[3]

Some Liberal Religionists do not wish to abandon religious myths. They compare a myth to the model of the scientist or to a scientific hypothesis. After all, they argue, the cosmology of the scientists is based on unproven theories—why not hold on to the biblical cosmology, which is easier to understand than that of the scientists? The comparison is not apt, and it constitutes an unfortunate effort to rehabilitate discredited myths. The model or hypothesis of the scientist is tentative and subject to constant testing and verification. It will be discarded when found untrue or useless. The biblical myths have long been shown to be untrue, but instead of discarding them, protagonists seek their perpetuation. If the protagonist is a Religious Liberal, he will try to suggest new and contemporary meanings; he will try to pour old wine into new bottles. Thus, one will be told that the myth of the Garden of Eden conveys the message that knowledge is a burden to man. That is true, but why should it be desirable to convey this insight through a mystical analogy?

It seems that those who cling to the myths, knowing them to be untrue, do so out of nostalgia and sentimental attachment. The bond with the past is stronger than the stern demand for naked truth. This attachment is not unlike that of children who are loath to abandon the belief in (or the pretense of) Santa Claus. The story of the stork dropping the baby through the chimney is nice. However, few parents today perpetuate the myth.

Bulfinch, in his preface to the celebrated collection of mythological stories, refers to them as "false marvels and obsolete faiths," but he recommends the myths because they "tend to cherish on our minds the idea of the sources from which we spring."[4] Bulfinch, being a Traditional Religionist, does not include any biblical story. To him, the ancient pagan stories of the creation are myths, the Scripture story is "accurate information."[5]

Professor Ethel Sabin Smith, in her book *God and Other Gods,* tells of many religious myths which suggest parallels to Western scripture. It is clear that people in all ages and in all countries have spun stories and built myths. Sometimes, stories and myths originated out of a human need to find an explanation for what appeared to be the mysteries of life. Examples include the myths about the creation of the world and the origin of man. The myths of immortality and Judgment Day may also have sprung from this human puzzlement or despair. However, more often than not, the myths are probably the product of an exuberant imagination which caused people to tell historic tales in a fanciful and poetic manner. This is the stuff of which the Irish shanachie was made, who reveled in ancient Gaelic history. Reverting to Bible stories, one thinks of the Great Flood which was probably an historic event. The Bible story is only one of many versions. Noah, the likeable souse and womanizer, comes off better than God; the latter is depicted as a blunderer (although claiming omniscience) who found it necessary to drown his own creation. In Greek tradition, Zeus became so disgusted with the iniquities of the human race that he drowned the world in a great flood from which only Deucalion and Pyrrah were saved in an ark which landed on Mount Parnassus. Some myths are sheer poetic invention, such as the tale of Job.

Religion is not the only field in which myths grow. There are historical myths, like the famous one about our ancestors who came to America to establish religious freedom. True, they wanted it for themselves, but they fiercely suppressed the religious freedom of dissenters. Medical myths would provide another set of examples, many of which are known as old wives tales. What all these myths, including religious myths, have in common is that they are designed to enhance the reputation of, and respect for, American history, a medical remedy, or a religious event, as the case may be, and to strengthen the faith of the listener in the mythical fact.

Numerous hypotheses about the cause and the cure of cancer have been advanced and discarded. New ones spring up all the time. It is not surprising that some despairing sufferers cling to some unproven theories. However, science refuses to budge and insists, to this day, that there is no hard evidence on which we can rely, and, consequently, science does not underwrite or ratify any of the unproven hypotheses. If myths are to be given the status of scientific hypotheses, then why should they not be treated with the same caution and reserve? Why should religionists regard myths as a form of truth or as a medium which is better able to convey a religious truth than truth itself?

To many people, it is unthinkable that religion should be stripped of its myths. It would be like stripping a person of his or her clothes. This seems horrendous. Liberal Religion, however, wants the naked truth.

It is possible that the fondness for myths is grounded in a nostalgic fondness for uncertainty and ambiguity which frequently fires religious fervor. A religious person can never entirely escape such uncertainty and ambiguity. However, Liberal Religion distrusts uncertainty and ambiguity; it therefore must abjure myths rather than accept and promote them.

Let us review some examples of biblical myths: the myth of the fall of man in paradise is a religious horror story; the myth of the Virgin Birth is worthless; and the alleged immaculate conception of Jesus does not add to the stature of Jesus.

The myth of the Virgin Birth—more accurately referred to as the immaculate conception of Mary—is told only in two of the Gospels. It is not a uniquely Christian myth,because it occurs in many parts of the world.[6] And yet, quite a few theologians of Traditional Churches have been discriminated against in America and Europe because they expressed doubts about the truth of this myth. Tillich calls the myth of the Virgin Birth quasi-heretical because it deprives Jesus of a human father and, therefore, of his full humanity.[7] The myth also contradicts the biblical statement that Jesus was a descendant of Abraham and David, who were ancestors of Joseph.

The biblical myths of the Creation have no greater religious value than the many other unscientific stories about the origin of the world and man. Not even the notion that the world was made out of chaos is new. The Greek poet Hesiod had anticipated it. Professor Charles Long has compiled an anthology of forty-five myths of creation. The biblical story in Genesis is one of them. Professor Eliade, in his anthology of religious history called *From Primitives to Zen,* reprints over thirty different myths of creation and origin. The myth of Adam and Eve is repugnant and apt to alienate a thinking person from religion. The myth of the Judgment Day may frighten some people into good behavior and is, in an obvious way, religiously acceptable to those whose lives are guided by the fear of God. If, as has been suggested, the Easter myth is one of liberation, then that story can be told straightforwardly without embroidery.

The paucity of religious language and the unwillingness to use blunt terms make it hard for some Liberal clergymen to communicate the teachings of Liberal Religion without resorting to ancient stories and myths. The perpetuation of myths has frequently been justified as a means to make it easier to convey the message of religion. Thus, the Roman Catholic maverick, Professor Küng, argues that most people cannot comprehend religious values without myths. He writes: "it is obvious that the biblical Christmas and Easter stories are more comprehensible and easier to remember than any amount of abstract propositions on divine sonship and passing through death to life. Even today, in the eye of rational, causal, and functional technical thinking, might not a vivid narrative form of proclamation still be absolutely necessary, and certain ancient formulae—mythological in the widest sense—still be useful?"[8] The answer to that question is "yes," useful to the teaching of Traditional Religion but unnecessary for Liberal Religion, which rests on unadorned truth. "Unadorned" does not mean ugly; truth has a beauty of its own. More will be said about Christmas and Easter in Chapter 21.

The myths about the Greek gods have no religious value today. The famed classicist Edith Hamilton describes them thus: ". . . the jovial company of the *Iliad,* who sit at the banqueting board in Olympus, making heaven shake with their shouts of inextinguishable laughter are not a religious gathering. Their morality even is more than questionable, and also their dignity. They deceive each other, they are shifty, and tricky in their dealings with mortals. In Homer's pages, they are delightful reading, but not in the very least edifying."[9] Hamilton then points out that this Greek mythology is far removed from Greek religion.[10] Hamilton does not deal with the poet and singer Orpheus, whom most of us know only through

Gluck's opera *Orpheus and Euridice.* He was an attractive but purely mythical figure. Orphic religion and theology, which developed in the sixth century B.C., paved the way for Traditional Christianity and, therefore, is an important myth. Will Durant described it thus: "The doctrines of hell, purgatory, and heaven, of the body versus the soul, of the divine son slain and reborn, as well as the sacramental eating of the body and blood and divinity of God, directly and deviously influenced Christianity which was itself, a mystery religion of atonement and hope, of mystic union and release. The basic ideas and ritual of the Orphic cult are alive and flourishing amongst us today."[11] Durant demonstrates that myth and religion are related but that myth is not religion, at least not as Liberal Religion conceives religion.

Additional examples of nonreligious mythology are the Nordic myths reflected in Richard Wagner's *Nibelungen Cycle* ending with the *Götterdämmerung,* when the world of the Nordic gods collapses. In his book *Myth and Reality,* Eliade points out that all myths are grounded in the belief in supernatural beings.[12] At the end of that book, Eliade illuminates the subject of myths by writing about what he calls the myth of modern art. Modern art often defies one's understanding. One does not want to admit such lack of understanding; the myth is such that one pretends admiration.

The worst feature of the myth is that it corrupts the young. The Sunday school teaches the myth as truth. Plato has already warned that misrepresenting the nature of the divine is a great fault. Tales which are lies are inadmissible, says Plato, "whether they are supposed to have an allegorical meaning or not. For a young person cannot judge what is allegorical and what is literal. Anything that he receives into his mind at that age is likely to become indelible and inalterable."[13] Plato may have been an unacceptable paternalist in his general philosophy, but in this warning against untruth, he is undoubtedly right and his warning must be heeded by Liberal Religion.

The Liberal Church does not reject a myth when it is told as a mythical story, just as it does not reject poetry or when it enjoys as great art the painting of the myth of the Last Judgment in the Sistine Chapel. However, Liberal Religion cannot favor the twilight of the myth. The roots of Liberal Religion are firmly planted in reality and in clear truth. An ancient hymn expresses it thus: "Abide not in the realm of dreams, O Man, however fair it seems, but with clear eye the present scan and hear the call from God and man."[14]

The German professor Rudolf Bultmann (1884–1976), one of the giants of Protestant theology, shocked his professional colleagues by demanding that the Bible, and especially the New Testament, be demythologized. This was first expressed in an essay called *New Testament and Mythology.* It was published in 1941 and translated into English in 1953. Dietrich Bonhoeffer thought that Bultmann did not go far enough.[15] He and Bultmann had a profound influence on John Robinson before the bishop wrote *Honest to God.* These theologians deplored it that their co-religionists (Bultmann and

Bonhoeffer were Lutheran, Robinson an Anglican) still clung to the three-tiered view of the world, which divides the earth into surface, underworld, and heaven. This concept reflects the authors' knowledge of the Bible, and the biblical myths are based upon that knowledge. Bultmann notes that: "there is nothing specifically Christian in the mythical view of the world as such. It is simply the cosmology of a pre-scientific age."[16] This is not the place to review Bultmann's work to which the theology of Liberal Religion is deeply indebted. Bishop Robinson makes this summary statement about Bultmann's teaching: "In order to express the transhistorical character of the historical event of Jesus of Nazareth, the New Testament writers used the mythological language of pre-existence, incarnation, ascent and descent, miraculous intervention, cosmic catastrophe, and so on . . . which makes sense only on a completely antiquated world-view."[17] William James wrote, "For our ancestors, dreams, hallucinations, revelations, and cock and bull stories were inextricably mixed with facts."[18]

What about legends? The difference between myths and legends is not easy to discern. It may be said that a legend is an embroidered historical or quasi-historical tale, not tinged with religion, and therefore less seductive, in a religious sense, than a myth. The stories about King Arthur and Camelot are typical legends. The tale of John Murray's stay at Barnegat's Bay is a charming legend, if not held out as truth.[19] The Biblical narrative of the Great Flood, which reflects an historic event and recurs in many non-Biblical traditions, can also be ranked as a legend. And yet, when Charles Darwin told the captain of the *Beagle* that the measurements of the ark, as described in the Bible, were insufficient to house all animals of that period, the captain thought this an offense to God.

Symbols

The symbols to which this section is addressed are religious symbols. There are many other kinds, for instance, mathematical symbols, political symbols, advertising symbols, stock exchange symbols, and sex symbols. All these symbols communicate a shorthand message in their particular field. Symbols are abbreviations. So it is with religious symbols, which requires that we comprehend their meanings. A symbol becomes meaningless if it does not communicate what it abbreviates. And yet, it is said that religion, being an abstract concept, cannot be understood without its symbols. What this means, of course, is that what is being abbreviated cannot be understood without the abbreviation. But this would be to stand causality on its head. The explanation for such an unusual phenomenon is at times a desperate desire to hold on to the old cherished symbols, a desire not unlike the wish to clothe religion in old myths, no matter how tattered. Professor

Charles H. Long "insists" on the primacy of symbols in religious life.[20] Professor Robert B. Tapp, conceding that many Unitarian Universalists reject symbolism, asserts nevertheless that the act of churchgoing is group symbolism.[21]

The oldest religious symbol in the Bible is circumcision. It was the mark of the Hebrew male which Jehovah demanded.[22] Later, Paul rejected the symbol as superficial and devisive (Rom. 2:12 and 4:11). When a young child is dedicated in a Liberal Church by touching it with water and a rosebud, the water symbolizes purity and the rosebud symbolizes the unfolding life. These are not religious symbols in the traditional sense, because neither water nor rosebud symbolize a religion, not even a religious belief. If a departing traveler is given a St. Christopher medal, the gift symbolizes and implies the religious belief that the medal invests him/her with the protection of the Saint, and that he/she will travel safely. No such religious belief attaches to the water and rosebud. This insight does not detract from the beauty, the meaning, or the religiosity of the celebration of the child's dedication.

Conclusion

The views on myths which are presented here are not only controversial, as stated at the beginning of this chapter, they are downright unpopular, even among Religious Liberals. This is a prime example of the ambiguity endemic to so much of religious thinking.

Liberal Religion is firmly rooted in reason and truth. Logic and consistency, therefore, require that we discard myths which dilute or embroider the truth. It may well be, as Father Küng writes, that the Easter and Christmas stories are easier to communicate through myth than without it.[23] Father Küng speaks from the viewpoint of the preacher. His remarks may illuminate why even ministers of Liberal Religion, at times, prefer a myth. However, Liberal Religion will lose its peculiar identity and integrity if it ceases to rely on the naked truth and reason. Children like to receive their codliver oil diluted in a glass of orange juice. Liberal Religionists should not want to be so treated. Nor should they want to perpetuate a myth just because their less enlightened ancestors liked it.

While Liberal Religion is austere and unsentimental in its religious message, it is by no means averse to fairy tales and poetry, provided the flights of enjoyable fancy are not presented in lieu of the truth or as truth itself.

The trouble with religious symbols, as Paul Tillich has stated, is their tendency to replace that to which they are supposed to point and to become the ultimate. They then become idols.

The cross is the religious symbol of Christianity. Donald Harrington has shown that the cross symbolizes religious love as well as religious hatred and cruelty.[24] An outstanding example of religious symbolism is represented by a monument in Salt Lake City which is described as a monolith. It was erected by the Fraternal Order of Eagles, a group that arranged for similar monuments in other parts of the country. On the monolith are inscribed the Ten Commandments, letters of the Hebrew alphabet, the Star of David, other symbols said to represent the seeing eye of God, and a likeness of Jesus Christ said to represent peace. Since the monolith was built on property owned by the city, some citizens initiated a lawsuit on the grounds that the city had no business propagating religion. The lower court agreed, but the decision was reversed by the Federal Court of Appeals. The Appeals Court ruled that what was symbolized here was not religion, but the American way of life.[25] The Supreme Court of California, in another case, said that the Salt Lake City monolith was indeed a religious symbol, but it was too partisan because it contained no such symbols as the Coptic, Universalist, and Scientology crosses; the Buddhist wheel; the Shinto trii; the Zoroastrian vase of fire; the Jain swastika; the Confucian yang-yin or the Unitarian flaming chalice.[26] These two court decisions present opposite views of the meaning of religious symbols. In addition, the California decision contains an interesting catalog of religious symbols, although it mistakenly refers to a nonexistent Universalist cross.

People like symbols. But symbols inspire not only love, loyalty, and allegiance, they also inspire fear and hatred. They are devisive.

Liberal Religion needs no symbols.

8

Jesus and Christianity

In May 1963 delegates of the American Unitarian Association and of the Universalist Church of America met in Syracuse, New York to discuss merger and a set of common bylaws. One of the hotly debated issues was whether Jesus or the spirit of Jesus belonged in the bylaws. Opponents said that Jesus was not so unique for the new denomination as to exclude the simultaneous mention of Moses, Buddha, Mohammed, and others. The bylaw provision finally agreed upon refers to the universal truths taught by the great prophets and teachers of humanity in every age and tradition, immemorially summarized in the Judeo-Christian tradition.[1]

Some scholars have made great and sincere efforts to prove that Jesus never existed. These efforts served no useful purpose because even if Jesus never existed, he had become the central character of the Christian religion and, as such, enjoyed tremendous influence and importance in the Western culture. The preponderance of scholarly opinion is that Jesus existed. To raise the question at all, and apply historic research methods in this connection, was (and is) understandably offensive to those who consider Jesus as part of the Godhead and beyond human research. The scholars are divided as to whether Jesus was an ordinary teacher and religious reformer or one who believed that the end of the world was near and that a new supernatural world would soon begin. The latter is called the eschatological view. Albert Schweitzer wrote an exhaustive history of the *Life of Jesus* wherein he explained that Jesus believed and held to the eschatological view. The fact that the world did not come to an end proves that Jesus was fallible. On the other hand, his teachings spread and survived which only serves to prove his greatness. An English summary of Schweitzer's findings is contained in his

123

autobiography from which the following excerpts are quoted as elucidating the place of Jesus in Liberal Religion.

> The religion of love which Jesus taught and which made its first appearance as an element in the late Jewish eschatological world view enters later on into connection with the late Greek, the medieval, and the modern world views.[2]
>
> What is decisive is the amount of influence over mankind won by the spiritual and ethical truth which it has held from the first.[3]
>
> He does nothing dogmatically. . . . Nowhere does he demand of the hearers that they shall sacrifice thinking to believing.[4]
>
> He kindles the fire of an ethical faith. Thus the Sermon on the Mount becomes an incontestable charter of Liberal Christianity. The truth that the ethical is the essence of religion is firmly established on the authority of Jesus.[5]

Since Jesus believed the end of the world was near, he was interested in making men worthy of life in the other world. He was interested in improving man's ethical behavior. He was not interested in social reform.[6] The greatness of Jesus' teaching is its timelessness; its value survives even though it was not intended for the future.

The Christian tradition is not content with this greatness. It has built a vast superstructure above Jesus. Christianity teaches that God has foreseen the fall of man, and therefore decided to descend to earth in the person of his son Jesus for the purpose of delivering the world from evil and corruption. This was accomplished by the crucifixion in which Jesus shares the fate of God's creatures. It is through this miraculous event that human beings are redeemed and death is forever abolished. Christian faith is based on this premise. And yet, as Alan Watts has pointed out, historically, Christianity is a religion in which anxiety plays a far greater part than faith.[7]

Christians are not a homogeneous group. Not only is there a difference between Roman Catholicism and Protestantism, but Protestants themselves are divided into many denominations each of which is jealous of its uniqueness. They do not even agree on a proper Bible text. For instance, in the Scottish Presbyterian Church one finds a book entitled *The Psalms of David* "according to the version approved in the Church of Scotland." In the eyes of Liberal Religion, this kind of parochialism is one of the weaknesses of Traditional Religion.

The followers of Reverend Jim Jones, who committed mass suicide and killings in Guyana in 1978, obeyed their pastor's command and promise that they "would meet in another place." Established Christianity was embarrassed. One of its foremost leaders, Reverend Billy Graham, wrote, "It is true that he came from a religious background, but what he did and how he thought, have no relationship to the views and teachings of any legitimate form of historic Christianity. We have witnessed a false Messiah . . . ."[8] Christianity cannot thus disclaim the consequence of its teaching.

It is worth noting that what we know today as Christianity is the surviving view of innumerable creeds which Jesus inspired. Many of these creeds were antagonistic and condemned by the prevailing orthodox Christianity.[9] While it is not appropriate in the present context to dwell on the stormy history of the early Church, mention must be made of the Gnostics. They seem to have been the religious liberals of their time. They seem to have looked upon Jesus as a great teacher rather than a dying savior. They doubted the resurrection story and did not consider it religiously important. The Gnostics had an elitist view of themselves. The Church fathers condemned them as heretics. One of them named Irenaus (130–202 A.D.) is said to have regarded Gnostics as the crazies of the second century.

Nobody in the Liberal Church believes Jesus to be the incarnation of God, or part of a divine trinity. The idea that the ingestion of wine and bread at the communion table in some way constitutes the absorption of the mystical body of Christ is a myth, not unlike the Orphic myth and other ancient myths which made believers think that by eating their God they could possess him and become godly themselves. One of the antiphons in the Roman Catholic liturgy reads, "Whoever eats my flesh and drinks my blood, will live in me and I in him."

When Jesus rode into Jerusalem it was, like the 1965 march in Alabama and the similar march in Washington, a challenge to the establishment, except that Jesus was certain that the establishment would not let him get away with it. Those in power would crucify him. He was a courageous man who died in order to spread his ideas.

This was greatness. The greatness need not be embellished with Traditional Religion's idea that Jesus' death washed away human sin, once and for all. Considering all the evil in the world (for instance the Thirty Years War and the atrocities of Hitler's holocaust), it is rather astonishing that Traditional Religion should cling to such an incredible notion. And yet it does. Examples from the *Anglican Book of Common Prayer* are: "Lamb of God who takes away the sins of the world" and (from the baptismal service) "that the child may enjoy the everlasting benediction of heavenly washing."

Traditional Religion had diminished the greatness of Jesus in other ways as well. Paul robbed him of his humanity and made him into a divinity. This is understandable because, at the time of Jesus, people in and around Palestine were expecting a supernatural deliverer, the hoped-for Messiah. Paul wrote that Jesus had the nature of God, yet he did not think of himself as the equal of God (Phil. 2:16), but Paul himself taught otherwise. When Jesus preached some people called him the Son of God. Jesus rebuked such appellations (Luke 4:41) and referred to himself as the Son of Man, which in today's language would be "a common man." When he criticized the rigid observation of the Jewish Sabbath rule, Jesus said, "The Sabbath was made for man, not man for the Sabbath, and so the Son of Man is master even of the Sabbath" (Matt. 12:8). The Gospels, which one must remember were written many decades after Jesus' death, are, of course, not consistent. In some parts they report that God called Jesus his beloved son, that Jesus was a divinity (Mark 1:1, John 5:23), and that he predicted his resurrection (Matt. 17:23).

If Jesus had been a divinity, he would have inspired veneration, but he would not command respect for his human courage, compassion, and wisdom. Paul Tillich writes that the doctrine of the Virgin Birth deprives Jesus of a human father and, therefore, of his full humanity.[10] The blind and mindless veneration of Jesus is probably the reason why Traditional Christians know so little about the person of Jesus. Minutes before he expired on the cross, Jesus is reported to have exclaimed, "My God, my God, why have you forsaken me?" and this is supposed to indicate the depth of his despair. Actually, Jesus was merely reciting the twenty-second Psalm which begins with the quoted phrase but ends up with an expression of contentment. In those days, devout Jews would recite a familiar writing by just uttering the opening words of a piece.

The traditional portraits of the crucifixion depict Jesus as quiet and content, without indicating any suffering. The exception is the great painting of Mathias Grünewald (1480–1528) which is part of the Isenheimer Altar and exhibited in Colmar, France. It very movingly depicts the great suffering of Jesus on the cross—and his humanity, which Traditional Religion suppresses.

In the West, Jesus is usually portrayed as a white Caucasian, which demonstrates that God and Christ in Traditional Religion are mirror images of the believer. While Gaugin lived in Tahiti, he painted the birth of Christ in which Mary is depicted as a Polynesian woman in a South Sea surrounding. The painting now hangs in Munich, Germany. Most pictures of Jesus show him as a man who wore sandals (the common footwear of his day), a beard, and long hair. For that reason, he has been compared with the hippies and flower children of our recent history. However, even if he had been clean shaven and unsandaled, he would have to be regarded as a radical foe of the establishment. He was a small businessman (Mark 6:3) who, at the age of thirty, decided to become a preacher (Luke 3:23).

The cheap conventional pictures depict Jesus as a young man with flowing blond hair and a face of almost feminine beauty. This is supposed to convey his message of gentleness, compassion, and love. Actually, Jesus does not seem to have been a soft man, but a powerful itinerant rabbi and preacher. More will be said about this presently. Max Weber says that what gave Christianity its extraordinary superiority over its competitors was "that this extremely masculine cult excluded women."[11] Judging by the composition of the average contemporary congregation, this sounds strange. And yet, one remembers Paul saying, "mulier tacet in ecclesia" ("let women be silent in church"). This male exclusiveness carries over into the present prejudice against female ministers.

The Christian Churches prefer to depict Jesus as an ever forgiving mild-mannered man. He was nothing of the kind. The Bible reports that he despised hypocrites (Matt. 23:13), would never forgive violation of the Holy Spirit (Matt. 12:31), and that he had not come to bring peace but the sword (Matt. 10–34). It has been suggested that this last reference to the sword is entirely out of character and, therefore, an alien and erroneous interpolation in the Bible report. This does not appear likely. Jesus was obviously a very strong personality who had no patience with the old ways. He was bent on reform at all costs. If persuasion would not succeed, coercion symbolized by the sword would be used to bring about the desired spiritual revolution. That is what Emerson probably meant when he said, "Whenever man comes, there comes revolution."[12] This strong spirit, whether called holy or not, is of the essence of Liberal Religion.

While he wanted people to live up to the law of Moses — "I come to fulfil the law, not to destroy it" (Matt. 5:17) — he denounced the corruption in the administration of the Jewish law and the rigidity of its application. That is why he drove the money changers from the temple (Matt. 21:12). He denounced the rigid observance of the Jewish Sabbath laws, saying, "the Sabbath is made for man, and not man for the Sabbath" (Mark 2:27). Christianity began as a Jewish reform movement and ended up as a new religion which most Jews regard as traitorous.

Christianity is often propagated as the religion of love. This is supposed to be the distinctive feature of the New Testament as compared with the Old Testament. In the Sermon on the Mount, Jesus said, "you were told an eye for an eye and a tooth for a tooth, but I tell you, not to resist injury, and to turn the other cheek" (Matt. 5:38). Jesus also preached that, in accordance with Hebrew teaching, man must walk humbly with his God and be merciful. Even in its early and purest stage, Christianity limited brotherly love to the circle of fellow believers, as it was with other Traditional Religions.[13] Over the centuries, Christians, like the Jews and the followers of Islam, have been neither loving nor humble. All Traditional Religions have been unloving and arrogant. Christians in particular have forfeited the claim of being followers of Jesus. The German classicist Gotthold Ephraim Lessing (1729–1781) wrote that the religion of Christ and the Christian religion are two entirely different matters.[14] This is, of course, the deist position as discussed in Chapter 3.

The Mormon Church was founded by its prophet Joseph Smith in 1830 with the assertion that, in the past eighteen centuries, Christianity had been corrupted. The famous Salt Lake City based church resulted. But the Smith descendants disdain the Mormon Church as unchristian. They have their own Reorganized Church of Jesus Christ of Latter Day Saints, in Independence, Missouri.

One of the great themes, if not the central theme, of the Christian religion is the story of the risen Christ. The Resurrection story is not as unique as most Christians think. In ancient Greek religion, Velchanos, the son of Zeus, rose from his grave and his resurrection was cause for religious celebration.[15] Jesus, as Christ, meaning the "annointed one," is supposed to have walked out of his tomb three days after his burial. He allegedly walked the countryside for several weeks, and then ascended into heaven. Such ascension to heaven was not novel. The Prophet Elijah is reported to have gone into heaven in a fiery chariot (2 Kings 2:11). Nobody is reported to have seen the living Jesus after his burial, but his disciples were sure that the wondrous event had taken place. Paul also believed it and considered it as conclusive evidence that Jesus was the Messiah whose appearance had been foretold by the ancient prophets. In the Gospels, which were composed after Paul's death, Jesus is made to predict his resurrection (John 11:25). Any person who has watched a performance of the late monologist, Ruth Draper, or a performance of a sound and light show, will know how the existence of an actual event can be evoked without it really happening. The Resurrection of Jesus and his ascension into heaven appear to be the result of such powerful suggestion.

The Resurrection of Christ inspires Christians to believe that they, too, will be resurrected. In 1744 an English deist published a book entitled *Resurrection of Jesus Considered,* in which he asserted that the story was a hoax. He was sent to prison for this boldness.[16] The Apostle Paul was well aware that people might ask how dead people could possibly be raised to life. In his first letter to the Corinthians he calls that a stupid question, and he then proceeds to answer it in a manner which some will call sophisticated and others will call double talk: ". . . whatever you sow in the ground has to die before it is given new life, and the thing that you sow is not what is going to come . . . the thing that is sown is perishable but what is raised is imperishable . . . flesh and blood cannot inherit the kingdom of God, and the perishable cannot inherit what lasts forever . . ." (1 Cor. 15:36 seq.).

In Liberal Religion, the greatness and the influence of Jesus does not depend nor does it rest upon the story of the risen Christ.

Considering that less than a majority of the world's population are Christians and that vast parts of the earth, not to mention the Universe, have developed and are developing without worshipping Jesus Christ, it is a colossal arrogance of Pope John Paul II to refer to Jesus Christ as the center of the Universe and of history. These are the exact words of the pope's encyclical *Redeemer of Man.* They reflect the traditional attitude of Traditional Christianity, which is repugnant to the Liberal Church. It is no less repugnant because the pope and Traditional Religion are probably not consciously arrogant.

Like the Moslems, the Liberal Church reveres Jesus as a great prophet. His teachings are transmitted through the Gospels. Nowhere in the Gospels is there a claim that Jesus was the Lord or the Son of God. He spoke of God as his father (for instance, "in my father's house there are many mansions"), but he also admonished the crowd in the Sermon on the Mount to pray to "our father" (Matt. 6:9). Obviously, he regarded all men, including himself, as God's children.

Long after Jesus' death, Paul spread His teaching and, through his missionary efforts and travels, built the cult into the Christian Church. Paul, not Jesus, is the founder of the Christian Church. Paul talked, preached, and wrote for twenty-five years throughout the eastern part of the Roman Empire until he died in 64 A.D. The Gospels were written later; the first was the Gospel of Mark, published in 70 A.D. It is astonishing, but nevertheless true, that this simple fact is disregarded by Traditional Religionists who speak of Jesus as the founder or author of their religion. Even Liberal Religionists occasionally fall into this error.[17] It was also Paul who invented the myth that Jesus is "our Lord" and that he was the Son of God.

The part of the Bible called Acts (the Acts of the Apostles) tells the story. Originally written by Luke, apparently it was later edited and translated in a variety of ways which have occupied scholars but are of no interest to us here. The Jesus cult was originally a Jewish commune (Acts 2). Its members were inspired by what they called the Holy Spirit. They believed that Jesus had been resurrected from the grave and had gone to heaven. Many Greeks joined the sect, being converted by what they conceived to be the Holy Spirit. The Apostles, foremost among them Peter and Paul, proclaimed faith in Jesus as the culmination of the Jewish religion and the fulfillment of ancient prophecies. Peter devoted himself mainly to the conversion of Jews, while Paul went on missions abroad. Obviously, the Jewish establishment was upset. When Stephen, a convert from the Hellenic religion, complained to the Sanhedrin that the religious establishment had always resisted innovations and the prophets, he was stoned to death (Acts 7–59). The Bible says that Paul approved the killing and, for that reason, Paul has been denounced as a murderer. This was before Paul's own conversion and prior to his missionary travels abroad, during which he established Christian communities and taught his new adherents that Jesus was the Son of God. Like all religious teachers and cult leaders to this day, Paul found it convenient to convey his message by clothing it with divine authority.

According to the laws of Abraham, adherents of the Jewish religion must be circumcised (Gen. 17:10). This did not suit the Gentiles. Paul therefore proclaimed that faith in Jesus Christ was more important than circumcision, thus antagonizing the Jewish religious establishment. Yet Paul did not tire of his effort to preach in the synagogues. The following of his speeches is cited to demonstrate that the Jesus worship was originally a purely Jewish matter.

Men of Israel and friends of God listen: the God of our nation Israel chose our ancestors and made our people great. He made David their King

of whom he approved in these words: I have selected David son of Jesse, a
man after my own heart, who will carry on my whole purpose. To keep his
promise, God has raised up for Israel one of David's descendants, Jesus as
Savior, whose coming was heralded by John when he proclaimed a baptism of repentence for the whole people of Israel. Before John ended his
career, he said, "I am not the one you imagine me to be; that one is coming
after me and I am not fit to undo his sandal." My brothers, sons of Abraham's race, and all you who fear God, this message of salvation is for
you. . . . (Acts 13:16)

The Lordship of Jesus—his divine qualities as the Son of God—are
clearly inspired inventions of Paul, long after the death of Jesus. The idea
that Jesus is part of the trinity is an even later invention of the Church.

Reminding us that Jesus was a carpenter by trade, and that his disciples
were artisans (fishermen, tentmakers) the sociologist Max Weber calls early
Christianity a religion of artisans. This explains, Weber states, the rapid
expansion of Christianity.[18] Artisans, he says, are attracted to cults and
avoid purely ethical or purely rational religions.[19] Weber also says that
Christianity is primarily designed to appeal to the underprivileged. Christianity directed its promise most emphatically to the poor in spirit and
worldly goods.[20] However, there were no proletarian instincts in the doctrine and teachings of Jesus. He was entirely indifferent to mundane matters because he was convinced that the end of the world was near.

In the Gospels, Jesus is treated as a physical descendant of Abraham
and David. These two are described as ancestors of Joseph, the husband of
Mary. The Gospels, in many of their contradictions, also tell that Joseph
was not the real father of Jesus. Mary allegedly conceived while still a
virgin. This was accomplished through the Holy Spirit who, according to
Luke, came upon Mary and "covered her with his shadow" (Luke 1:35).

The myth of the Virgin Birth reoccurs in other religions because it apparently was thought to lend special grace and authority to the person who was
conceived by a virgin. Science today knows that certain lizards can reproduce
through unfertilized eggs. However, those so born are only female.[21]

The Liberal Church does not need the unscientific underpinning of a
Virgin Birth in order to have respect and reverence for Jesus and his teachings. The Virgin Birth is a myth which is questioned even by modern scholars of the Traditional Religion. That Jesus should have been the Son of God
is likewise an irrelevancy to Liberal Religion.

At the time of Jesus, the Roman Empire, of which Judea was a part,
seethed with cults and there were many divinities for whom virgin birth was
claimed and those whose blood was said to wash away sins. But it was only
Jesus whose veneration was elevated to a world religion, and this was due
solely to the unflagging zeal of Paul. In the Roman Empire, and even in
Palestine at the time of Jesus, there were many reformers whom the Roman
authorities considered dangerous and were therefore put to death.

There is a short story by Anatole France which tells of Pontius Pilatus, the former governor of Judea, strolling in the gardens of Rome with a friend who, like himself, had served in Palestine. They chat about the unrest in that country and the friend talks in particular of that man Jesus whom Pilate condemned to the cross. "Jesus," responds Pilate, "I do not remember any Jesus."

The Liberal Church rejects the dogmatism of Paul, his faith in the Lordship of Jesus, his myths of the Virgin Birth and the Resurrection, as well as his demand for uncritical, irrational faith in the supernatural power of Jesus.

The Liberal Church accepts the simple ethical teachings of Jesus once they are removed from the legends and stories which the Gospel authors, their editors, translators, the Apostles, and others after them have spun around this simple and straightforward man. This is what Thomas Jefferson aimed at when he edited the so-called Jefferson Bible. Albert Schweitzer followed the same approach.[22] Therefore, the small group whose members call themselves Unitarian Christians must be regarded as belonging to the Liberal Religion. However, some of the Unitarian Christian ministers in the U.S.A. desire membership for themselves or their congregation in the National Council of the Churches of Christ. Since that organization requires that its members acknowledge the Lordship of Jesus Christ, the desire for membership is not compatible with the principles of Liberal Religion. The wish to be accepted by the National Council jeopardizes the religious integrity of a Unitarian Christian.

In many respects, Christianity today has become a habit rather than a religion. The mindless mouthings of Christianity intrude on numerous public invocations. Worse still, it has become a sales tool. There are Christian ashtrays, Christian doggie sweaters, and Christian underwear. Such items can be found in the Christian Yellow Pages, a telephone directory designed "to aid the Christian in locating a Brother in the Lord." (No Sister is mentioned.) All this is elaborated in a midwestern newspaper story which is aptly headlined: "Jesus Sells."[23] Liberal Religion abhors such callous pretense of religion.

In conclusion, it bears repeating that in spite of its enormous influence in the world, Christianity has failed to bring about more peace, and that the teaching of Jesus did not have a noticeable impact on the conduct of men.

9

Satan, Heaven, and Hell

While Satan, heaven, and hell are common concepts in almost all cultures, and are indispensable concepts in the scheme of Traditional Religion, Liberal Religion regards these concepts as useless, mythical baggage. In order to understand the position of Liberal Religion, it is necessary to review the historical and contemporary meanings of these words. Such a review will also shed further light on the meaning of Liberal Religion.

Even those who do not believe in Satan may refer to someone as "devilishly clever" or enviously refer to another person as a "lucky devil." Satan was a familiar character to the Jews at the time of Jesus, and he is mentioned in the Gospels on several occasions. When Jesus approached the Apostle Peter, he said, "Get out of my sight, you Satan, for you do not side with God, but with men" (Mark 8:33). It is interesting to note that in the juxtaposition of God and man, Satan is identified with man. In the Book of Revelation, the city of Pergamum is called the place "where Satan has his throne" (Rev. 2:13). This refers to the fact that Pergamum had a temple dedicated to emperor worship. In the gospel of Nicodemus (one of the books which the Church fathers rejected when they put the Bible together), there is a vivid account of Jesus' descent into hell after his crucifixion and before his resurrection. In this account, Jesus discourses with Beelzebub, the prince of hell. In popular usage, Satan is sometimes called Beelzebub.

Satan also goes by the name of Lucifer, which is a Latin word meaning "light bearer." This seems a curious name for the "prince of darkness," as Satan is often called. Alan Watts suggests that it is a mistake to regard Satan as evil; rather he should be understood as the symbol of the dark side of life, "of shadow revealing light by contrast," corresponding to "what the

133

Chinese call yin as distinct from yang, the dark negative and feminine aspect of life."[1] Why femininity is negative, is not clear.

In the Book of Job, one encounters Satan as one of the sons of God who came "to attend to Yahweh" (Job 1:6), indicating that he was not equal, but a subordinate to God. In Isaiah, Satan (Lucifer) is mocked as the fallen angel (Isa. 14:12). This concept is perpetuated in Milton's *Paradise Lost.* In that poem, Satan is the serpent in Paradise, who seduced Adam and Eve. In the "Prologue in Heaven" of Goethe's drama *Faust,* the Devil is personified as Mephistopheles and the serpent is referred to as his cousin. The Devil himself is again subordinate to God. There is an interesting parallel between the biblical Book of Job and Goethe's work. In both, God challenges Satan to seduce the earthling into disobedience and insubordination, and in both instances Satan gains a temporary victory, but loses in the end.

Milton and Goethe are not the only authors who have made use of the person of the Devil. Stephen Vincent Benet has given us the tale of *The Devil and Daniel Webster.* This and similar stories are found in *Speak of the Devil.*[2] In addition, there is Bernard Shaw's *Don Juan in Hell,*[3] one of the most titillating satires about Satan. In the thirty-fourth canto of Dante's *Divine Comedy,* the Devil is depicted as a composite of Judas, Brutus, and Cassius.

The power of the Devil is ingrained in Western culture. When Niccolo Paganini (1782–1840) dazzled his audience with his incredible virtuosity on the violin, there were witnesses ready to swear that they had seen the Devil himself standing at his side to assist with the more difficult passages.

Some sober Traditional Religionists consider the belief in a supernatural Satan as a mere superstition, although they recognize the existence of biblical demonology. Some traditional Protestants, in particular, seem to believe that Satan is a Jewish invention later superseded by Christ and unnecessarily perpetuated by the Roman Catholic Church.[4] And yet, Martin Luther himself reported several personal encounters with the Devil.[5] The true Traditionalist would respond to the Protestant critics with the Beaudelaire quote, "the lowliest trick of the devil is to persuade you that he does not exist."[6]

After the mass killing and suicide which occurred under the inspiration of the Reverend Jim Jones in November 1978 at a religious community in Guyana, the Baptist Evangelist Billy Graham announced that the tragedy was brought about by Satan. Wrote Mr. Graham, "God is at work in the hearts of millions, but so is the devil."[7] According to that statement, God and Satan are competitors; in the Guyana case, it was Satan who prevailed. Satan, it follows, is on the same level as God; in other words, Satan is a god. One cannot conceive good without evil. It is therefore logical that if one believes in a supernatural anthropomorphic God, one can also believe in a supernatural anthropomorphic Devil. Such equivalence of power is by no means unusual.

It appears that Reverend Billy Graham, who assumes a duality of supreme power existing between God and the anti-God Satan, represents the view of most Traditional Christians. Satan is a real person with supernatural attributes; he is the anti-God. A detailed exposition of this view is contained in the book *The Devil* by Giovanni Papini, an Italian Roman Catholic. Papini explains that despite baptismal renunciation Satan is the real master of man.

Many persons actually worship Satan and there are cults devoted to him. In the United States, there even exists a Church of Satan and a Satanic Bible. The highlight of the Satan Cult and the Church of Satan is the Black Mass, a celebration which nonadherents find disgusting.[8] The Satan worship is said to originate from the so-called mystery religions of the Hellenic world, and the Mithras religion, all of which were synthesized in Christianity.[9]

If Satan, rather than God, is responsible for all evil, the traditional concept of God as *all good,* is strengthened. In Leviticus, the duality of the supreme power is expressed in a double sacrifice. Aaron, the high priest, is instructed to cast lots upon two goats, one to be slain for Yahweh, and the other (the scapegoat) to be sent alive into the desert as an offering to the Devil (Lev. 15:10). This incident has been edited out of the King James version of the Bible. However, Satan, as an independent operator, is encountered when he tempts Jesus without success (Mark 1:13) and references to him abound in the Gospels. One of King David's minor offenses was that he caused a census to be taken although God did not want it. But Satan told him to do it anyway. Traditional Religion's belief in the Devil is typically expressed in the biblical exhortations "Be sober, be vigilant because your adversary the devil, as a roaring lion, walketh about seeking whom he may devour" (1 Peter 5:8).

Liberal Religion has no regard for Satan. It rejects the idea of duality of power, as that idea implies supernatural powers. Liberal Religion knows, of course, that man has good as well as evil impulses. But man is not inherently evil. Neither baptism nor other rituals can change the nature of man. Liberal Religion endeavors, through its ethical teachings, to cultivate the good impulses and to weed out the bad ones.

According to biblical tradition, God created both heaven and earth out of chaos. God lives in heaven and, according to Christian teaching, Jesus sits at his right hand. The Roman Catholic dogma states that the Virgin Mary, after her death, was bodily raised to heaven, where she now stays with God, Jesus, the saints, and the angels. When the clergyman at a Christian funeral recites from John's Gospel (John 14:2) "at my father's house are many mansions. I go to prepare a place for you," the mourners think of heaven.

All good Christians expect to go to heaven after death. Jews are less specific but the devout believe in a life "beyond," and presumably they picture this to be heaven.[10] The alternative is hell. The psalmist sings joyfully: the wicked shall be turned into hell for their misdeeds.[11] There the sinners suffer as shown in Michelangelo's painting in the Sistine Chapel of the Vatican. The painting depicts the Last Judgment at which, according to Christian tradition, all humans are resurrected and either rewarded with life in heaven or punished with misery in hell. An exception to this juxtaposition of heaven and hell is found in the famed Swabian Pilgrim Church at Wies. There, Jesus is depicted as mounting the seat of the Last Judgment from which he sends all people not to heaven and hell, but through one single door leading to eternity. All other paintings in this richly decorated Rococo church conform to established doctrine, which may be the reason why the deviation in the Last Judgment representation was overlooked. Even in that painting, Chronos, the ancient god of time, lies slain at the door to eternity, his hour glass broken, symbolizing that Christ has overcome death as proclaimed by Paul.

Reference has already been made to Milton's *Paradise Lost,* and Dante's theological romance (as Benedetto Croce called it), *The Divine Comedy.* In the ninth line of the third canto Dante tells us that the inscription above the gate of hell reads, "abandon hope all ye who enter here." Bernard Shaw, in his play *Man and Superman,* contends that this very inscription makes hell attractive. "For what is hope? A form of moral responsibility. Here, there is no hope and consequently, no duty, no work, nothing to be gained by praying, nothing to be lost by doing what you like."[12] Shaw, in this satirical play, not only makes hell attractive, but calls heaven an "angelically dull" place. It is interesting that Shaw's equation of hope and duty, and its relation to religion, is shared by a middle American scientist and liberal religionist Ralph Burhoe. He wrote, "Man's basic feelings of hope and duty have been shaped for thousands of years by religion. . . ."[13]

According to the Apostle's Creed, Jesus descended into hell and eventually ascended into heaven. Professor Küng seems to regard this as a mythological statement but he emphasizes that the concept of hell is sound theology and means separation from God.[14] In the book of Revelation, heaven is described as a city of pure gold (Rev. 21:19) and hell is a lake that burns with fire and brimstone (Rev. 20:10).

The traditional ideas of heaven and hell are so irrational that many theologians today consider them to be merely symbolic concepts. They are fuzzy and vague like so many ideas in Traditional Religion. But, apparently such fuzziness is desired. Father Andrew Greeley, the bad boy Peck of the Roman Catholic Church, discusses hell and limbo and criticizes St. Augustine for his doctrine that unbaptized babies will go to hell. They, like other sinners, merely go to purgatory, says Father Greeley, from where they have a chance to go to heaven. "Whether such folk get another chance or not is something best left to the mercy of God," is the cleric's straddling conclusion.[15]

Another modern Jesuit scholar is quoted as saying that the traditional view of heaven and hell is about 95 percent mythology. And what about the remaining 5 percent, one must ask.

No astronaut has encountered any heavenly population. It is not known whether Traditional Religionists worry about the possibility that modern intercontinental missiles might do harm to heaven, the "Heavenly Father," or to its other presumed inhabitants.

The idea that there must be a dwelling place for deceased people in some other world is both ancient and widespread. It is older than the Judeo-Christian tradition. It touches on the problem of immortality which is discussed elsewhere (Chapter 11).

Heaven and hell are not part of the religious vocabulary or the belief structure of the Liberal Religion. However, there is no objection to using the words as linguistic symbols. "Heaven," then, is shorthand to describe a state of happiness and contentment ("I am in seventh heaven") and "hell" denotes alienation, misery, or general unhappiness. Liberal Religion rejects the biblical geography of a three-tiered world but it enjoys Haydn's music in Addison's English adaptation of Psalm 19, which praises the "spacious firmament on high." It ends with the following four lines:

> In reason's ear they all rejoice
> And utter forth a glorious voice
> Forever singing, as they shine
> the hand that made us is divine.

Recognizing that a divine power made the beauty of the heavens as we look at them does not mean that one considers the heavens as the dwelling place of a supernatural God, of supernatural beings, or of deceased persons. But, Liberal Religion will always recognize that music and other creative arts have been inspired by Traditional Religion, and the Liberal Church will not deny itself these fruits of Traditional Religion.

10

Sin, Redemption, and Salvation

A discussion of these topics must begin with the unequivocal assertion that each person is responsible for himself or herself. Liberal Religion insists that one is master of one's own life. This is what James L. Adams calls the notion of personal sovereignty.[1] Such a notion is heresy in Traditional Religion which teaches the lordship of God and that humans cannot achieve salvation without the intercession of the divine savior. Indeed, according to Traditional Religion, man cannot accomplish anything good, except with the aid of God. Some Traditional Religionists go so far as to say that good is not accomplished with the aid of God but by God alone. According to this teaching, man accomplishes nothing.

Liberal Religionists commit sins like their brothers and sisters of Traditional persuasion. The greatest sin, in this author's view, is the wasting of food. We live in a world in which food is plentiful and yet there is want. The waste of food, therefore, shocks the conscience. This, however, is not the common concept of sin. The first sin, according to Western thinking, is disobedience to God, which occurred for the first time in paradise when Adam and Eve disregarded God's injunction and were forced out of Eden. This, according to Erich Fromm, was the beginning of history.[2] In the Christian tradition, this was the original sin, which afflicted all future generations and still stains all newborn babies. It was, in traditional parlance, the fall of man. Everybody, therefore, needs salvation and redemption. As Paul wrote, sin entered the world through one man, meaning the male (Rom. 5:12). Contrary to popular misconception, neither Eve nor the serpent is held ultimately responsible.

To the Liberal Church, the Bible myth is preposterous. The Bible condemns the desire for knowledge; the Liberal Church praises it. The Bible disparages Adam and Eve's sexuality. The Liberal Church recognizes it as a natural matter which one cannot disapprove of without at the same time disapproving of Nature and the Creation. God's alleged curses are monstrous. Women are condemned to bear children in pain and to be ruled by their husbands. Man (the male) is punished by being condemned to work. These curses spotlight the obnoxious character of the doctrine of original sin.

The doctrine is not found in the Bible but was invented by St. Augustine several centuries after the death of Jesus. For Augustine, as for many theologians since, the idea of a primordial sin helped explain the existence of evil in a world supposedly created by a good (personal) God. Liberal Religion is not in this quandary which scholars call theodicy. To this day original sin remains an integral part of Christian dogma. The French Jesuit, Father Russo, in a review of Teilhard de Chardin's work, says that "we know original sin through revelation." (The nature of revealed religion has been discussed in Chapter 2.) Liberal Religion will have none of this. Besides, few people believe that they are born sinners and cursed with some fatal ancestral blemish.

When Westerners speak of the Redeemer and the Savior, they think of Jesus of Nazareth. Many of them do not know that the terms have Old Testament origin. "I know that my redeemer liveth" is a line in the book of Job. One may think that it is a prophecy about the coming of Jesus, but it is not. The last stanza of Psalm 19 reads, "Let the words of my mouth and the meditation of my heart be acceptable in thy sight, O Lord, my strength and my redeemer." It is clear that the ancient Hebrews considered Yahweh as their redeemer and savior who loved and forgave them. Isaiah (Isa. 43:3) proclaimed, "I am the Lord thy God, the holy one of Israel, thy savior."

In the story of the Bible, Adam's fall is not even called a sin. The concept of original sin, which corrupted all future descendants of Adam, is a later invention. The remedy for original sin is baptism, and persons who are not baptized are not saved. The unbaptized must go to hell, or at least purgatory; the Bible says so (Mark 16:16). Traditional Christianity gives mankind a second chance. If they believe in Christ as the Redeemer who died on the cross for all believers, all sins will be forgiven, not only the original sin, but also all sins committed during one's lifetime. There is no salvation outside the church—*extra ecclesiam nulla salus*. While the traditional Protestant churches—following the teachings of Paul, Luther, and Calvin—adhere strictly to this doctrine, the Second Vatican Council of the Roman Catholic Church has loosened and broadened the redemption doctrine. According to the pronouncements of the Vatican Council II, redemption is open to all—even Jews, heretics, and atheists—if they are in good faith, which means, if they do not know any better. This development in Roman Catholic theology is remarkable and resembles the doctrine of universal salvation which was the keystone of the Universalist religion. The Universalists, when they were still committed to the Christian tradition, believed that Jesus, by his death on the cross, saved not only those who believed in him, but all mankind.

Christians are taught that God, being omniscient, was fully aware of Jesus' forthcoming crucifixion and, indeed, willed it. In the often recited words of John: "God so loved the world that he gave his only begotten son that whosoever believe in him should not perish but have everlasting life" (John 3:16), Christians believe that the soul of the most wanton criminal has been saved in advance by the God-ordained blood sacrifice of Jesus.

That the crucifixion of Jesus is regarded as salvation and redemption is but an extension of the ancient custom of the blood sacrifice. Instead of pleasing God with an animal sacrifice, Jesus allowed his blood to be shed like that of a sacrificial lamb. That is the theory, as expressed in the ancient traditional hymn of Isaac Watts (1674-1748):

> Not all the blood of beasts
> On Jewish altars slain
> Could give the guilty conscience peace
> Or wash away its stain.
> But Christ the heavenly lamb
> Takes all our sins away
> A sacrifice of nobler name
> And richer blood than they.

To sing this hymn with conviction requires the blind faith which Traditional Religion expects from its followers but is lacking in Liberal Religion.

Traditional Religion is based upon the notion that all men are inherently evil and sinful. One cringes when exposed to the frequent confessions of evil, sin, and guilt which abound in Traditional Religion. The psychologist William James, citing Spinoza, says that only sick souls wallow in remorse of evil and sin. He calls for healthy-mindedness, and suggests that the Catholic method of confession and absolution is a device to that end.

The words "save" and "redeem" are often used interchangeably. Jesus is adored as Savior and Redeemer. In his *Encyclia Redemptor Hominis (Redeemer of Man)*, Pope John Paul II said that the redemption of Jesus Christ is a mystery. A mystery defies rational analysis and explanation.

The quest for salvation is common to all humans who are hurt by the physical, psychological or social suffering which life inflicts. It is particularly important to those who suffer from estrangement and alienation in the existential sense. Not surprisingly, the socially disadvantaged are especially attracted by the promise of salvation. One of the lures offered by Traditional Religion is easy salvation, albeit in life after death.

The urge for salvation is a universal religious impulse. In that sense, all religions, including Liberal Religion, are salvation religions. The motivation, the means, and the achievement differ widely. Primitive religion was born out of fear of threatening outside forces and the desire to propitiate these forces from which one wished to be saved. This carried over in modern Traditional Religions which developed rituals and dogmas for the purpose of achieving reconciliation with the supernatural powers. The divinity was propitiated by sacrifices, rituals and prayers, and, in modern Protestantism, by mere faith. The death of Jesus, as savior of all men, made salvation convenient and easy for Christian believers. Easy because, quite obviously, guaranteed salvation and forgiveness weakens the demand for morality in the conduct of one's life, and it tends to extinguish the guilt feeling which is sometimes required in order to induce a person to attain a higher standard of morality. One of Luther's strong arguments in favor of reformation was the condemnation of the sale of absolutions from sin. He then proceeded to exchange absolutions not for money but for the profession of faith. There can be no salvation except by faith, according to Luther. Ethically, this was an improvement; religiously, it was not.

Liberal Religion does not allow such easy escape. It demands that every person heal himself or herself. This means integration with the evolutionary process of the Creation, into the social and physical environment in a manner which will end all feelings of estrangement and alienation, as exemplified by those Australians who felt like a part of God.[3] Like Buddhism, this often requires a personal volition and an intelligent effort, which Traditional Religion dispenses with. The will power required of a Religious Liberal presupposes, as a matter of course, self reliance and not reliance on a supernatural power. That is why Emerson, in his essay on self reliance, calls prayer a "disease of the will." The view that one's sin can be washed away by baptism or vicariously by the blood of Jesus, that forgiveness for sins can be obtained by rituals in the Judeo-Christian tradition is incompatible with Liberal Religion. Salvation can only be effected by the person who is responsible for the sin, the sinner himself/herself. Liberal Religion holds that salvation lies within us. As the angels say in Part II of Goethe's *Faust,* as they carry Faust's soul to heaven:

> Wer immer strebend, sich bemüht
> der können wir erlösen
>
> (Whoever makes an effort to strive on,
> We can redeem and save.)

The story of Faust is that of a person who is dissatisfied with his life and his achievements. In Part I of Goethe's work, he strives for perfection of his private life; in Part II, he moves to the public sphere, and dies while engaged in the reclamation of land from the sea for the public good. This is his finest hour.

Salvation must be understood as a healing process. Since the healer must also be the sufferer, it is sometimes called salvation by character, in contra-distinction to salvation by water or blood. This self-healing process is some-times a difficult task, about which psychiatrists and psychologists may have much to say. John Hayward, a theologian, cites the Greek and the Jewish approach: "The Greeks suggested that there is in man's mind a resource for ultimate serenity and harmony through wisdom. The Jews suggested that a serene and harmonious life occurs in the degree to which one gives himself to a loving care and support of his fellow man. There is no absolute cleav-age here. Greek wisdom implies not only the enlightenment of divine revela-tion, but also the application of human intelligence. But whereas the Greeks tended to emphasize the possibility of man's individual salvation through wisdom, the Jews stressed the obligation of man's social salvation, through justice and love."[4] Greek rationality is closer to Liberal Religion than the described Jewish approach to the salvation problem. However, since most of our sins are sins against the community of men, the Jewish path to salva-tion is necessary in order to restore and preserve peace.

The Salvation Army merits special mention here. It is, of course, built on Traditional Religion and aims at conversion to traditional faith. How-ever, instead of dwelling on gloom and sin, it emphasizes gaiety with drum and tambourine. Its founder, Edwin Booth, understood the superficiality of saving when he postulated: save yourself, keep saved, and thereafter save others. Social service to the underprivileged is more characteristic of the Salvation Army than any theology.

Social salvation implies reconciliation with the community. Reconcilia-tion is a concept which occurs often in Christian theology. It is very familiar from Charles Wesley's Christmas hymn "Hark the Herald Angels Sing":

> Peace on earth and mercy mild
> God and sinners reconciled.

Reconciliation with the community is necessary, and equally needful is one's reconciliation with one's self, if one is to live in harmony with the Uni-verse, which may but need not be called God. The same applies to forgiveness. Liberal Religion does not accept the idea that, as a result of Jesus' violent death, one's sins have been forgiven in advance. Forgiveness and reconcil-iation can only be obtained through individual efforts of the sinner. Professor Hayward refers to this effort as a creative act, and he says that, theologi-cally, such creativity is regarded as redemptive.[5] It is important that one understand what is meant when the words "sin," "salvation," and "redemption" are used.

As for salvation from the general misery of life, as experienced or merely perceived by the individual, there are two ways of achieving it: flight from the world or flight into the world. Flight from the world is pursued by the

hermit, who believes he can achieve salvation by living a contemplative existence of prayer and abnegation. This is also the Buddhist response to the
quest for salvation which ideally ends in complete self-rejection and Nirvana.

The Liberal Church prefers the other alternative: flight into the world,
which requires affirmation of the creation, participation, and integration.

Ojata, writing about Zen Buddhism, compares its teachings to that of
the German medieval mystic Meister Eckhard. He cites Eckhard's disinterest
in the world.[6] Liberal Religion disapproves of such disinterest and postulates reverence for the ongoing life. Buddhism, and especially Zen, preaches
that man can only find salvation if he avoids confrontation with the world.[7]

This turning away from the world is one of the causes for the apathy
which has been deplored in the preface to this book. It is incompatible with
the life affirmation of Liberal Religion.

Buddhism has been called the salvation doctrine for intellectuals,[8] and
many Liberal Religionists like to think of themselves as intellectuals. The
distress and the misery of the intellectual person is generally less external
than the suffering of others. Liberal Religion assumes that a rational person
can use his or her intellectual powers to become reconciled to the environment without seeking a Buddhist Nirvana.

Lastly, mention should be made of the doctrine of predestination.
According to this doctrine, one's fate and salvation is predetermined by
God and foreordained regardless of one's conduct in life. The theologian
Rudolf Otto, in a chapter entitled "The Numinous in the New Testament,"
provides a lengthy explanation of predestination, which amounts to the
assertion that God's will must prevail, no matter what man plans to do.
Before man makes a plan, God has already determined what is going to
happen. Otto cites Christian and Moslem scripture, but he concedes that the
doctrine defies rationality.[9] It makes faith indispensable. It is closely related
to the doctrine of original sin. Luther and Calvin maintained that original
sin completely destroyed freedom of choice and so they accepted predestination. Puritanism was steeped in predestination. Puritans nevertheless
insisted on a rigorous lifestyle in order to live up to what they conceived to
be God's will and to prove that God was justified in granting them the grace
of predetermined salvation. Liberal Religion rejects this doctrine altogether
because it conflicts with its tenets of self-reliance and self-responsibility.

11

Death, Immortality, the Soul, and the Last Judgment

Theologians make the problem of death and immortality enormously complicated. It is hard to do justice to all their doctrines.

To the Religious Liberal, it should be very simple. Death is the termination of a person's life. Mortality is ordained both by the needs of evolution and the nature of protoplasm—that substance in all cells which gives life to them for a limited period of time. Life with a capital "L" continues. A dead person has no further life in the beyond. One's immortality is to found in one's descendants, works, and lasting influence on others. That is all there is to it, and this chapter could end right here.

However, for the Traditional Religionist and many other people, the matter is not so simple. There is the dread of death which began with primitive religions, and remains with us to this day. The psalmists lament the terrors of death. In the Old Testament, God counsels man to choose life as good, in contrast to death which is evil (Deut. 30:15). Adam and Eve are reported to have been immortal in paradise, but when they were driven out as punishment for their disobedience to God, they became mortal (Gen. 4:19). Paul wrote that death is the enemy of man and the punishment for sin (1 Cor. 15:26, Rom. 5:12). That is why Christians are happy to believe that Jesus' death atoned for their sins and thus guarantees them eternal life. This attitude is reflected by the familiar lines from the order for the burial of the dead in the *Anglican Book of Common Prayer*:

> I am the resurrection and the life, saith the Lord, he that believeth in me, though he were dead, yet shall he live, and whosoever liveth and believeth in me shall never die.

145

The longing for life after death seems to be common to many cultures. In the Old Testament, the dead continued to live in Sheol, which is at times incorrectly translated as "hell," because dead people, regardless of merit, were believed to live in Sheol. The ancient Greeks expected the souls of the dead to live in Hades, after being carried over the river Styx, and small coins to pay the ferryman were stuffed in the dead body's mouth. The same expectation is evident in the pre-historic age. Many objects of use and value were found in the graves at Mycena. The subterranean apartments which the Egyptians built for the Pharaohs bespeak their belief in everlasting life after death. Dante described life after death in purgatory, hell, and heaven. Michelangelo painted the spectacular events after the Resurrection and on Judgment Day. The ancient Vikings placed a favorite horse or even a ship in the graves of their dead, for use after death. Their warriors went fearlessly into battle, convinced that after death, they would live gloriously in their special paradise called Valhalla. The Eastern religions hold that one's lifetime is only part of a long series of successive lives. An injustice suffered in one life is balanced out by previous or future incarnations. The devout Jewish writer Wouk describes the Judeo-Christian attitude as follows: "The basic popular answer of Judaism and Christianity and Mohammedanism (sic) is to stretch out the accounting period into an unknown future beyond death."[1] The sentence is quoted verbatim because of the apparently characteristic concept of accounting which is also mentioned by the Roman Catholic Hans Küng: "After the Babylonian exile, people (the Jews) were becoming less and less satisfied with the ancient answer that all accounts were settled within the present life between birth and death, in terms of appropriate rewards or reprisals."[2]

It seems that the Jewish religion is somewhat ambiguous about immortality, but there was no such ambiguity during the time of the Babylonian exile (538–328 B.C.) when Daniel wrote, "And many of those who sleep on the land of dust shall awake, some to everlasting life, and others to everlasting reproach and contempt" (Dan. 12:12). According to Traditional Religion, all accounts will be settled on Judgment Day. On that day, all will be resurrected with bodies and souls reassembled. God will sit in judgment, as depicted by Michelangelo in the Sistine Chapel. A dying person who lived an unhappy life but was always ethical, may find comfort in the thought that on Judgment Day he or she will obtain a just reward. And the believing scoundrel may tremble in death at the thought of Judgment Day, and therefore yield to an importuning clergyman at his deathbed.

The idea of Judgment Day antedates the Judeo-Christian tradition. The ancient Egyptians believed that Osiris would sit in judgment of each soul.[3] The Persian prophet Zoroaster proclaimed in the seventh century B.C. that, on the day of last judgment, every individual passed across the Bridge of Separation whence the wicked fall in the pit of torment and the righteous proceed to paradise.[4]

Liberal Religion disdains any such ideas as unmitigated fantasies which have no basis in reality and merit no credibility.

At funeral services and at least once a year on Easter Sunday, Traditional Christian preachers hold out to their congregations the promise of life everlasting. Paul said that Jesus had abolished death as a result of his blood sacrifice (2 Tim. 1:10). The prospect of life after death and of the Resurrection, even as Jesus is believed to have been resurrected, is of immense comfort to the true believers of Traditional Religion.

In the Christian religion, the Resurrection of Jesus is central. However, the resurrection idea as such did not originate in Christianity. It is rooted in an older Jewish tradition.[5] The prophet Elisha is reported twice to have resurrected a child from death.[6] And there is another account of the resurrection of a man who touched the bones of the deceased Elisha.[7]

William James suggested that, for most people, immortality is the essence of religion, and one who does not believe in immortality has no religion.[8] The scientist Carl Sagan suggests that the human fear of death has produced the "hypothesis that the soul lives on after the body's demise."[9] That the fear of death is widespread appears to be fact. That Traditional Religion exploits this human fear is an inescapable conclusion.

Professor Küng endeavors to make the idea of the afterlife more palatable to a modern, rational person. He says that life after death is not simply a continuation of the old. "Even to speak of life after death is misleading; eternity is not characterized by 'before' and 'after.' It means a new life which escapes the dimensions of space and time, and a life within God's invisible, imperishable domain."[10] That this is beyond rationality and reasoning power becomes clear in the following passage of Küng: "The Resurrection faith is not an appendage to faith in God, but a radicalization of faith. It is a faith in God which does not stop halfway, but follows the road consistently to the end. It is a faith in which man, without strictly rational proof, but certainly with completely reasonable trust, relies upon the fact that the God of the beginning is also the God of the end and that as he is the creator of the world and man, so too he is their finisher."[11]

It is important to know this view, but the Religious Liberal does not have such reasonable trust. One of its fallacies is to conceive of God as a power outside the world. The traditional belief is that the dead person leaves this world and "goes home" to live with God. In Liberal Religion, death is regarded as a natural phenomenon which neither Jesus nor any other person or power can abolish. Küng and other theologians of traditional persuasion seem to believe that God owes it to man to abolish death, that God would be disloyal if he did not.[12] This notion is related to the traditional belief in God's tremendous love and goodness which makes it unthinkable that God should allow eternal death.

The Religious Liberal has reverence for life and for the Creation without expecting to take part in it for longer than his or her individual lifespan.

Very few people will, like Albert Schweitzer and the Jain sect in India, spare the life of an insect that crosses one's path or is an annoyance. However, we grieve if a loved person dies and that grief may be overwhelming if death occurs prematurely. We do not blame God, nor do we lose our reverence for life.

The custom of having elaborate funerals, and especially that of providing expensive coffins, may be in part attributable to social pressure; but it seems reasonable to assume that the unwillingness to face the reality of death plays an important part in these funeral habits. Liberal religionists, who regard death as a natural event, prefer memorial services to elaborate or even simple funerals. Instead of spending money for wilting flowers, they prefer to make a contribution for the relief of living people. It is gratifying to know that this aspect of Liberal Religion has begun to influence people outside of the fold.

Liberal Religion teaches that immortality is achieved not literally but by the lasting influence and impressions which the deceased person leaves behind. In that sense, the forty living members of the Academie Française, being eminent persons, are called "the Immortals." Supersalesman Duveen convinced a number of rich American businessmen in the early part of this century that they could achieve immortality if they would buy and donate valuable paintings to the public. Duveen thus succeeded in laying the groundwork for the National Gallery of Art in Washington, D.C.

According to newspaper reports, when Pope Paul VI died, Cardinal Cooke, the Archbishop of New York, prayed: "May he now share in the joy of the risen Lord in the company of the Apostles, and all those holy shepherds in whose footsteps he walked so valiantly and so selflessly." Religious Liberals will grant that Pope Paul VI was valiant and selfless in his lifetime. That should insure his immortality among the surviving and future faithful Roman Catholics. It is not necessary, and indeed it is absurd, to imagine that the dead pope now strolls around in heaven with other deceased clerics.

One recalls the funeral prayer of a rabbi in which God was implored to bestow his choicest blessings upon the soul of the departed. Apparently this representative of Traditional Religion assumed that God distributes his blessings to the dead in various qualities: ordinary, choice, and choicest, like merchandise in a department store. In Liberal Religion, a dead person has no use for blessings. His memory, of course, may be a blessing to future generations, if they recall his good deeds.

Jesus promised the downtrodden that they would receive their reward in heaven, where they will sit at a banquet table with Abraham, Isaac, and Jacob (Matt. 8:11). This reflects the compensatory doctrine which permeates the Bible and which may explain the above mentioned utterance of the cardinal and of the rabbi. The Old Testament is replete with bargains between Jehovah and his people, and the Christian message contained very definite elements of a compensatory doctrine in the sense of the future equalization of human fates. The promise of life after death is therefore indispensable for Traditional Religion.

This is repugnant to Liberal Religion. Honesty, decency, and goodness carry their own rewards on earth and during one's lifetime.

Suicide

In the words of Camus, suicide is not legitimate.[13] When Camus wrote this, he had in mind people who commit suicide because they are unhappy and seemingly unable to cope with the problems of living. The generalization does not apply to a desire to end one's life because of an incurable illness. Here, the principle of freedom of choice must govern. Some people today execute an instrument known as a "Living Will," in which they direct that in the case of an incurable illness, no physician or hospital should be permitted to apply life-supporting remedies which would defer the termination of life. The law in most states has not yet recognized the efficacy of such a Living Will, but Liberal Religion postulates respect for a person's desire to terminate life under the described circumstances.

Canon Law has held, since 1958, that no one is required to use extraordinary means to prolong life. This has been interpreted as sanctioning the withdrawal of a respirator or other life supporting devices from a terminally ill person. Liberal Religion is happy to be in the company of the Roman Catholic Church on this issue.

The Soul

The frequent references to the "soul" of a departed person, often spoken of as the immortal soul, raise the question of what that expression really means.

The soul is a lady. Said Thomas a Kempis (1379–1471), "Blessed is the soul that heareth the Lord speaking within her." The word "soul" denotes an incorporeal aspect of the human being, the essence of such being's spirituality as distinguished from the physical body. When black people speak of soul food, or a soul brother, they mean that which characterizes the spirit of black people. The word "soul" is also used as a representative word for the person who is supposed to possess the soul, as when it is said that a village has a population of 3,000 souls. Thales (640–546 B.C.) believed that all matter, plants and metals, as well as animals and men have an immortal soul.

Traditional Religion believes that the soul, as the spiritual component of man, is separated from the body upon death, but will be reunited on Judgment

Day. In the interval, the soul leads an independent existence. Those in Traditional Religion who recognize or are reconciled to the physical disintegration of the body believe that at least the soul of a deceased person goes to heaven or hell, as the case may be. All Souls Day (November 2) is a day on which Roman Catholics and some Anglicans offer special prayers for the dead. In his book of lectures entitled *Varieties of Religious Experience,* William James deals with what he calls "the sick soul."[14] These lectures do not describe the soul. They tell of the spirituality of the religious optimist and the religious pessimist. The latter, according to James, has a sick soul because he is preoccupied with evil and with sin. Healthy-minded people, James says in a subsequent lecture, are born only once, but the sick souls must be born twice to attain happiness.[15]

Liberal Religion does not object to the word "soul" as representing the spiritual aspect of man, but it holds that the soul is integrated with the body and therefore, quite naturally, dies with it. The immortality of the soul in Liberal Religion is the same as the immortality of the entire deceased person: the stronger the person's spirituality, the more will his/her influence survive. The defiant statement "I am the captain of my soul" means that one's spirituality is not dictated by any overlord but only by one's own being and volition.

Emerson's reference to the "over soul" is addressed to the spiritual climate which pervades the world or the society in which one lives. "Within man is the soul of the whole."[16]

The dualism of body and soul, which was invented by the Greeks, is incompatible with Liberal Religion. Emerson denounced the doctrine of the immortality of the soul, and the idea that body and soul are severed from each other, as inventions of Jesus' disciples. James Luther Adams wrote: "Freedom, justice, and love require a body as well as a spirit. We do not live by spirit alone. A purely spiritual religion is a spurious religion."[17]

PART TWO

PRACTICES

12

The Democratic Process in Human Relations

In 1943 the Unitarians accepted the democratic process in human relations as one of the five principles upon which they could agree. To this day it is still one of the most important tenets of Liberal Religion. Democracy is based on the doctrine that all members of a given community are equal, and that a majority shall determine the rules by which the community is governed. Majority rule is the primary principle of the democratic process. Equality is its premise, and rotation in office is its generally accepted, but not necessary, by-product.

Democracy has never been practiced in a pure form. "Democracy" is a Greek word denoting government by the people. Around 500 B.C., Cleisthenes, an aristocrat himself, is reported to have introduced democracy into the state of Attica,[1] of which Athens was then the capital. But only 15 percent of the population were eligible to vote.[2] Plato (427–347 B.C.) disliked democracy; he thought that the democrats were as bad as the plutocrats.[3] Aristotle (384–322 B.C.) had a somewhat better opinion of the democratic principle, but he was afraid that it would give too much power to the irresponsible poor. He proposed to restrict the voting franchise to the landowners and the members of the middle class.[4] In the United States, women gained the right to vote only in 1920; the voting rights of blacks were recognized in the 1960s. Democracy in the United States has been, and still is, a matter of persistent faith and steady distrust. The rugged individualists of old-fashioned capitalism have no use for democracy. Some conservative politicians insist that the United States is a republic but not a democracy. Winston Churchill is reported to have said that democracy is a most inefficient form of government but that no better form has yet been invented. Religion is not, as a rule,

153

a democratic institution. The democratic process in human relations cannot be expected to prevail in those Traditional Religions which are based on hierarchical or episcopal principles. Thus, the pope or his agents in the curia determine the policies and beliefs of the Roman Catholic Church; the Bishops rule the dioceses and the rectors govern the various parishes. The Anglican Church, which is the Episcopal Church in America, is similarly organized on an authoritarian basis. John Calvin was a nasty despot. The Puritans despised democracy. The cleric John Cotton (1584-1652) wrote: "Democracy I do not conceive that ever God did ordeyne as a fit government either for church or commonwealth. If the people be governors, who shall be governed?"[5]

The Puritan church, to which John Cotton belonged, was not an authoritarian episcopal church, but belonged to another branch known as the Congregational Churches, where the congregation is the highest authority. Most adherents to Traditional Religion in the United States, who are organized in Congregational Churches, are theologically adverse to the democratic principle because they consider Jesus Christ as their Lord. However, theological belief in the Lordship of Jesus does not necessarily prevent a congregational church from practicing the democratic process.

John Cotton correctly perceived that Traditional Religion and, most particularly, Christianity are inconsistent with the ideal of democracy. A religion which is based on the submission to God or Jesus is not compatible with the belief in individual freedom of choice and absolute majority rule. We thus face the historical paradox that many Americans sincerely devoted to democracy are also devoted to the Lordship of Jesus. Traditional Religion—Christianity in particular—teaches fellowship but not democracy.

Liberal Religion does not conceive of Jesus as an overlord; it believes strongly in the democratic process in human relations. Just the same, the process does not always flower. There are three main reasons for this.

First, the full operation of the democratic process requires participation of all members in the group, and this is often lacking. Failure to participate is a serious problem in politics, as well as in the life of a religious organization. A substantial number of group members do not participate; they stay home or they "go fishing." Consequently, the decision made by a majority of those who vote does not necessarily reflect the will of the majority of the group.

The second reason why the democratic process frequently fails to function properly in many religious societies is that the clergy often exercise an undemocratic influence. The minister is, of course, the spiritual leader of the congregation. It is therefore difficult sometimes for the minister, as well as for the individual members of the religious society, to recognize the line separating spiritual leadership and worldly concerns. The result is that, as a practical matter, even a liberal minister may become a pastor—which means shepherd—and the members may become sheep instead of independent participants in the democratic process. The democratic process, if properly understood, does not want to strive for man's conformity or for coercion.

The third reason why the effectiveness of the democratic process often suffers is that the majority fails to take the wishes of the minority into consideration. Thomas Jefferson said in his first inaugural address, "All will bear in mind this sacred principle, that though the will of the majority is in all cases to prevail, that will to be rightful must be reasonable; that the minority possess their equal rights, which equal law must protect and to violate would be oppression."[6] Jefferson here demands that the majority must always be reasonable, which is perhaps asking too much. Failure to follow Jefferson's advice, however, is one of the reasons why the democratic process sometimes malfunctions. It may lead to divisive internal factions or, in the case of religious societies, to resignations which sap the strength of the society. In any event, since Liberal Religion is dedicated to the democratic process, all members of a Liberal religious society or group must accept the decisions made by a majority of its members who participate in the voting process.

This is also true when democracy functions through representative government. Where the voters elect representatives in a democratic manner it behooves them to respect their representatives as their decision-making leaders. And yet one knows that representatives in parliament, as well as elected trustees of a religious society, often encounter a spirit of distrust which is inappropriate. There are these anarchistic spirits which cannot reconcile themselves to any order or power structure, democratically elected or not. To them, the words "law and order" are synonymous with despotism. This is profoundly false. Democracy does not denote disorder. The democratic freedom, which the Greeks expounded and which Liberal Religion wants to emulate, is a disciplined, self-controlled freedom.

Faith in democracy can be compared to the faith in God. Even those who do not have any such faith often pretend it. Political entities which have no use for democratic principles like to adorn themselves with its name. East Germany calls itself the German Democratic Republic, which is reminiscent of such other Marxist states as, for instance, the People's Democratic Republic of Yemen. Marxist as well as Fascist governments arrange from time to time for a political vote, even though the results are foreordained. Such elections are a charade staged by those in power to gain a semblance of the respectability which the democratic process enjoys in the world.

Religious bodies crave the same respectability. They must take care that their voting process does not degenerate into the same type of empty charade.

13

The Dignity of Man

The dignity of man is central to Liberal Religion. The word "man" is used here in its broad biological sense, embracing male and female. The concept is also referred to as the supreme worth of every human being. This religious tenet is simply an extension of the reverence for the Creation of which man is part. Liberal Religion does not regard man as a miserable sinner who can only be saved by faith in and through the grace of a supernatural power outside the natural order. This is not the only way in which Liberal Religion differs from Traditional Religion with respect to the nature of man. Traditional Religion holds that man is inherently corrupt. Had the American Declaration of Independence contained a condemnation of slavery it would not have been adopted by all the states. The old-time religionists would never have allowed it. Traditional Religion believes, to paraphrase George Orwell, that some men are religiously more equal than others. This prejudice is based on a racial bias, which in turn stems from an instinctive distrust of those who are or look different. In a barnyard of brown chickens, a lone white chicken will be picked upon mercilessly. So it is with unthinking men. Hitler utilized this primitive streak of nature. Enlightened political leaders like Alexander the Great and Napoleon succeeded because they valued persons of varied parentage. Racial and national distinctions meant nothing to them. This theme was touched upon in that part of Chapter 2 which deals with the outworn concept of "chosen people." It is epitomized in the following verse from the ancient Greek playwright Menander (243–292 B.C.) as quoted by Edith Hamilton:

> Mother—you are killing me with all these pedigrees
> Reading off lists of all our grandfathers

You won't say, will you, there is a man alive
Who hasn't got a grandfather? I tell you
A man who is good by nature — Mother mine
Even if he is born in Ethiopia
Is nobly born.[1]

Slavery is incompatible with the dignity of man and therefore repugnant to Liberal Religion. In many parts of the world, slavery emerged as the result of warfare. For instance, in ancient Rome, the slaves would have been the masters had they not lost the battle, and the masters would have been slaves, if they had not won. In the United States, slavery did not originate from warfare but from the slave trade. The slave traders were native African exploiters, shrewd Moslem traders, and stout American Christians. Almost all American abolitionists belonged to the Liberal Church. The leaders of the traditional established churches opposed abolition.

The Traditional Religionists of South Africa have justified racial discrimination by asserting that the black nations are descendants of Ham, whose crime, according to the Bible, was that he discovered his father, Noah, in a drunken stupor, naked. Thereupon Noah cursed Noah's son, Canaan, and said that Canaan should be the slave of his (Noah's) other sons (Gen. 10:25). Apparently, the clerics of the South African church found no better Bible justification for apartheid. They must have searched hard. One likes to think that they had a bad conscience.

Traditional Religion has poisoned the status of women all over the world and relegated them to an inferior position. If an unmarried woman consorts with a married man or a celibate priest, she is branded as a fallen woman, but no blemish is attached to the male. The religion of Islam demands that women wear a chader, an all covering tent-like black overgarment. No female with bare arms may enter a Roman Catholic church. Apparently, it is feared that a woman without a chader or a woman whose arms are bare will entice onlooking males to uncontrollable lust. An orthodox Jewish male will not shake hands with any woman for fear of contamination, and he will not share a meal with a woman of another faith. Most Protestant theological seminaries do not welcome female students. In the Roman Catholic Church, women are ineligible for the priesthood. Augusta, the wife of the last Kaiser of Germany, used to say that women should deal only with the three K's: Kinder, Küche, and Kirche (children, kitchen, and church). All of this is revolting to Liberal Religion because it is not compatible with the dignity of every human being, which will not allow any discrimination on the basis of sex.

Adherence to the supreme worth of every human being dictates Liberal Religion's attitude towards modern feminist movements and their objectives. Women deserve to be liberated from the odious Bible based tradition that they are inferior to males. The ideal biblical wife is Sarah, because, as the Apostle Peter wrote, she obeyed her husband Abraham and called him "lord" (1 Peter 3:6). Paul taught that the husband is the head of the wife (Eph. 5:23). Today, prostitutes are arrested and their male customers go free. Liberal Religion condemns this attitude even though many women like it. In opposing the adoption of the Equal Rights Amendment to the United States Constitution, one woman was heard to say, "I am against it because it may force me to work instead of allowing me to depend on my husband's earnings."

It may be questionable whether there is any real need to adopt a special amendment to the United States Constitution in respect to sex discrimination. It did not require an amendment of the Federal Constitution to have the state of Wyoming, then still a territory, grant suffrage to women in 1869, and to elect a female governor in 1924. Wyoming, thought of as part of the typical masculine Wild West, has as its state motto the words, "Equal Rights." American courts steadily outlaw practices which deprive females of the same social and economic privileges enjoyed by males. Nevertheless, for the Liberal Religionist, the Equal Rights Amendment (ERA) cannot be controversial. If a qualified female wishes to do the work of a longshoreman, or if she wishes to be a warrior in the trenches, the doctrine of the dignity of man demands that her wishes be respected.

The opponents of ERA, under the leadership of Phyllis Schlafly, seem primarily concerned about the absolute right of a married woman to be supported by her husband, even if she is financially able to support herself. Many states have enacted their own ERA legislation. In none of these states have any of the dire predictions of the ERA foes become true. None of them has established unisex toilets, college dormitories or prisons. Women have actually benefited and gained in dignity. For instance, in Maryland and Pennsylvania, household property used to be considered the property of the husband. The local ERA legislation changed this. The household property is now presumed to belong in equal shares to both husband and wife. In New Mexico, a community property state, husband and wife are common owners; but before the local ERA only the husband had control of the property. The conclusion is inescapable that the tenets of Liberal Religion, recognizing the dignity of man, require that we support the Equal Rights Amendment.

The idea that women are inferior in relation to men can be traced to the teaching of Traditional Religion regarding the fall of man in paradise. God's curse that, as a punishment for Eve's transgression, all women must suffer pain in childbirth, has been literally accepted by numerous physicians who have refused to alleviate a woman's birth pangs. Bible-believing women have been known to refuse any anesthetic when their babies are born.

The doctrine of the dignity of man also applies in the field of sexuality. Sexuality is a private matter unless it is flouted in public and intrudes upon public life. Therefore, it is incumbent on the Liberal Religionist to respect the private lives of homosexuals, and to oppose public discrimination on the basis of sexual preference. Traditional Religion seems to enjoy the exposure and persecution of homosexuals whether they constitute a public nuisance or not. Traditional Religion believes, of course, in the innate depravity of man and its adherents revel in providing evidence to justify that belief by practicing sexual snooping. All aspects of other people's sex lives are scrutinized. One recalls that it required two decisions of the United States Supreme Court to outlaw the Connecticut statute which made it a crime to sell contraceptives, a statute which, as the Jesuit Father John Courtney Murray put it, could only be enforced by police invasion of the bedroom.[2]

For the traditionalist, birth control and abortion are natural objects of contempt. The test-tube baby, which was conceived in a vitrous dish, is regarded as an outrage. In all of this the dignity of man is violated. One wonders whether these traditionalists themselves lead exemplary lives. This, however, is an issue for psychiatrists and psychologists; it is not a religious problem.

That the Traditional Religion's attitude indicates an unhealthy interest in human sexuality seems to be demonstrated by the fact that the detractors of the test-tube baby do not object to the so-called embryo transfer in cows, which is a widespread practice in the cattle industry. The principle there is the same as in the case of the test-tube baby, namely, interference with the natural reproductive process. Cows, it would seem, do not arouse the snoopers of Traditional Religion.

If parents are divorced or separated, courts usually award custody of a young child to the mother unless there is evidence that the child would suffer psychological damage from staying with her. Two Illinois court decisions in this field illustrate the insidious role of Traditional Religion in its lack of regard for the dignity of man. In the first case—which is regarded as a leading case—the mother cohabited with a man, not her husband, which violated the law against fornication. The child did not suffer and the court, therefore, ruled that the mother should keep custody of the child.[3] In the second case, the man with whom the mother lived, was married to another woman and the crime, therefore, was adultery. This outraged the court and, although there was again no showing that the child suffered any harm, the mother was deprived of custody. Adultery must be judged differently than fornication, ruled the court, because adultery violates a fundamental tenet of Judeo-Christian law and beliefs. The Bible is cited in the court decision as its authority.[4]

Christian preachers in America did not blush when they preached the white gospel to the slaves. The Liberal faith in the inherent dignity of man does not allow any distinction between races, nor any distinction between believers and nonbelievers. There are no chosen people or elects in the Liberal Religious scheme of things. What is objectionable is the arbitrary distinction between fornication and adultery used to justify the above court rulings.

When it comes to judging their own, the judiciary is not always so severe. A Pennsylvania judge who was married and lived with another married woman in an open illegal relationship was said to bring the judicial office into disrepute. The court refused to censure the judge.[5]

14

Justice

The Hebrew Prophet Amos (approx. 750 B.C.) cried for justice. His message was and still is closer to the human experience and wants than Jesus' preachment of universal love and Buddha's postulate of wisdom. In that sense, Amos was a more important religious figure than either Jesus or Buddha. The justice with which Amos was concerned, and which is important in Liberal Religion's theology, is social justice. This is more than legal justice but less than the higher justice of the so-called "Natural Law," which the Catholic Church and many other groups proclaim. In the context of this writing, it would be inappropriate to discuss these legal concepts other than summarily and other than by accentuating the approach of Liberal Religion.

Religion, especially Traditional Religion, is much concerned with punitive justice or retributive justice. The evildoer will be punished by God. Punitive justice is a part of legal justice.

The task of legal justice, or positive law, is to devise ground rules for daily social intercourse, even as Moses did for his tribe in the desert. The ground rules for social intercourse, like traffic regulations, need not be just. What is important is that the rules are generally understood, observed, and enforceable. The law must be certain. Therein lies what Martin Luther King, Jr., called its majesty.[1] Certainty is more important than abstract legal justice. If everybody knows the consequences of every act or omission in social intercourse, the law has achieved perfection. Even then, it will be subject to the frailties of administration by mere humans.

The Constitution of the United States provides for a modicum of legal justice by requiring that all citizens are entitled to the equal protection of the law and to what lawyers call, due process of law. This still does not mean that all laws must be just. The attainment of legal justice is especially difficult in the Anglo-American orbit, which glories in the common law tradition. The weakness of this system is that it is based upon decisional law which grows out of the facts of individual cases and a myriad of precedents. What the Constitution requires is that the laws must be administered with equal force or equal clemency for all. In the interpretation of the Constitution, judges have sometimes invoked an unwritten, so-called higher law. This approach is rooted in the Declaration of Independence which speaks of inalienable rights that override any other laws. Hitler used the same theory in order to overturn the laws of the Weimar Republic. Such higher law is also invoked by the Catholic Church in its opposition to any form of abortion. This higher law is generally known as "Natural Law." It represents the age old search for absolute justice which, according to Saint Thomas Aquinas, flows from the law of God. The doctrine of natural law will be discussed presently.

Liberal Religion rejects the illusion of absolutes, as was pointed out above in the chapter on truth. However, we do believe in social justice, as demanded by the Prophet Amos, and other liberal religious thinkers to this day. Social justice is more than the observance of the laws promulgated by Moses. It is a social system which allows every human being to live in dignity and to develop according to his or her own potential. Liberal Religion is imbued with the conviction that harmony with the Creation can only be achieved if human potential is developed in socially beneficial and personally fulfilling ways. The principle of social justice conflicts, at times, with the economic system. In that case, Liberal Religion requires the economic system to yield. Affluence and economic power, so often denounced as economic evils, are not necessarily bad. If appropriately used, they can serve the ends of social justice. If the child of a poor family is undernourished and therefore suffers brain damage, a gross injustice has been perpetrated. Liberal Religion demands that no child in any part of the world be permitted to languish in such a condition. There are many other threats to the development of the human potential, for example, anti-abortion laws, wars, and nuclear pollution, all of them inimical to social justice. The organization of the Fellowship for Social Justice (now defunct), the UU Service Committee and the UU United Nations Office are manifestations of religious concern for justice.

The extreme position of legal justice is expressed in the ancient slogan: *Fiat Justitia et pereat mundi,* which means, "Let justice be administered even if it destroys the world." The position of social justice is emphasized in the often cited sarcasm of Anatole France: The law is impartial. It prohibits the beggars as well as the rich men to sleep under the bridges of Paris. Liberal Religion demands social justice for the beggars by insisting that the community provide opportunities which afford the beggars a place to sleep in an appropriate shelter, and do away with the need for begging.

Paul Tillich, in his *Systematic Theology,* points out that the concept of justice is ambiguous. "Justice implies equality, but equality of what is essentially unequal is as unjust as inequality."[2] Religiously, the beggars are the equals of the rich men. Viewed in this light, the law against sleeping under bridges is just. Practically, the beggars are not equal to the rich. Therefore, the law is not just; certainly it violates the demands of social justice.

One of the great injustices in contemporary society is the spread of unemployment. Quite apart from its physical hardships, unemployment is degrading and humiliating for those who are affected. The Puritans believed that idleness of a person capable of work was inevitably his own fault. This typical Calvinistic attitude has not disappeared. Students of economics and sociology have learned that unemployment is primarily a consequence of the prevailing political economy. While some individuals may be "welfare chiselers," most unemployed persons are not, therefore, suffering voluntarily. We cannot do them justice, as Liberal Religion demands it, without recognizing this fact of life.

The Liberal Church has no monopoly on social concern. The concern for the unemployed is but one facet of Liberal Religion's intolerance of economic injustice. Most Liberal Religionists favor social programs which alleviate what they conceive to be the harshness of the economic system. Some Liberal Religionists favor socialist economics, but Liberal Religion as such, has no simple answer to the economic problems of the world. Nor should this be expected. However, the struggle against economic injustice is part and parcel of the social justice which Liberal Religion demands. For instance, Liberal Religion recognizes that the lawless crime wave threatening our social fabric is largely born of slums, ignorance, poverty, bad health conditions, race discrimination, and a lack of economic opportunity. Liberal Religion will, therefore, support all efforts to eliminate and diminish these causes of injustice.

Absolute justice is difficult to obtain, especially since it is also hard to reach a consensus as to what is just. A contemporary illustration is found in the present distress of the American automobile industry. The auto makers plead for a relaxation of the law requiring the installation of antipollution devices. The closing of manufacturing facilities leads to unemployment and idle plants for the steel industry and other automobile suppliers. The resolution of the problem, in a democratic society, must be left to the lawmakers.

It is true that the legislatures are not all wise and all just and that the positive law, therefore, is often the cause of discontent and unhappiness. It is also true that such discontent and unhappiness is not uniform. The feelings of an automobile manufacturing executive differ from those of the wife of a worker who has been laid off. This was demonstrated in 1937, when workers occupied the General Motors plants in Detroit in what probably was the first sit-down strike.

Since ancient times, people have endeavored to achieve justice by defying the positive law and invoking a so-called higher law, commonly called

"Natural Law." The doctrine of natural law is part of the Roman Catholic dogma, but it exists also outside of Roman Catholicism, and has appeal to some Religious Liberals.

This is not the place to discuss in depth, and to do justice to, the many lawyers, theologians, and philosophers who have devoted much thought and learning to the doctrine of natural law. Its essence is this: Above the law which is found in the statutes, ordinances, and judicial decisions, there is a higher law possessing a religious quality. When the law of Rome prohibited Christian worship, the young church went underground and announced that laws which conflict with the Christian faith need not be obeyed. This was the first step to civil disobedience.[3] The name "Natural Law" evolved because it was thought that, as the sun rises every morning, so nature had provided a higher law for every contingency, even though such law may be hidden from human recognition and must be searched for in case of need. The author of the law of nature is, of course, God. It is the same law to which Sophocles alluded in his play *Antigone*. When Antigone defied King Caron's decree, which forbade the burial of her slain brother, she announced allegiance to "the infallible, unwritten laws of Heaven." It is also mentioned in the digest of laws which the Roman emperor, Justinian, compiled and which named God as author (*Deo autore*). Under the doctrine of "Natural Law," the human legislators and judges are regarded as finding the law, not giving or creating it. Former Chief Justice and republican standard bearer Charles E. Hughes supported the doctrine of higher law by his dissent in *United States v. Macintosh*.[4] Macintosh was a former Canadian army chaplain whose application for naturalization was denied because he refused to commit himself to bearing arms in defense of the United States of America, as the statute requires. He desired to reserve the right to determine the morality of any future armed conflict. Chief Justice Hughes would have allowed the naturalization because Macintosh was motivated by religious scruples. The Will of God, the Chief Justice wrote, was superior to the will of the state. This argument spotlights the problem. The will of the state is expressed by the statute which was enacted by the democratically elected representatives of the people. As to the Will of God, firstly it assumes the existence of a personal God and, secondly, even if that were not so, every Tom, Dick, and Harry might have a different idea what that will is.

There are two primary difficulties with the "Natural Law" doctrine as it relates to Liberal Religion. First, it lends itself (and invariably leads) to arbitrariness, depending upon one's religious or political bent. It undermines the certainty and stability which the law requires. When the Founding Fathers of the United States issued the Declaration of Independence, they invoked the "God of Nature" and declared certain unwritten, inalienable rights. All successful revolutions are based on such natural law. In this particular case, Americans applaud because they all approve. When Hitler came into power, he and his followers claimed that a higher law justified their misdeeds. Hitler declared that, under this higher law, the good of the German people was to become the standard of right and wrong. He then proceeded in detail to decree the content of the higher law. This remained in force so long as Hitler lived, then it became invalid. The authority which the victors of World War II adopted in the Nuremburg trials was also based on some higher, heretofore unknown law. The Russians, who participated in this legal exercise, probably would not ascribe this law to God. The Roman Catholic Church is opposed to the United States Supreme Court decision on abortion. This opposition is based upon "Natural Law." The Right to Life Party, which, in the state of New York, has more adherents than the Conservative Party and the Liberal Party, agrees and also relies on the higher law of God.

The second problem with the "Natural Law" doctrine is that it conflicts with the doctrine of democracy to which Liberal Religion is committed. In a democratic system, the democratically elected legislators make the law. True, the legislators cannot anticipate every contingency that may face a judge. However, if a judge is confronted with an unforeseen contingency, and if there is no time to defer the decision until after the legislature has met again, it is not asking too much that the judge make the decision within the framework of the existing legislation without indulging in personal predilections as to what God would want. If the judge is a devout Christian, the risk of such a decision is particularly great because Paul, the founder of the Christian religion, had no particular respect for the law. He held that man is made upright by faith rather than by law. Examples of Paul's disdain for the law are found in his letter to the Romans (Rom. 4:29) and his letter to the Galatians (Gal. 3:25).

The doctrine of "Natural Law" has no legitimate place in a democratically organized society.

There is more to be said about religion and the law. It will be found in the chapter dealing with religious liberty.

It is not compatible with a liberal theology to recognize a law which is superior to the law enacted by democratically elected legislatures or proclaimed by properly appointed or elected judges. Liberals are often ambivalent on this issue. For instance, during the Vietnam War, some indignant citizens refused to pay taxes in defiance of the duly enacted Internal Revenue Code; and others, without claiming objection to any war, refused to fight in this one. The objectors claimed that they were acting in accordance with some higher, unwritten law. Conceptually, this is the same attitude as that proclaimed by Hitler.

At one time, Liberal Religionists were leaders in the contest for social justice, but that leadership has since been lost. Today, many Traditional churches are concerned with social justice. This is all to the good and pleasing to the Liberal Church. It would, of course, be desirable, and it would strengthen the position, as well as the self-esteem of Liberal Religion, if it could regain the leadership position of the religious concern for social justice.

What is stopping the Liberal Church, and why has it lost its leadership position? There are, naturally, many reasons. Foremost among them is a slackening of spirit. This is the general malaise of our times. It can only be cured if we recognize it for what it is and then rouse enough willpower to change the situation. We will then be able to deal with a second factor—the lack of courage to innovate.

To illustrate, liberal organizations have traditionally allied themselves with the labor movement. Today, the labor movement in many respects has become conservative, dictatorial and/or dishonest. It takes special courage for a Liberal Religionist to speak out against such flaws in the organization and policies of labor.

Similarly, liberals are almost automatically and by instinct in favor of the underdog (a typical American trait, and a part of the American tradition, which has been liberal in nature). And yet, we must recognize that some of these underdogs are undesirable characters. Liberals must not blink at this fact.

The worst is that many religiously liberal churches are unwilling to live up to the ideals which they preach. They are too property minded. If they own property—and quite a few do—they might be willing to spend the income thereof to promote the ideals of social justice—but capital? Never. It is hard to eradicate the conservative notion that capital must be hoarded to insure future income.

15

Freedom of Belief

Liberal Religionists cherish the idea that they enjoy individual freedom of belief. It was one of the famous five points of Unitarianism developed in 1944, and still is a pillar of Liberal Religion. It is also a greatly misunderstood principle. Some Liberal Religionists think, and even proclaim, that their religion allows them to believe anything they please. This is profoundly false. There is no absolute freedom. There are limits to the freedom of belief, limits imposed by the standards of Liberal Religion which are discussed throughout this writing. Anti-rationalists such as William Jennings Bryan have no place in a liberal religious community.[1] Ever since Servetus wrote *The Errors of The Trinity,* it has been impossible for any Liberal Religionist to regard Jesus as anything but a great teacher. (Indeed, Liberals have reverence for Jesus just because he was a mere man.) Likewise, a racist who exalts one race over another does not belong, because such a belief violates the principles of the dignity of man (see Chapter 13) and social justice (see Chapter 14). These examples will suffice to indicate the broad and few limitations on freedom of belief found in Liberal Religion.

This raises the question as to whether anyone could be expelled from a congregation in the Liberal Church. While many answer the question in the affirmative, in order to preserve the integrity of the Liberal Church, others are opposed because expulsion reminds them of the burning of heretics and smacks of censorship, practices which are obnoxious to Liberal Religionists. In any case, the question is theoretical because a believer in the Trinity, or one who believes that the Bible is the revealed word of God will, as a rule, have left the Liberal Church long before the matter has come to the attention of those concerned with a possible problem or expulsion. Some people

167

join liberal as well as nonliberal religious societies for the sake of expediency (see Chapter 18), or for the sake of ecumenism (see p. 59).

In order to understand the principle of freedom of belief, one must appreciate the fact that it evolved as a protest against compulsory religious restrictions. Traditional churches are societies of believers in preordained unalterable sets of belief. A person is born into such a society and is expected to believe in what has been handed down. There is no room for individual freedom of belief. One knows, of course, that some Christians do not believe in the Virgin Birth or in other particulars of their church's dogma. That deviation from dogma indicates the extent to which one is not true to his or her church.

An orthodox Jew who was challenged about the rationality of one of the rules by which he lives, replied that all these rules were ordained by God and the individual cannot pick and choose between God's commandments. That makes sense from the viewpoint of Traditional Religion, but not in the Liberal Religion.

The Nicene Creed, professing faith in the Trinity, and the Apostle's Creed, professing faith in God, which are recited in many Traditional Churches, are the foremost examples of obligatory beliefs to which Liberal Religion objects, primarily because their validity rests solely on the fact that they have been handed down by ancient authority. Liberal Religion demands that all religious tenets must be tested in the crucible of contemporary free inquiry. That is what individual freedom of belief means. While most Religious Liberals deny the existence of a supernatural God, they are ready to change their mind if further inquiry proves them to be incorrect. This explains why many Religious Liberals resent the word "creed." The Nicene Creed and the Apostle's Creed have instilled in them a veritable allergy against the world.

Unlike the Traditional Churches, the Liberal Church welcomes and includes agnostics, atheists, and humanists who hold to their beliefs as a result of individually exercised freedom of belief. The World Council of Churches and the United States National Council of Churches demand that all their members must accept the Lord Jesus Christ as God and Savior. The Liberal Church's principle of individual freedom of belief precludes such a limitation.

As stated in Chapter 2, Liberal Religion does not consider the Bible as the revealed Word of God, and it gives individual freedom of belief free reign to accept or reject the Bible as a whole or any part thereof. In particular, Liberal Religion, with its principle of freedom of belief, is very critical of the black or white, good or evil, absolutist attitude of the Bible. In Traditional Religion, Jehovah, Jesus, or Allah is always right, and those who disagree are considered enemies of religion. This Liberal Religion cannot accept. The Liberal Church also rejects Calvin's position that toleration is an evil because it allows private judgments to exist outside the authority of the Scripture.[2] Such private judgment is just what the tenet of individual freedom of belief claims as a religious entitlement.

Such historic events as Traditional Religion's resistance to scientific discoveries, the burning of heretics, and the listing of forbidden books are repugnant to Liberal Religion and the principle of freedom of belief. That principle is essential to the ongoing search for truth discussed in Chapter 6. The mind of man cannot search for truth without complete freedom. William Ellery Channing (1780–1842), "the great awakener," put it this way in his sermon on spiritual freedom: "I call that mind free which jealously guards its intellectual rights and powers. Which does not content itself with a passive or hereditary faith, which opens itself to light whenever it may come, which receives new truth as an angel from heaven."[3]

There is another facet to the freedom of belief principle. Robert Hutchins, the famous late Chancellor of the University of Chicago, wrote: "The mind cannot be free if it is slave to what is bad. It is free if it is enslaved to what is good." This may sound fine when one hears it for the first time. Upon reflection, however, the statement is incompatible with Liberal Religion because it assumes the existence of an authority who determines what is good and what is bad. The Traditional Church assumes just such authority, the Liberal Church does not. A person may worship evil as a member of the cult of Satan. If he or she arrives at that religious stance while exercising the right of freedom of belief, he or she does not measure up to the standards of the Liberal Church; it cannot be said, however, that his or her mind is not free. An individual may be a sincere communist. Liberal Religion considers communism an evil which suppresses freedom and violates the principle of human dignity. But it does not follow that the mind of the person believing in communism is not free. The importance of the free mind principle of the Liberal Church lies in the fact that it imposes no value judgment and leaves the individual completely free to believe even what the rest of us consider evil. The Roman Catholic radio and television priest, Bishop Fulton Sheen, observed once that freedom is the right not to do what you please or what you must, but what you ought. Precisely the opposite is taught by the Liberal Religion. Individual freedom of belief means that the mind of believers may roam in all directions, without preconceived notions or dictates as to what it ought to do.

In an unpublished sermon entitled "The Faith Behind Freedom," the late Lon Ray Call said in 1951: "Without this principle of the free mind in religion, we would still be mumbling pious phrases that have no logical meaning, checking our minds at the church door, saying things with our lips we do not believe in our hearts, paying the ecclesiastics to get our loved ones out of hell and living in fear of hell ourselves. But, fortunately, we have the free mind in religion, or at least, some of it, and we shall have more! We cannot stop where Channing stopped . . . ."

At the beginning of this chapter, it was pointed out that the principle of freedom of belief is often misunderstood and leads some people to assert that they can believe in anything, such as voodoism, fascism, or racism. This freedom should not be curtailed, but it must be understood that its exercise may lead the believer right out of the Liberal Church.

In an effort to make this clear, it has been said that freedom of belief is not so much an article of faith for Liberal Religion as it is a method by which Liberal Religion arrives at its faith. This statement overlooks one crucial point: the method of arriving at a religious faith is also an element of its substance. The substance of Traditional Religion has no room for a method of freedom which seeks and determines religious faith. The existing dogmas preclude what Donald S. Harrington has repeatedly cautioned Liberal Religionists against: the exaltation of freedom of belief as an article of substantive faith. This position is summarized in his Denver address, "The Faith Beneath Freedom."[4] In this address, Harrington seeks to prove that freedom of belief must inevitably lead to a rejection of agnosticism and atheism and to an affirmation of theism. One may doubt this conclusion without disagreeing with the basic assertion that freedom of belief is not a spiritual or religious license to believe anything that comes to mind.

When the Vatican forbade Father Küng to continue teaching Roman Catholic theology, its official statement contained the following: "In their research, the theologians, like scholars in other fields, enjoy a legitimate scientific liberty though within the limits of the method of sacred theology" and "theological research and teaching should always be illumined with fidelity to the magisterium . . . ."[5]

"Magisterium" is the word for the authoritative power of the Roman Catholic Church to announce religious truth. Professor Küng was censored because he disregarded the magisterium. He was condemned because, as the official declaration also stated, he was a "cause of disturbance in the minds of the faithful" and "serious harm to some essential points of Catholic Faith." It is one thing for the Church to disassociate itself from Küng's teaching, but it is another to censor him for stirring up the minds of his listeners and readers and to prevent the latter from exercising freedom of belief. The magisterium leaves no room for freedom of belief. It dictates belief. Liberal Religion abhors such dictation. It encourages and postulates free inquiry which is essential to freedom of belief. Father Küng's experience is similar to that of Albert Schweitzer, whose application for a lectureship at the University of Strassbourg was almost rejected because his research was not orthodox and might "confuse the students."[6]

A logical and almost inevitable consequence of the doctrine of freedom of belief is the principle of freedom of choice. The principle is often referred to in the current controversy over abortion. It is said that a woman should have freedom of choice concerning her body. Liberal Religion agrees with this, except for overriding interests of the community or third parties. According to the present knowledge of science as adopted by the Supreme Court of the United States, an unborn fetus becomes a third party after three months of pregnancy.[7] Thereafter, a woman's freedom of choice ceases to be the controlling principle. (This does not mean that other principles may not justify abortion.) Freedom of choice is also important if the question of suicide or other termination of life arises. This has already been discussed in Chapter 11.

The assertion of freedom of belief as a tenet of Liberal Religion requires the courage to exercise that freedom and, where it is hindered, fight for it. That courage is sometimes lacking. If that courage fails, Liberal Religion fails. Such failure cannot be avoided by professions at a worship service, nor by debates with like-minded people. These rituals cure the evil as little as the incantations of the medicine man heal a broken bone. The cure consists of straightening the bone and then exercise. Not many persons are able to be barnstormers like Moses, Jesus, and Gandhi. But, an individual can stand up for freedom in a thousand little ways: in the Parent Teacher Association, in a sewing circle or bowling club, at Rotary meetings, in political assemblies or at a tea party. When the issue of compulsory school prayers is debated, Religious Liberals must have the courage to stand up and be counted as opponents. The racketeering in business, in labor unions, in political parties, and in public life frequently constitutes suppression of individual liberty by powerful organizations or individuals. It often goes unchallenged because people do not wish to bother, or are afraid. Liberal Religion disapproves. If Religious Liberals do not raise their voices and exercise their freedom, they are delinquent. In the 1950s, Senator Joseph McCarthy terrorized America and suppressed freedom. The voice of Liberal Religion was not heard, although some of the few opponents of McCarthy may have been Religious Liberals. In 1953, the American Civil Liberties Union had great difficulty in hiring a meeting hall in Indianapolis because of public opposition by certain powerful ultra-conservative groups. Finally, it was not a Liberal Religionist but a Roman Catholic pastor who made the basement of his church available. The incident aroused national interest and was the subject of a CBS broadcast. The prediction that its commercial sponsor, Aluminium Company of America, would suffer grievous financial losses turned out not to be true. But even if it had been otherwise, the broadcast would have been a shining example of how freedom can and must be exercised. Another example is experienced in the family and the upbringing of future citizens. Religious Liberals must teach their children the meaning of freedom and how to stand up for freedom without fear. The parent who lets his child do what it pleases, even if the parent disapproves, fails to exercise his parental freedom of choice and thereby sets a bad example. This entails the risk that the youngster will develop into a willful bully, a self-indulgent weakling, or a mental robot. In any of these cases, the youngster will be incapable of being a citizen of a free society.

Freedom of belief is a hollow phrase if those who profess it do not act in accordance with the beliefs they hold.

16

Social Concern

In 1965, when the Reverend Martin Luther King, Jr. organized the protest march from Selma to Montgomery, Alabama, religionists from all quarters, Traditionalists and Liberals, flocked to Alabama and participated. Among this interdenominational crowd, none stood out more visibly than a squad of nuns from St. Louis.[1] The weary marchers spent their last night at a Roman Catholic institution.[2] The Board of Trustees of the American Unitarian Association transferred its regular meeting from Boston to Selma where it met in a rectory.[3] A large number of Unitarian ministers were swept up in the singing of fundamentalist hymns, as well as in an orthodox Jewish religious service.[4] One of them, Unitarian minister James Reeb, became a slain martyr of the cause of racial integration.[5]

The Selma event is recalled here as an example that Traditional, as well as Liberal Religionists are occupied with social concerns. However, one has doubts whether the nuns of St. Louis would have been so enthusiastic about racial equality if the blacks in Alabama had not been Christians. It is noteworthy that the archbishop of Alabama forbade his constituents' participation in the march. Another outstanding participant in the Selma event was the Methodist Foundation for Social Action. Its members, all Traditional Religionists, are reputed to be on the so-called "liberal" edge of Methodism.

While few people belittle social idealism, there are many who believe that it is an entirely different concern from that of religion. They hold that social concerns are no business of the churches and temples. They do not want to hear sermons on social concerns. Fundamentalists are particularly disturbed about the expression of social concerns by religious institutions. The notorious former Georgia governor, Lester Maddox, told a rally at

173

Shelton College, "get away from social reform and go back to the word of God."[6] One is inclined to scoff at the Maddoxes of this world as rather ignorant demagogues, but even more sophisticated religious people share that view. Religion, they protest, should concentrate on personal piety and devotion. Liberal Religion must reject this attitude. Social concern is an essential part of Liberal Religion. Personal piety and devotion which do not lead to social engagement are sterile. The hostility of many Traditionalists to the emphasis on social action is not compatible with biblical religion. The Old Testament says (Lev. 18:9): "When you reap the harvest of your land, you shall not wholly reap the corners of thy field neither shalt thou gather the gleanings of thy harvest. And thou shalt not glean thy vineyard neither shalt thou gather every grape of the vineyard, thou shall leave them to the poor and stranger."

At the present time, the foremost concern centers on disarmament. This is not only caused by the universal yearning for peace, but more so by the vast expenditures of developed countries for armaments. Even churches which are not interested in pacifism now feel, to put it in popular language, that the survival of God's Creation is at stake and that God's resources are sinfully diverted from human needs to military production.

Almsgiving is one of the four basic commandments of the Islamic Religion, and many Christian churches have poor boxes to collect money for the less fortunate. The principal concern of Pope John Paul II is said to be the alleviation of the lot of poor people.

As Max Weber has pointed out, a distinctive concern with social reform is characteristic of the Hebrew prophets. This concern has carried over to the New Testament. It is immaterial whether the Hebrew prophets were politically motivated as Weber suggests.[7] Islam, Judaism, and Christianity take poverty for granted. Their social concern is not to be scoffed at. However, it is more important to be concerned with the causes of poverty and ways to abolish it. Liberal Religion tends towards this broader concern.

Traditional Religionists worry about the pagan religion of the heathen. They send out missionaries to convert them to the "true faith." Pearl Buck, daughter of a missionary, tells in her book *Fighting Angels,* how the Christian missionaries in China did not agree what the "true faith" is and how they competed hotly with each other. The Mormon Church even sends its young people abroad in order to convert those whom they believe to be erring Christians. Most Americans are familiar with the door bell ringing activities of the Seventh Day Adventists. At this writing, a bill before the Indian Parliament aims at forbidding efforts of missionaries to convert people from one faith to another.

Liberal Religion scorns such conversion efforts. The missionaries of the Liberal Church are the teams of the Unitarian Universalist Service Committee which bring health care and teach practical skills to people in need, both abroad and in the continental United States. This is done regardless of the religious orientation of the aided people and without any effort at conversion. The Unitarian Universalist Service Committee exemplifies the social concern of the Liberal Church movement. It follows the larger example of the Quaker Service Committee which has been justly praised for its worldwide charities administered without any effort to influence the religious faith of the recipients.

The Quakers maintain a home near the United Nations headquarters in New York where they arrange meetings for representatives of nations who are officially not on speaking terms. These informal meetings are designed to promote international understanding, peace being one of the fundamental objectives of the Quaker religion. This, like the activities of the Service Committees, can be truly called "social action."

The Quakers seem to be the only religious group which has a genuine, active concern for peace and a desire to practice pacifism. Most Traditional Religionists consider pacifism an impractical pipe dream. Their statesmen protest that they want peace, but peace with honor. This generally implies dishonor to the enemy and, therefore, not real peace. The "Collect for Peace in the Morning" prayer in the *Book of Common Prayer* rather belligerently says, "Defend us, thy humble servants, in all assaults of our enemies, that we, surely trusting in thy defense, may not fear the power of any adversaries . . . ." That is not pacifism, but it is in the biblical tradition. The phrase "Prince of Peace," although generally associated with Jesus, originates in the Old Testament when Isaiah prophesied that a messiah would bring peace and put an end to the wars in the kingdom of Judah (Isa. 10:6). Traditional Religion generally demands armed defense of the faith as a religious obligation. Islam has been spread by aggressive war. The teaching of Gandhi, the great pacifist, did not prevent his disciple and successor Nehru in 1961, from forcibly ousting Portugal from Goa and two other islands. The American war in Vietnam was pursued by leaders who professed Christianity, one of whom (Nixon) professed pride in his Quaker heritage. Another noteworthy aspect of this was that many so-called war resisters were not pacifists. They did not object to all wars, only to this one. The U.S. Supreme Court rejected such selective conscientious objection.[8] Liberal Religion is ambivalent about this issue and about pacifism. However, it will not participate in any denigration of pacifism. It recognizes that pacifism springs from the sincere desire for universal peace, and that without universal peace all efforts to build what, for want of a finer phrase, we call the kingdom of God on earth, must come to naught.

Related to the issue of pacifism is the social concern about the present armaments race. Liberal Religion favors disarmament. It condemns the overkill approach which requires huge expenditures for weaponry that is capable of destroying life on the earth several times over. Quite apart from any religion's aversion to killing, it is felt that large sums are wasted for unnecessary weaponry while not enough money is made available for much needed public improvement to alleviate the misfortunes of disadvantaged people.

An urgent social concern today is the potential damage to human life posed by the development of nuclear energy, genetic engineering, and a deteriorating environment. These were the principal topics of a conference on science and religion, held in 1979, at the Massachusetts Institute of Technology under the auspices of the World Council of Churches. Owing to the restrictive membership of the World Council of Churches, Liberal Religion was hardly represented at that conference. Liberal Religion has, of course, long allied itself with science (see Chapter 6). It has no theological problems with science. However, it shares a growing concern about the social impact of unbridled scientific development, especially in the nuclear field.

While all religions have some social concerns, Liberal Religion has an all-encompassing concern for the whole of humankind, which it places above all religious rites. It is not unreasonable to blame the precepts of Traditional Religion for the present deterioration of the human environment and the spoilation of the entire ecological system. For centuries, people were indoctrinated with a Bible text requiring them to subdue the earth and its creatures (Gen. 1:28) and to put all things under their feet (Psalm 9:6). Small wonder, then, that men have pursued technical perfections and prosperity regardless of the consequences of the quality of life. Liberal Religion rebukes this Bible teaching. It postulates that men must integrate themselves into nature, becoming part of it instead of its master.

This does not mean that Liberal Religion opposes efforts to improve the quality of life. On the contrary, Liberal Religion wants such improvements. Were it not so, it would be conservative rather than liberal. The current controversy over birth control illustrates this point. Traditional Religion is conservative and believes that nature must be allowed to take its course without human interference. The opposite view of Liberal Religion, on the other hand, can claim the support of Father Teilhard de Chardin. The late Jesuit scientist wrote: "We have allowed our race to develop at random and we have given too little thought to the question of what medical and moral factors must replace the crude factors of natural selection . . . it is indispensable that a nobly human form of eugenics . . . be discovered and developed."[9]

Traditionalists oppose birth control and particularly abortion because they are thought to be contrary to the Will of God. At this writing, there is much agitation in America about the matter of abortion. People disagree as to when human life begins. Conservatives say it begins at the moment of conception. Others, backed by the U.S. Supreme Court assert that life does not begin before the fetus becomes viable, i.e., when the fetus is capable of living outside the mother's womb.[10] Science has been unable to support either contention, and the issue is, therefore, essentially a religious one. The Supreme Court has ruled that, as a matter of constitutional law, a fetus is not a person before it becomes viable. The Court also ruled that a mother is entitled to the constitutional freedom of choice, and may freely decide on an abortion until her right collides with an overriding public interest. This occurs when the fetus becomes viable. Medical science to date has determined that this usually happens twenty-eight weeks after conception, and sometimes as early as twenty-four weeks after conception. The U.S. Supreme Court, as a practical matter, therefore ruled that it is constitutionally permissible to regulate abortion procedures during the second trimester of pregnancy, and that abortion may be absolutely prohibited during the third trimester, except to preserve the mother's life. The proposition that abortion during the first trimester of pregnancy constitutes murder of a baby, has nothing to commend itself in science, in constitutional law, in common sense, or in Liberal Religion. The political propaganda of the misnamed Moral Majority and other anti-abortion people distorts the controversy by asserting that Liberal Religion favors abortion. Liberal Religion is not pro-abortion; instead, it asserts the principle of human dignity which requires that a woman shall have the freedom of choice and shall be the sole judge of what happens to her body, so long as no viable life is killed.

While any kind of birth control seems anathema to Traditional Religion, Liberal Religion is guided by the simple principle of freedom of choice. Experience shows that even devotees of Traditional Religion often exercise that freedom of choice. Theologians in the Traditional Churches, therefore, have carved out exceptions to the ban on birth control. Liberal Religion will not allow any restrictions of the principle of freedom of choice. The opponents of this principle have organized themselves under the name of the Right to Life Party. This is a curious name for a group which favors capital punishment and scorns any form of anti-war activity.

The status of the human embryo is also involved in the controversy about test tube babies. These are babies who grow from human eggs fertilized in a vitreous dish and are then implanted in the womb of a mother. In 1978, the first test tube baby was born in England and it caused a religious stir in the United States. Traditional Religion is so opposed to what it calls scientific tampering with human reproduction that the American government, through what was then the Department of Health, Education, and Welfare (HEW), banned all grants for research on in vitro fertilization. That stopped all experimentation in the United States. In 1979, the Ethics Advisory Board of HEW recommended resumption of this research on a limited scale.[11] Forbidding or limiting scientific research violates basic tenets of Liberal Religion. Therefore, the story of the test tube babies, while unimportant in itself, has become significant in two respects. It accentuates the difference between Traditional Religion and Liberal Religion in relation to the search for truth, and the respect for scientific research. Secondly, it highlights the fact that, in Liberal Religion, human reproduction and, indeed, sexuality, do not enjoy any immunity from human observation.

Test tube reproduction has long been commonplace in American agriculture. Calves have been and still are produced this way. Embryos are implanted in so-called scrub cows. This has something to do with farm economics, and there is no known protest from Traditional Religion.

One of the reasons why most Religious Liberals are opposed the new draft of the Federal Criminal Code is that the code attempted to punish behavior which may be regarded as sinful but does not victimize anybody, such as public drunkenness, possession of drugs for one's own use, and consensual sex acts between adults. Here again, the principle of human dignity comes to the fore and causes the Liberal Church to express social concern.

The issue of women's rights was discussed in Chapter 13. It is not controversial in Liberal Religion, which condemns any kind of discrimination in human relations. The ratification of the Equal Rights Amendment is of social concern to Religious Liberals. However, this does not mean that male chauvinism is nonexistent among Religious Liberals. These male chauvinists are simply out of tune with the theology of their faith. The ordination of women as ministers in the Liberal Church, while not commonplace, raises no issue in the minds of its members.

Liberal Religion does not approve of public intrusion into personal sexual preferences and habits. Traditional Religion and conservatives seem to revel in such intrusions. In 1978, Garrett Evangelical Theological Seminary, a Methodist school connected with Northwestern University in Illinois, expelled two homosexual students on the grounds that they could not be ordained because they, as homosexuals, were not fit to be ministers. At about the same time, the Episcopal bishop of New York, ordained an avowed lesbian as a full-fledged minister in the Episcopal Church, causing a storm of protest and a promise on the part of the bishop not to do it again. The cities of Wichita, Kansas; St. Paul, Minnesota; and Miami, Florida had enacted ordinances prohibiting discrimination against homosexuals in housing and employment. These ordinances were repealed in referendums initiated by Traditional Religionists who asserted that the ordinances condoned an immoral way of life. The leader of the intransigent group in Wichita was a Baptist minister who seemed to believe that homosexuals have no civil rights. Judging from his many utterances on the subject, Pope John Paul II seems to be preoccupied with sex. He said, in 1980, that a husband must not lust after his wife. Liberal Religion does not regard this as a religious let alone a social concern.

Traditional Religion is entitled to regard active homosexuality as sinful and wrong. However, a number of clergymen of Traditional persuasion have attempted to establish an atmosphere of tolerance and even respect for homosexuals. In 1979, the Reverend Paul Shanly, a Roman Catholic priest in Boston who had gained a national reputation for his work with homosexuals and their families, was transferred to a suburban parish, and this has been regarded as a signal of the intransigence of Traditional Religion.

Marriage is a matter of social concern because it is an integral part of the social fabric. Its popularity seems to be waning. To understand Western traditions, it is important to go back to the Apostle Paul. In his first letter to the Corinthians, Paul dealt extensively with marriage. He said it is not a sin, even though an unmarried person can devote his entire attention to the Lord's work, while a married person will presumably be concerned with worldly affairs. This explains the Roman Catholic dictate of celibacy for priests and religious orders. Liberal Religion does not share this view because it regards worldly affairs as God's work. Nor does Liberal Religion share the prejudice which Traditional Religion holds against mixed (inter-religious) marriages. This prejudice also goes back to Paul who wrote that a widow was free to remarry, as long as her new husband was a Christian.

The Roman Catholic Church has recently loosened the strictures against mixed marriages. Jews are particularly disturbed about mixed marriages because they feel that these marriages tend to diminish adherence to Judaism. Empirically, this concern may be justified. Religiously, it is not. One of the most moving stories in the Old Testament is that of Ruth, a lady of foreign blood who is shown to be a most faithful daughter-in-law. The biblical story of Ruth is a veritable tract against nationalism, racism, and religious prejudice. The practical result of such prejudice is often that the marriage is performed by a minister of Liberal Religion, and that both marriage partners are lost to the Traditional Religion from which they have come.

Censorship is a social concern. Thought must be free, and so must the communication of ideas. In this, the Liberal Church is at odds with Traditional Religion. Thought control is inherent in any religious or political system that prescribes acceptable behavior. In that respect, there is little difference between Russian Marxism and the Traditional Church, which demands adherence to a religious dogma. Anybody who does not conform is punished and treated as a heretic. The Liberal Church does not know heresy. The late Episcopal Bishop Pike was tried for heresy after he had expressed doubt about the doctrine of the Virgin Birth. In 1979, the German Lutheran pastor Paul Schulz was defrocked for similar offenses. Father Melish was ousted from his Episcopal rectory in Brooklyn when he refused to obey his ecclesiastic superiors who had demanded that he separate from his son and assistant, who was associated with left-wing political causes. The ecclesiastical censor's restraint on Father Teilhard de Chardin, the Jesuit scientist, has already been mentioned. Liberal Religionists are shocked by such censorious occurrences, but these sentiments are quite inappropriate. A clergyman who insists on remaining with a hierarchical denomination deserves no particular sympathy for doing so, and he cannot complain when the hierarchy acts in accordance with the tenets of its religion. The eminent Roman Catholic theologian Hans Küng has apparently not yet been disciplined by his church.

Zealous parents' groups sometimes seek to foster conservative ideology by eliminating textbooks from school libraries. Liberal Religion resists intellectual straightjackets for students. The censors do not want the youngster to know about evolution and about the social ills and conflicts of our time. Censorship is repressive. Some contemporary feminists would like to prohibit the publication of pornography, even if such literature does not violate criminal law. These feminists urge that pornographic literature is offensive to womanhood. It probably is, and the sensitivity of these women is understandable. However, Liberal Religion is socially concerned with freedom of expression. Even persons of poor taste must be accorded this freedom. Legal sanctions are not to be tolerated unless and until the criminal law has been violated.

Liberal Religion is greatly concerned with the preservation of all civil rights and all civil liberties. Many of its adherents are members of the American Civil Liberties Union which numbers among its founders such liberal clergymen as John Haynes Holmes and Rabbi Stephen Wise.

As a final example of social concern, unemployment should be mentioned. Lack of work is one of the principal causes of poverty and other social ills. The Puritans believed and taught that lack of work was necessarily the result of slothfulness. This may or may not have been true at that time. It is not true today, and yet the puritanical public attitude has not disappeared. Many successful people feel that, since they have succeeded, anybody who has not yet done so has only himself or herself to blame. We know that many unfortunate people are the victims of economic, social, and even genetic conditions which are beyond their control. They need our social concern.

The foregoing random catalog of social concerns is intended for illustrative purposes, and not as a dogmatic statement. The overriding principle of freedom of belief gives every Liberal Religionist the right to disagree.

The concern of Liberal Religion is frequently expressed through the formation of social action committees and the resolutions which these committees adopt and publish. The danger here is that an adopted resolution may seem to bind all members of the committee, the congregation, or the larger body. This, of course, is not the case.

There are other pitfalls in the adoption of such resolutions. Most social action committees of Religious Liberals confine themselves to the adoption of resolutions. The process preceeding the adoption of these resolutions is very educational for the participants and it is certainly indicative of their social concern. However, it is not social action. As Bernard Shaw observed about the French Revolution, it was not won by "virtuous indignation, caustic criticism, conclusive arguments, and instructive pamphleteering, even when done by the most earnest and witty literary geniuses."[12]

One of the weaknesses of these so-called Social Action Resolutions is that they frequently call on governments (even foreign governments) to take action. This is sometimes nothing short of ludicrous since governments are not likely to pay any attention to these resolutions. Another weakness is that resolutions are sometimes adopted by persons who are not familiar with the facts to which the resolution is addressed. Liberal Religionists have a commendable zest for helping the underdog and for condemning exploitation, unfairness, and overbearing attitudes. This zest sometimes overshadows the principle of rationality which Liberal Religion cannot abandon without jeopardizing its integrity. For instance, a few years ago, the Annual Assembly of the Unitarian Universalist Association voted by an overwhelming majority to disapprove a bill which would have enacted a new Federal Criminal Code. The condemnation may have been justified, but almost none of the voting delegates had studied or even read the proposed code. Liberal congregations and even their social action committees are not infrequently remiss in this respect. This bespeaks zeal but not rationality. Worse still, the zeal sometimes develops into zealotry.

It must be recognized that such zealotry leads at times to liberal idolatry or dogmatism, which must be guarded against. Cautions James Luther Adams, "Liberalism has sometimes retreated into a superficial and provincial backwash of progress ideology, sometimes into the mere privatization of religion, and sometimes into up-to-date but provincial zeal for the spirit of the times."[13] The result, says Adams, is a thinning of liberalism into moralism, and the loss of the religious dimension.

The ritual of passing resolutions is questionable, but social concern remains an important part of Liberal Religion.

Running like a red strand through all these social concerns is a devotion to individual liberty. According to the tenets of Liberal Religion, the individual is and must be subordinate to the community and the environment; the liberty of the individual is necessarily limited. It is limited by the social order which communal living requires. That is the meaning of ordered liberty which Liberal Religion espouses. It has a long history. In Anglo-American history, it goes back to the Magna Carta (1215), to the Petition of Rights (1628), the Habeas Corpus Act (1679), and the Bill of Rights in the American Constitution (1791).

Liberal Religion used to be a leader in the field of social concern. Henry Bellows (1814–1882), the long time minister of All Souls Unitarian Church in New York, founded the Sanitary Commission, a forerunner of the American Red Cross. Dorothea Dix (1802–1887) was instrumental in prison reform. Horace Mann (1796–1859) reformed education in America. Susan B. Anthony (1830–1906) championed women's rights. John Haynes Holmes (1879–1954) and Rabbi Stephen Wise (1874–1949) were co-founders of the National Association for the Advancement of Colored People and of the American Civil Liberties Union.

Liberal Religion can be proud that the ideas of these forebears have become part of the American mainstream. Like others, the people of Liberal Religion are in danger of becoming complacent and sick with apathy. The spiritual environment of Liberal Religion is a natural breeding ground for innovative ideas and progressive action. It is to be hoped that the present and future generations of Liberal Religionists will again be the standard bearers of innovation in the ongoing evolution of our social problems.

The greatest social concern of Liberal Religion is religious liberty, to which the following chapter is devoted.

17

Religious Liberty

Historical Perspective

Religious liberty was a revolutionary concept when the first and only Unitarian king, John Sigismund of Transylvania (1540–1571), proclaimed that all religions are entitled to the same respect. Unitarians, therefore, claim that they inaugurated the idea and they have been in the vanguard of the struggle for religious liberty ever since. It has been, and often still is, a struggle in the face of religious beliefs which insist that all dissenters are heretics—evil heretics. One favorite fairy tale in American history, still used by public orators and read in newspaper editorials, is that our ancestors came to America to establish religious liberty. Quite the opposite is true. The early settlers would not tolerate dissent from their own religious dogmas.

Toleration was the most one could expect in those days. Although toleration to this day is regarded as a virtue, it is, in reality, the lowest form of civilized community living. Tolerance means suffering. The desirable form of community living is not by sufferance but one based upon respect for the diverse views of one's neighbors. The only American colony founded on tolerance was Maryland. This was due to the fact that the proprietor, Lord Baltimore, was a Roman Catholic, and most settlers were Protestants.

Genuine religious liberty in the church and civil government existed only in the Rhode Island plantations which were formed by the rebel Roger Williams. The Dutch colony of New Netherlands (later New York) obtained the most liberal patent issued to any American colonial settlement. In 1645, the governor granted all settlers of Flushing the right "to have and enjoy liberty

183

of conscience according to the custom and manner of Holland without molestation or disturbance from any magistrates, or any other ecclesiastical minister that may pretend jurisdiction over them."[1] The quoted language indicates what people feared at that time. The reason for the liberal grant was purely economic—the need for more settlers. However, when Peter Stuyvesant came to be governor of New Amsterdam in 1652, he paid no attention to the grant and persecuted all nonconformist Catholics, Baptists, and Quakers. The Quakers, a fiercely independent sect in all American colonies, suffered most from the persecution. This led the inhabitants of the Flushing area to adopt the Flushing Remonstrance in 1657, the earliest American document concerning religious liberty. For some unfathomable reason, it is not mentioned in our history books. One sentence of it reads:

> The law of love, peace, and liberty in the states extending to Jews, Turks, and Egyptians, as they are considered the sonnes of Adam which is the glory of the outward state of Holland, soe love peace and liberty, extending to all in Christ Jesus, condemns hatred, war, and bondage.[2]

Roger Williams's work is better known. In 1644, he published in England "The Bloody Tenent of Persecution."[3] The point of this essay is that civil government can be sustained without the church, and that the church does not need the support of the civil government. The essay is preceded by twelve arguments. Two of the twelve should be quoted here because they brand orthodoxy as a threat to peace.[4]

> *First,* that the blood of so many hundred thousand souls of Protestants and Baptists, spilt in the wars of present and former ages, for their respective consciences, is not required nor accepted by Jesus Christ, the Prince of Peace. . . .

> *Eighthly,* God requireth not an uniformity of religion to be enacted and inforced in any civil state, which inforced uniformity (sooner or later) is the greatest occasion of civil war, ravishing of conscience, persecution of Christ Jesus in his servants and of the hypocrisy and distraction of millions of souls.

Religious Liberals are proud of these antecedents which culminated in the Act of Establishing Religious Freedom, drafted by Thomas Jefferson for Virginia and later introduced in the Federal Constitution. Religious Liberals respect all religious beliefs and disbeliefs. They say with Thomas Paine that infidelity does not consist in believing or disbelieving, but in professing to believe what one does not believe.[5] By that definition, many contemporary churchgoers are infidels.

The Virginia Legislature rejected a proposal to name Jesus Christ as the "author of our religion" on the ground that the statute was intended to protect "the Jew, the Gentile, the Chinese and Mahometan, the Hindoo (sic) and the Infidel of every denomination." In the 1960s, the late Senator Ralph Flanders had a similar idea when he introduced the so-called "Jesus amendment" to the United States Constitution. Fortunately, the amendment was never adopted. It shows, however, that the urge to foist a particular religious faith on the public is ever present and religious liberty is never secure.

Religious Liberals have a stout ally in one of the most conservative American religious groups, the Seventh Day Adventists. The Adventists are championing the cause of religious liberty through their magazine, *Liberty,* and its splendid editor, Roland R. Hegstad.

The Federal Constitution adopted Jefferson's doctrine of religious liberty as the law of the land. For that reason, the inherent disdain of some Traditional churches for religious freedom is not quite apparent in the United States. Also, persecuted groups among Traditional Religionists, such as the Roman Catholics and the Jews in the United States, could assert themselves only by claiming religious liberty in the United States. The same zeal for religious liberty does not exist in countries where the Roman Catholics or the Jews are in control of the government and are unfettered by constitutional provisions. In the Moslem countries, religious liberty is unknown.

It is noteworthy that church attendance in countries where religion is supported by the government, such as in England, the Scandinavian countries, and Germany (see Chapter 18), is far below the level of attendance in the United States where the principle of religious liberty forbids government support.

The concluding sentence of Article VI of the U.S. Constitution says that "no religious test shall ever be required as a qualification to any office or public trust under the United States." More important than Article VI is the clause in the First Amendment of the Bill of Rights which reads:

> Congress shall make no law respecting an establishing of religion or prohibiting the free exercise thereof.

This clause applies to federal as well as to state and municipal laws. The first part, known as the Establishment Clause, commands the government to be completely neutral in the field of religion. The second part, known as the Exercise Clause, commands that citizens can engage in or refrain from engaging in religious observances as they please. Thus religious liberty means freedom *of* religion, as well as freedom *from* religion. Freedom *from* religion means that forced compliance with any kind of religious practice is strictly forbidden.

This, of course, is contrary to Paul's teaching that the government is the agent of God and to the Calvinistic doctrine which charges civil magistrates with upholding the rule of God as taught by the dominant church.[6] When the Reverend Roger Williams challenged the Calvinistic view, he was expelled from the Massachusetts Bay Colony.[7] It took another 150 years until Jefferson's view of religious liberty took hold. Jefferson said that it is not the business of civil magistrates to care whether a man believes in one god, twenty gods, or no god at all.[8]

The Contemporary Scene

A man quits his job because his employer assigned him to armaments work, which he refused to do because it violated his religious beliefs as a Seventh Day Adventist. Is he entitled to unemployment benefits? The Supreme Court of Indiana said "no." The Supreme Court of the United States reversed the Indiana court. The United States Supreme Court held the man was entitled to the unemployment benefit out of respect for his religious liberty.[9]

Liberal Religion is fortunate that the founders of the American Republic embedded the principle of religious liberty in the Constitution. Unlike the homogeneity found in other countries, the pluralistic society of the United States and the diverse backgrounds of her people make life without religious liberty unthinkable. In view of this, and the strong command of the Constitution, one might expect that there are no serious problems with religious liberty. This, however, is not the case. Religious liberty is under constant attack. Religious Liberals must be ever vigilant in its defense.

In 1952, Justice Douglas, who had a reputation for being radically libertarian, illustrated the problem when he wrote the majority opinion of the Supreme Court in the almost forgotten Zorach decision. The Court was called upon to decide whether New York was within constitutional bounds when it decreed that public school students should, upon request, be released during regular school hours for sectarian religious instruction under a program supervised by the public school teachers. The Court said that this did not impinge religious liberty. Justice Douglas wrote: "We are a religious people whose institutions presuppose a Supreme Being. When the State encourages religious instruction or cooperates with religious authorities, it follows the best of our traditions."[10] This ruling violated religious liberty because, as Justice Black wrote in his dissenting opinion: "The State makes religious sects beneficiaries of its power to compel children to attend secular schools. . . . It is only by wholly isolating the State from the religious sphere and compelling it to be completely neutral, that the freedom of each and every denomination and of all non-believers can be maintained." Also dissenting was Justice Jackson, a devout Episcopalian, who wrote: "It is possible to hold a faith with enough confidence to believe that what should be rendered to God does not need to be decided and collected by Caesar. The day that this country ceases to be free for irreligion, it will cease to be free for religion."

The high ringing phrases of Justices Black and Jackson reflect the ideals of Liberal Religion. However, Justice Douglas, in this instance, was probably closer to the popular view which has not changed since 1952, and which poses a challenge to Liberal Religion.

Jefferson postulated that there should be a wall between church and state. Religious Liberals believe passionately in this wall. However, conservative religious groups are making constant efforts to break the wall down, and not without success. As Chief Justice Burger wrote not long ago, apparently with some personal satisfaction, "The line of separation, far from being a wall, is a blurred, indistinct, and variable barrier."[11] This development, while distressing to Religious Liberals, must be understood in the light of two sets of circumstances. First, Traditional Religion apparently feels insecure; it craves constant support from civil authority, and it does not believe in what Mr. Justice Jackson said. Secondly, the people of the United States, even those who have no particular concern for religion, have a great liking for the outward trappings of Traditional Religion, and they do not want these trappings abolished.

Certain religious customs are deeply rooted in American life to the point of hypocrisy. The Congress employs chaplains to pray even though few members of Congress pay attention to the prayers. Recently a judge perceived a secular purpose in such prayers.[12] The Constitution forbids the use of a religious test as qualification for office, yet the presidential oath, administered by the Chief Justice of the United States, customarily ends with the words, "So help me God." Many meetings are opened with an invocation and closed with a benediction, at which those present willy-nilly bow their heads. When this happens outside of a religious assembly, or outside the family circle, it is religious compulsion, not religious liberty.

Americans are apt to think that all of them are either Roman Catholic, Protestant, or Jewish. They overlook religious minorities, such as Buddhists in the state of Hawaii and elsewhere, the nonconforming American Indians, and others whose religion is not based (or no longer based) on the Judeo-Christian tradition. Thus, when a court complaint was filed against the Port Authority of New York and New Jersey because that governmental body had built and maintained at John F. Kennedy Airport three chapels for the three principal religions, people did not understand the grievance. The Federal District Judge ruled that this was not a violation of the Establishment Clause, because the Port Authority did not aid but merely "accommodated" religion. He then dismissed the complaint on a technical ground, and the Appeals Court confirmed this.[13]

The Pledge of Allegiance is another illustration of the government's blindness to the religious rights of those who do not adhere to the Judeo-Christian majority view. The Pledge of Allegiance was written in 1892. In 1954, President Eisenhower signed legislation inserting the words, "under God" in the oath. He explained that the phrase "under God" would "strengthen the spiritual weapons which forever will be our country's most powerful resource." These words probably reflected the view of the legislators who voted for the insertion and the views of many others who, to this day, believe that the invocation of God improves the speaker's morality and, in any event, can do him or her no harm. The constitutional guarantee of religious liberty was simply overlooked for those who, like the Buddhists, do not believe in God, those who do not like to invoke divine power in a prescribed or routine fashion, and those who simply object to the use of the word "God."

Given the popular preference for religious practices, it is not astonishing that ambitious politicians and zealous clerics constantly attempt to extend compulsory religion. In order to circumvent the constitutional command, the protagonists of the attack on religious liberty often couch their proposal in the cloak of voluntarism or private financial support.

At the time of this writing, the school prayer issue is red hot even though the Supreme Court has ruled that prayers, as well as Bible reading in public school are forbidden by the Constitution. The proponents complain that, as a result of the judicial insistence on the separation of church and state, "God has been expelled from the classrooms." This, they contend, is the cause for the decay in public morals, the increase of crime, and the other evils of contemporary civilization. They insist that public school children, before receiving instruction, should say or listen to a prayer. They propose that this be voluntary and that exceptions be made upon the request of the child or his (her) parents. Teachers are not given this choice. No less a religious minded person than former President Carter has pointed out that the proposal of voluntarism is quite unrealistic because children always want to conform. The proposed voluntarism is a hoax. In 1980, the highest court in Massachusetts invalidated a statute requiring teachers to invite students in public schools to lead their classes in prayer. This has not discouraged the conservative forces to try their luck elsewhere. The mainline churches are opposed to school prayers, not only on constitutional grounds, but also because they believe, as Liberal Religion does, that religious education is the responsibility of the family and of the religious institutions.

Fearful that any school prayer bill, if enacted, might be invalidated by the courts, the foes of religious freedom have filed a bill (the so-called "Helms amendment") which would deprive the Federal courts of jurisdiction in such matters.

The Federal Constitution is the source and fountainhead of religious liberty in America, and the Supreme Court is its guardian. It is, therefore, understandable that all controversies in this field are resolved by court decisions. Anyone concerned with religious liberty is compelled to deal with the legal decisions which reflect the ongoing struggle. These decisions are made by judges who, being human, are not always consistent. Four general principles can be distilled from the case law as guidelines for the understanding of decisions related to religious liberty.

Four General Principles

1. *The Constitution protects religious beliefs and not religious conduct.*

On that ground, the Supreme Court declared illegal the practice of polygamy, although the Mormons contended that their polygamous practices were nothing but the free exercise of their religion.[14] In spite of this old Supreme Court decision, there are still Mormons in the United States who practice polygamy without hindrance. The activist character of Liberal Religion forces it to question the distinction between religious belief and religious conduct. Liberal Religion demands that a person must conduct oneself in accordance with one's religious beliefs. The courts do not quarrel with this attitude; they merely withhold constitutional protection from what they regard as conduct. The Supreme Court denied constitutional protection to polygamy on the ground that it offends the public order. "Suppose," wrote the court, "one believed that human sacrifices were a necessary part of religious worship, would it be seriously contended that the civil government . . . could not interfere to prevent a sacrifice?" The public interest is a legitimate limit to religious liberty. More will be said about the limits of religious liberty at the end of this chapter.

When members of the Krishna sect (International Society of Krishna Consciousness) annoyed the public in transportation terminals by pressing literature upon them and soliciting contributions, the courts ruled that such conduct cannot be prohibited because it would violate the free exercise of religion (Sankirstan), the tenet which requires Krishnas to spread their truth and to solicit money contributions.[15] This incident is cited to show that courts are not always consistent.

A group of Quakers asserted that they were deprived of their constitutional right to practice their religious convictions which forbade participation in or support of war. Their employer, they asserted, should not be allowed to withhold or be required to withhold that part of their income tax which was used by the U.S. Government to support the war effort. The U.S. Supreme Court ruled against the complaining Quakers apparently because the tax strike effort is held to be unprotected conduct.[16]

The Religious Liberty clause was invoked when a government agency sought to stop a child from distributing religious literature in violation of the state child labor law. A Massachusetts court ruled that the child's conduct was not constitutionally protected and that the child labor law must prevail.[17]

2. *In cases where the purpose of a statute or government action is not readily apparent, governmental action is permissible only if it meets three tests: (i) it must have a secular purpose, (ii) it neither advances nor inhibits religion, and (iii) it avoids excessive entanglement with religion.*

This threefold test stems from past school prayer and Bible reading cases which could not pass muster. It also came into play when the Supreme Court had to pass on a Kentucky statute requiring that the text of the Ten Commandments be posted in all public school classrooms, provided the cost thereof is borne by private contributions. The Supreme Court of Kentucky upheld the statute on the ground that the Ten Commandments reflect the American way of life and are approved by Christians, Jews, and Moslems. Confucionists, Hindus, Buddhists, Shintoists, Taoists, Zoroastrians and other religions were not considered. The U.S. Supreme Court ruled the Kentucky statute unconstitutional. It obviously advanced religion, which was not permissible for a government supported public school. It was, therefore, immaterial whether the government or private contributors paid for the printing of the posters. The statutory provision for private contributions was an obvious attempt to circumvent the constitutional mandate.[18] North Dakota school officials who posted a copy of the Ten Commandments were likewise judicially enjoined from doing so because the practice was motivated by none other than sectarian purposes.

3.   *A philosophical belief and personal preference which is not shared by an organized religious group cannot qualify for constitutional protection.*

This principle was invoked when Cherokee Indians protested the building of the Tellico Dam in the Tennessee Valley. They contended that the dam would destroy a place of worship and, hence, interfere with their constitutional right to the free exercise of religion. The court found that the Cherokees were demanding protection for personal preferences and not for the tenets of a religious group.[19] Although the Supreme Court has repeatedly expressed the principle, it has not consistently adhered to it.

When Mr. Seeger, who did not belong to an organized religious group, based his claim of exemption from the military draft on the grounds that he did not believe in a Supreme Being—as the Selective Service Act prescribed— the Supreme Court granted the exemption. The Supreme Court subscribed to the reasoning of the Federal Appeals Court which had said:

> We feel compelled to recognize that a requirement of belief in a Supreme Being, no matter how broadly defined, cannot embrace all those faiths which can validly claim to be called "religious." Thus it has been noted that, among other well established religious sects, Buddhism, Taoism, Ethical Culture and Secular Humanism do not teach a belief in the existence of a Supreme Being. Indeed, our country has long prided itself on the enormous diversity of religious beliefs which have been able to find acceptance and toleration on these shores.[20]

The writer of this opinion, Judge Irving Kaufman of the Federal Appeals Court in New York, was awarded the Thomas Jefferson Religious Liberal Award by the Unitarian Universalist Metropolitan District. Similarly, a Federal District Judge in Maryland wrote in 1968:

> Defendant's claimed belief occupied "the same place in his life as an orthodox belief in God holds in the life of one clearly qualified for exemption . . . these beliefs were not derived essentially by the application of reason and logic or were essentially the product of political, sociological or philosophical views. Rather, they appear to be a product of faith, albeit a curious almost perverse faith which glorifies man and his mortality but rejects the concept of an orthodox God."[21]

In these cases, the personal philosophical belief of a nonorganized individual was granted the constitutional protection of religious liberty.

4.   *A statute or governmental act does not violate the Constitution just because it coincides with the tenets of a religion.*

This principle can be distilled from two recent cases. The Supreme Court was presented with the question as to whether a state law limiting medicaid funds for abortion should be outlawed because it coincided with the position of the Roman Catholic Church. The Court ruled that the statute was constitutional.[22] A similar question was posed when two orthodox religious groups attacked the Smithsonian Institution's expenditure of public funds for an exhibit on evolution. The plaintiffs contended that this aided the religion of Secular Humanism, and they attempted to heat up this argument by stating that Secular Humanism also advocates the right to divorce, birth control, universal education, and a world community. The Court coldly rejected the plaintiff's argument by holding that the Smithsonian exhibit did not involve religion and neither disparaged nor promoted any religious belief.[23]

A number of other court decisions do not fit into the pigeonholes of the four principles, but, nevertheless, they tell us more about the problems of religious liberty.

The *Exercise Clause* of the Constitution was invoked when children of Jehovah's Witnesses refused to salute the American flag, and when a prospective notary public was denied appointment in Maryland because he was an atheist. Of far more reaching importance was the above mentioned interpretation of the Selective Service Act which grants conscientious objector status to those who object to military service on religious grounds. The statute required belief in a Supreme Being. The statute was probably intended to require belief in a Traditional deity, but the Supreme Court ruled that a sincere belief which is "parallel to that filled by the orthodox belief in God" qualifies for the statutory exemption. The Court thus granted a nontheistic religious person the same right to exercise his religion as the Traditional Religionist.[24]

Many states have enacted laws which forbid ministers to hold political office. Such laws are intended to assure a separation of church and state. However, they also deprive ministers of their free exercise of religion. Therefore, they are unconstitutional, and the Supreme Court has so held. However, the Vatican directed Father Drinan to give up his seat in the United States Congress. The Vatican does not want any priest to hold political office.

The free exercise of religion becomes an issue when the parents of a very sick child refuse to allow a hospital to administer a blood transfusion because their religions prohibits such medical practices. The Amish religion is opposed to high school education. When a Wisconsin court convicted some Amish parents for violating the state's compulsory school attendance law, the Supreme Court ruled that such a conviction would violate the Free Exercise Clause.[25]

Sabbath observance has also led to conflicts about the meaning and application of the Free Exercise Clause. In one case, the government refused unemployment compensation to a man who could not find a job because he declined to work Saturdays, as his church affiliation commanded. The Supreme Court ruled that the man was entitled to act in accordance with his religious belief and, therefore, entitled to receive unemployment compensation.[26] An orthodox Jew who would not work on a Saturday, demanded the right to open his store on Sunday instead. This violated the local Sunday law. The complaining Jew argued that he was hindered in the free exercise of his religion. Not so, ruled the Supreme Court. The Court said that the plaintiff suffered a hardship because of his religious observance of the Sabbath, but he was not prevented from free exercise of religion.[27] Liberal Religion cannot quarrel with either decision.

The Establishment Clause

The problems arising in connection with the Establishment Clause of the Constitution center primarily on the education of children. No problem arises if the religious education and instruction of children takes place in the home and in religious institutions such as churches, temples, or similar establishments. The difficulty arises if public and government supported institutions are used to impart religious instruction or for religious exercises, because, in situations like this, public as well as government funds and facilities are used to promote religion. This is the crux of the school prayer controversy which was discussed earlier in this chapter. A footnote thereto is offered by a recent court case involving prayer meetings organized by students and held in public classrooms. Students are, of course, free to organize prayer meetings and to engage in any religious exercise they wish. However, they are not allowed to do this in the classrooms of public schools. In forbidding it, the Federal Appeals Court in New York wrote, "We must be careful that our public schools where fundamental values are imparted to our children are not perceived as institutions that encourage the adoption of any sect or religious ideology."[28] According to a newspaper report, it is customary in Tennessee at football matches for high school teams to begin with a common prayer. The Attorney General of Tennessee ruled that the public school coaches who arranged for these prayers were violating the Constitution. This has not stopped the forbidden practice. Some of the allegedly devout people have threatened to shoot out the windows of anybody who complains.[29]

The personal God of Traditional Religion appears to be a needed educational tool for many teachers, as the following ancedote illustrates. A lady who taught a class of fourth graders succeeded in intimidating her students by telling them that God saw every infraction of the rules which escaped her and that God would mete out severe punishment. Another teacher complained in a letter to the editor that God was dead in the public schools and she asked desperately for something to cling to instead. She asked for some nonreligious rituals which could calm the spirits of the children and replace what she called "the sweet breath of a just and loving God." The present separation of God and child, especially the slum child, seemed catastrophic to her.

Religious liberty does not require that people, and especially school children, be kept ignorant of the religious influences which are ingrained in our culture. What is required is merely neutrality with respect to sectarian creeds. No particular religious viewpoint must be promoted. Some find it difficult to observe the distinction.

A New Jersey public school offered courses in transcendental meditation. It required two court decisions to stop this practice. The state of New Jersey also allowed a tax deduction to parents who enrolled their children in parochial schools. This was ruled illegal because it had the primary purpose of advancing religion.

Parochial schools are a source of constant friction. In particular, Roman Catholics and Orthodox Jews claim the right to educate their children in schools which emphasize their religious orientation. If these people merely wanted to exercise the right to practice their religion, no problem would arise. The difficulty is that parochial schools frequently demand support from the public treasury. Such support is granted in many ways: in the form of favorable tax treatment, school bus service, supplying textbooks, health care, or special government programs.

The parochial schools constitute a heavy financial burden on religious institutions that choose to establish them. At the same time, they afford financial relief to public school systems. This is one of the reasons why indirect support for parochial schools is not abandoned. However, as Leo Pfeffer has pointed out, parochial schools are on the wane because public interest in sectarian education is not as intense as it used to be.[30]

Some parochial schools have become a means of escaping racial desegregation because few children from racial minorities are sent to parochial schools, which charge tuition and are not free like the public schools. It seems that parochial schools in the suburbs prosper because well-to-do people live there. This gives a different slant to the government support of parochial schools. It raises the question, says Pfeffer, "of the morality of taking money sorely needed for the education of the poor and disadvantaged in order to finance separate and superior education for members of upper classes." And "even those committed to the survival of separate schools would not like to see them become a haven for those who are running, not to God, but away from the Negroes."[31]

Mention was already made of the Kentucky and North Dakota situations where courts outlawed, as a violation of the Establishment Clause, state laws requiring the posting of the Ten Commandments in public schools. A religious liberal cannot but be astonished that anyone in Kentucky, North Dakota, or elsewhere should regard the Ten Commandments as a suitable guideline for contemporary American children, considering that these commandments were designed to regulate the conduct of a band of primitive migrants. The state of North Carolina printed a "motorist's prayer" on its official road map. When this was challenged, the Court forbade it. A prayer, said the Court, is always religious and the government is not allowed to spread religion. In its defense, the state of North Carolina pointed out that the Supreme Court has sanctioned the words "In God We Trust" on coins and official documents. That is different, ruled the Court, because the slogan "merely reflects our history and has no theological significance. The Motorist Prayer has not acquired such historical legitimacy."[32] A religious liberal, while applauding the decision at hand, may find it difficult to understand the alleged difference. As the Constitution forbids any religious entanglement, a violation of the constitutional ban should not be condoned as historically legitimate because people have become accustomed to it. However, as was stated before, certain religious habits seem to be ineradicable in the American system.

The Establishment Clause is also an issue in the dispute about the Blue Laws or Sunday Laws which have been prevalent since colonial times in America and in other cultures. The original rationale of all these laws was that Sunday is the seventh day of the week and should be devoted only to divine worship. Of course, this was in support of religions which regard Sunday as the seventh day. The Jews and some Christian sects differ. Their Sabbath is Saturday. For Moslems, Friday is the day for divine worship and rest. It was, therefore, unavoidable that the Sunday Laws should be stricken from the statute books as a violation of religious liberty.

The Civil Rights Act

New problems in the field of religious liberty resulted from the American Civil Rights Act. That federal statute forbids discrimination in employment practices, a restriction which includes religious discrimination. The definition of the word "religion" is not a theological one, but tailored to the practicality of the problem. Religion is defined as "all aspects of religious observance and practices without undue hardship on the conduct of the employer's business." The constitutionality of the statute has been criticized because it requires the employer to make reasonable accommodations to an employee's religion. This can be regarded as assuring the employee of the free exercise of religion. It can also be regarded as forcing the employer to support a religion and thus violate the Establishment Clause. This is not the place to advocate a position on the constitutionality of the statute. For present purposes, it is more interesting to consider some factual situations in which the problem has arisen. In one case, a plant supervisor did not want to work on a Saturday because his church, The World Wide Church of God, forbade it. Another case involved a collective bargaining agreement which required the employee to hire only union members. The plaintiff objected to this practice because his religious beliefs prohibited union membership. In still another case, an employee was discharged because one of his job assignments was raising and lowering the company's American flag, which he refused to do because it was in conflict with his beliefs as one of Jehovah's Witnesses who regard the flag as an unholy idol.

Liberal Religion will, in all such cases, respect the religious beliefs of the employee. It must also respect the religious belief or disbelief of an employer who does not choose to have any regard for the religious beliefs of the employee. The question then is whether Congress, or any other government agency, shall have the right to make an employer respect his employee's religious beliefs. The Civil Rights Act affirms this right except in those cases where the employer can prove that accommodation to the religious preference of the employee would constitute a hardship to the employer. If Congress had not spoken, Liberal Religion might also take the opposite position and say that the law should not allow an employee to force his religious views upon an unwilling employer. Indeed, a lower court in California recently (May, 1980) held that an employer's religious liberty was violated by such a statute.

Tax Exemption

American statutes exempting churches from federal and municipal taxes are still upheld although they obviously aid in the establishment of religion.

All religionists enjoy this exemption without discrimination. But it is questionable whether such automatic and comprehensive tax relief is compatible with the principles of Liberal Religion. Some Liberal Religious institutions, therefore, make voluntary payments to the municipalities whose services they use. Automatic tax exemption leads to great abuses and is an incentive to fraud.

The tax exemption for religious institutions made sense when the church rendered services to the public which were not available elsewhere: for example, schooling, hospital services, care for the poor, etc. These are now government functions. There is no justification whatsoever for exempting churches from paying their fair share for municipal services such as fire and police protection. The cost of these services is customarily divided among property owners. If the owners of church property are released from their public obligation, then private owners must bear a disproportionate share of the burden. Thus, the taxpayers are required to support a church regardless of whether they believe in it. This violates the principles of religious liberty. Thomas Jefferson wrote in the preamble of his Act for Establishing Religious Liberty in Virginia, "to compel a man to furnish contributions of money for the propagation of opinions which he disbelieves is sinful and tyrannical."[33]

Parochial schools, like any educational institution, enjoy tax exemption. New York City recently decided that private schools should at least pay for the water and sewer service. This required the enactment of a state law, and the proposal was defeated. In the words of a newspaper report, "parents organized demonstrations, priests voted protest resolutions, nuns wrote letters to the Mayor, and rabbis lobbied in Albany." Traditional Religion proved to be unbeatable.

A storm broke loose when, in 1978, the U.S. Labor Department ruled that unemployment compensation taxes must be paid by all church schools employing salaried teachers.[34] Since these teachers are entitled to benefits if they become unemployed, the ruling makes sense. Liberal Religion does not sympathize with the fury of Traditional Religion.

Abuse

The mushroom growth of new church organizations has led to many abuses of the religious liberty principle, some of which are nothing short of scandalous. The Universal Life Church in California sells ecclesiastical degrees for a mere ten dollars. By paying that amount, anyone can become an ordained minister of the Universal Life Church. Most inhabitants of the little town of Hardenbergh, in the Catskill Mountains of New York, have availed themselves of that opportunity. As a result, 211 persons out of a total population of 250 became mail order ministers and have claimed real property tax exemption.

The legislature of New York has tried to abolish these abuses by prescribing that tax exemption can only be granted for property which is held in trust for the members of a religious group. In 1980 the state of New York commenced an action against the Life Science Church. The complaint charged that the church induced about 5,000 inhabitants of New York to spend an estimated 17.5 million dollars for the privilege of becoming ministers of the church for the purpose of qualifying for tax exemption. It was also charged that the Life Science Church promised its ministers fat commissions for soliciting new recruits.

It appears that state governments are becoming increasingly aware of this type of tax evasion which is practiced under the guise of religion. The Attorney General of California is very active in the effort to protect the public against financial machinations of certain religious organizations operating in his state. The occasional full page advertisements placed in *The New York Times* by the Universal Life Church of Pasadena indicate that this organization is fighting for its survival against unwanted state investigation. In July 1981 the Internal Revenue Service commenced a campaign against the increasing practice of purchasing certificates of ordination and thereby trying also to purchase tax exemption.[35]

An extreme example of the audacity with which the cloak of religion is used for private ends is the California based Bubbling Well Church of Universal Love. According to a newspaper report, this organization has only three members: John Herberts, who is president; his son Dan, the vicepresident; and his wife Catherine, the secretary-treasurer.[36] It was not shown that anybody else derived benefit from this so-called church, and tax exemption was therefore denied. Religious liberty means liberty for religion; it should not be used as a tax shelter.

Two more cases in the area of income tax illustrate the abuse of religious liberty: A Mr. Heller was a mail order minister. He then made what he dressed up as a tax-free contribution to his church and had the church pay his rent and electric bills. Thus, the cost of rent and electricity was converted into tax deductible expenses. The U.S. Tax Court nixed this charade. A man in Michigan resorted to a similar scheme. He made a contribution to a church which used the money to pay the cost of educating the donor's children.[37]

The Limits of Religious Liberty

Enough has been said to justify an investigation concerning the limits of religious liberty. These limits are, of course, not those which the snipers from the camp of Traditional Religion seek to impose. However, as earlier sections of this book indicated, Liberal Religion abjures absolute truths. No tenet is permanently etched in stone. The principle of religious liberty must yield when it conflicts with the public interest.

It is not always easy to determine the public interest. One's political, social, and religious beliefs tend to influence any attempt to ascertain the public interest. For this very reason, Traditional Religion and Liberal Religion frequently differ. Traditional Religion believes it to be in the public interest to indoctrinate school children. Liberal Religion holds that the religious education of children is a private matter and therefore the proper province of the family. More difficult are the diverse opinions within the community of Liberal Religion. For instance, some Liberal Religionists will feel that Quakers are entitled to refrain from paying a portion of their income taxes on the ground that their religion prohibits the support of war efforts. Others may feel that the public interest requires the government to be the sole judge as to the collection and disbursement of income taxes. However, there is probably a vast area in which there is no ideological dispute about what constitutes the public interest. For instance, some years ago, the children of Christian Science parents in New York were excused from attending biology classes when the germ theory was taught. The resulting inconvenience led to the elimination of the germ theory from the biology syllabus and the regents examinations. All children remained ignorant of the risk of spreading germs. Thus, the public interest in an aware citizenry was sacrificed in an effort to respect the religious liberty of the Christian Scientists. This position seems less persuasive when, for religious reasons, children are excused from lectures on evolutionary theory. Ignorance of evolution, it can be argued, does not endanger the public interest. Preserving life is generally considered a matter of public interest. That is why courts tend to disregard the wishes of a parent who objects to a blood transfusion for his child. And yet, on other occasions, the rights of the child are disregarded. For example, when the court upheld the religious liberty of Amish parents to withhold a child from high school, no inquiry as to the child's preference was deemed necessary.

The public interest test may offer a solution to the continuing strife over support to parochial schools. If the use of public funds is regarded as paramount for the public interest, some support for the parochial school can be justified because the maintenance of these schools by their sponsors saves the government some money. The government does not bear the main financial burden for educating the students in parochial schools. However, most adherents of Liberal Religion believe that the paramount importance of education in the public schools is the benefit which future citizens will gain by growing up with youngsters from various economic, religious, and racial backgrounds. From that viewpoint, any support of parochial schools, at taxpayer expense, is contrary to the public interest. The need to balance the principle of religious liberty with the demands of the public interest does not represent the present position of the courts. The courts have tended to support any aid to parochial schools so long as the proposed assistance, for instance bus service, is purely secular in nature. And, as above stated, the Federal Statute known as the Economic Recovery Act of 1981, treats tuition payments to parochial schools as tax-free gifts.

Complaints have been voiced against hospitals operated by the Roman Catholic Church because they will not allow birth control measures. This policy conforms to Catholic doctrine and therefore represents the constitutionally guaranteed free exercise of religion. However, many of the patients who clamor for birth control assistance are poor people from the neighborhood whose medical care is paid for with public funds. Government funds must not be spent to aid any religion or religious doctrine. The public interest therefore demands that hospitals which elect to withhold medical assistance on the basis of a religious doctrine must not be subsidized with government funds.

Automatic tax exemption for any organization which calls itself a church is certainly not in the public interest. It would be deplorable if adherents of Liberal Religion would blink at such tax exemption because they may benefit from it.

Liberal Religion must applaud a decision against tax exemption for the Bob Jones University in South Carolina. This is a religiously oriented university. Its religious beliefs condemn interracial dating and marriage, and violators are expelled. The Internal Revenue Service withdrew the tax exemption of this religious institution because its beliefs violated the public interest of the United States, which forbids racial discrimination. While the government must maintain an attitude of neutrality towards all religions, certain government interests are so compelling that conflicting religious practices must yield (see Postscript).[38]

18

Politics

Religion and politics are two topics which many persons seek to avoid in polite conversation because these subjects are frequently controversial and liable to create embarrassment. In many churches, even in some liberal churches, politics is taboo and not to be discussed in the pew or from the pulpit. Religion is regarded as a lofty matter, while politics is considered base. The polarity of religion and politics is alien to liberal religion. Politics has a religious dimension.

Dramatic contemporary proof is found in the Islamic revolution which is being carried out by Islamic clerics. The career and the reign of Oliver Cromwell in England is another historic example of the fusion between religion and politics. The organization of the leading American Colonies bore a religious stamp: Pennsylvania, that of the Quakers; Maryland, that of Roman Catholicism; Massachusetts, that of the Calvinist Puritans; Virginia, that of the Anglican Church.

At the center of every political activity is the public interest. Admittedly, the public interest is often distorted by self-seeking political practitioners. This does not diminish its importance. On the contrary, it must spur us on to greater, unselfish participation in the political process. Religious values and ideals can assist us in the effort to define the constitutent elements of the public interest. The values, ideals, and aims of Liberal Religion differ from those found in Traditional Religion. Some of these differences will be touched upon in this chapter.

Regardless of their differences, all religions aim at peace. The aim is hard to achieve because the world is full of problems and antagonisms. People try to overcome them by violence, either domestic revolutions or international wars. There are some people who believe that the second coming of Christ or some other messiah will bring the universal peace found in the removal of all frictions and antagonisms. Few people expect this to happen and even fewer have the patience to wait for the event. In the meantime, political solutions rather than violent solutions can bring relief. This we know from practical experience. In other words, politics aims at preventing violence and, for that reason alone, deserves the infusion and blessing of religion. More broadly speaking, politics is an instrument, if not *the* instrument, by which the Kingdom of God can be established on earth. This, of course, is one of the aims of Liberal Religion. The politics of the American Revolution and the American Constitution represent largely the religious views of the Founding Fathers. As Liberal Religion adheres to these views, it is really politically conservative, but in the 1980s the term "political conservative" has gained a very different connotation.

In the ancient religions, the gods were local deities existing only for the benefit of their local followers. They were interested in the political fortunes, especially the wars of their people. Thus, the Hebrews carried Yahweh along in their wanderings and Yahweh was deeply concerned with the political victories of the Hebrews. This carried over to modern times when God had become universal. During the last war, it was assumed by all warring factions that God was on their side; the weapons of each side were blessed and God was implored to destroy the enemy. Each national church wanted political victory for its followers. The American clergy prayed for the victory of American arms. The German pastors asked God to support the German cause. Both sides prayed for the victory to the God of their fathers, and it was supposed to be the same God. All this was in the accustomed religious tradition. Apparently, it occurred only to a few that this was a travesty of religion. William James tells of a friend who complained about the Christian God because He "is on the side of our enemies as much as He is on our own."[1]

Religion has been, and still is, supporting the established order, whatever it might be. Paul wrote that government authorities must be obeyed and all taxes must be paid because the state is an agent of God (Rom. 14:4). Any resistance to the established order is opposed. The Judeo-Christian liturgies contain prayers for the head of state. Luther vehemently condemned all opposition to the establishment. At the so-called prayer meetings at the White House, Mr. Nixon assembled clergymen and laypersons of all shades of Traditional Judeo-Christian religion, and they all supported the Nixon administration with their prayers. Traditional Religion is generally a pillar of the establishment. Carl Sagan refers to it as a "bureaucratic religion," a label, it is hoped, Liberal Religion will always avoid.[2]

Religion is often the foundation of the establishment. The sociologist Max Weber says that the religious influence on the establishment is all pervading:

Among these religious functionaries, whose pastoral care has influenced the everyday life of the laity and the behavior of political officials in an enduring and often decisive manner have been the counseling rabbis of Judaism, the father confessors of Catholicism, the pietistic pastors of souls in Protestantism, the directors of souls in the Counterreformation of Catholicism, the Brahim purohitas of the court, the gurus and goarins in Hinduism, and the muftis and dervish shaykhs in Islam.[3]

The Roman Catholic theologian Küng tells how the church and the clergy supported the colonial power establishment in exploiting the Asian people.[4] Franz Fallon wrote: "The Church in the colonies is the white people's church, the foreign church. She does not call the natives to God's ways, but to the ways of the white man, of the master, of the oppressor."[5]

In India, the Brahmans proffered divine justification for keeping the untouchables in slavery. Similar religious arguments were used to justify slavery in the United States and apartheid in South Africa. The historian Morison describes how organized religion gained by advocating slavery which was the mainstay of the establishment, especially in the South.[6]

Jefferson tells in his autobiography that the majority of the American population were dissenters, but the majority of the legislators favored the establishment and thus forced the people to support the established (Anglican) church.[7] Gibbon says of ancient Rome, "The various modes of worship that prevailed in the Roman world were all considered by the people as equally true, by the philosophers as equally false, and by the magistrates as generally useful."[8] The magistrates favored religion, any religion, because it tended to keep the population disciplined, law abiding, and virtuous. There can be no quarrel with this Roman attitude, so long as the establishment respects Liberal Religion's values.

Unhappily, this is often not the case. When the establishment embraces a particular religion in preference to others, and if it uses its power to stamp out or to restrict nonconformists, the Liberal Church becomes anti-establishment.

There are those in the Liberal Church who, as a matter of principle and visceral reaction, will join any anti-establishment movement or demonstration. This is often done without carefully evaluating the issues involved, a violation of the fundamental principle of rationality. That does not seem to trouble the anti-establishment religionists because they feel that the establishment has too much church support and a counterweight is needed. This is not a persuasive argument—it is religiously sloppy. To quote a liberal minister, "there is nothing quite so pernicious as a free swinging thinker with a lot of swing and precious little think."[9]

Not all of Traditional Religion supports the establishment. Some are anti-political, rejecting all worldly affairs; they have no interest in temporal events affecting their lives. As Weber said, "The power of the apolitical

Christian religion of love was not derived from interest in social reform, nor from any such thing as proletarian instincts, but from the complete lack of such concern."[10] People who feel that way are disgusted with politics. In the current arms race between the United States and Russia, they would rather quit the race than keep the upper hand or maintain parity with Russia. They would rather turn the other cheek, preferring to be martyrs or, to change the metaphor, they would rather be red than dead.

While many Religious Liberals may favor the last described attitude, this preference is derived from a very different religious motivation. Liberal Religion does not favor political passivity. The Religious Liberal is an activist interested in improving the environment, making this a better world to live in, and creating the best possible Kingdom of God on earth. Such an ambitious goal cannot be achieved by indifference. It requires rational involvement in political activities.

The word "politics" denotes the science, art, and practice of operating the government. The low esteem in which politics is held stems from the misbehavior of a few politicians. The proverbial bad apples are found in every calling be it law, medicine, or plumbing. However, one does not hold law, medicine, or plumbing in contempt just because of a few unscrupulous individuals. The objective of political philosophy, as Plato first said, is to devise a method of barring incompetence and knavery from public office and electing the best available people to rule for the common good. It seems clear that the church is an eminently proper place for this kind of political philosophy.

The German Chancellor Bismarck defined politics as the art of the possible. Skillful and successful as he was in domestic as well as foreign policies, Bismarck knew that he could not achieve his goals by battering his head against a stone wall of opposition, although he often knew how to undermine and weaken such a stone wall. This is what the Liberal Church has not always understood. In a country where the vast majority are committed to Traditional Religion, it is seldom possible to enact legislation which represents Liberal Religion's principles. But, it is possible gradually to spread these principles and thus to open the door to religiously progressive legislation. Italy offers a contemporary example of what this means. It enacted divorce legislation which would not have been possible if the majority of the legislators had not deviated from the traditional anti-divorce approach of their Roman Catholic Church. It is fair to assume that by doing so, the Italian legislators did not abandon their church. They genuflect before a church altar prior to joining a party meeting.

The recognition that politics is the art of the possible need not, and indeed should not, lead to a betrayal of basic principles. This thought opens up the difficult question as to where and how a dividing line can be drawn between compromise and betrayal of principles.

The theology of compromise is very troublesome because, as Max Weber says, "public political activity leads to a far greater surrender of rigorous ethical requirements than is produced by private economic acquisitiveness, since political activity is oriented into compromises, to craft, and to the employment of other ethically suspect devices."[11]

The following is offered as a working hypothesis for the religious dilemma:

> If one abandons an objective which is not of essential importance, it is a permissible compromise. If one abandons an essential principle, it is impermissible betrayal. What is essential depends upon one's outlook and, therefore, it all boils down to a subjective test of one's priorities.

To the Italian legislators of the Christian Democratic Party who voted in favor of divorce reform, the matter was obviously not of essential importance. So they compromised with their colleagues of the Communist Party. The late Adlai Stevenson was known as a staunch Unitarian. During his second presidential campaign in 1956, he was advised to be more down to earth than in the earlier campaign and to obliterate his image as an "egghead." He thereupon announced that one of his parents had been a Presbyterian and that he had now joined the Presbyterian Church without abandoning his Unitarian affiliation. From then on, during his presidential campaign, he alternated on Sundays between attendance at a Presbyterian Church and a Unitarian Church. Some liberals thought that it was a betrayal of principle to participate one Sunday in a worship of the Father, the Son, and the Holy Ghost, and on the next Sunday, in a worship which abjured the Trinity. However, religion was probably not of essential importance to Stevenson, and, if that is correct, what he did was not a betrayal of principle but a compromise.

The Stevenson anecdote illuminates one of the less admirable influences of religion on politics in the United States—the apparent need of presidential candidates to go to church every Sunday. It was said of General Eisenhower that he never went near a church until he became a candidate for the presidency. Only Abraham Lincoln, who was unchurched, seems to have had the spiritual fortitude to rebuff a delegation of churchmen who solicited his membership during his presidential campaign. He said he would join a church if he ever found one which simply practiced Jesus' command of love of God and love of neighbor. Lincoln was very much interested in religion and in theology, but he was not a Traditional Religionist.[12] For this reason he was accused of religious infidelity. This also happened to Thomas Jefferson, and it happened to William Howard Taft when he was a presidential candidate in 1908 against William Jennings Bryan. Bryan's evangelism highlighted the religious issue in the campaign. Taft was a member of the All Souls Unitarian Church in Washington, D.C., where he attended throughout his presidency. During the campaign, he stood on his Unitarianism without being defensive about it and, unlike Adlai Stevenson the elder, he did not compromise his liberal religion.

Politics without religion is unprincipled, and religion without politics makes religion too otherworldly and therefore sterile. Everyone is involved in politics, if not as a subject, then as an object. Therefore, all should be interested in having politics governed by the spirit of religion. Politics is so serious and important a topic that it should not be avoided, and the escapist attitude alluded to at the beginning of this chapter is not commendable. The biblical injunction, "Render unto Caesar the things that are Caesar's and unto God the things that are God's," must be understood as a command to take part in the things that are Caesar's, namely, politics. A congregation may wish to be apolitical in the sense that it does not wish to have politics discussed from the pulpit. This is tolerable. What is intolerable is an antipolitical attitude. Islam has always been more militant than Christianity. The revolution in Iran, under the leadership of the Ayatolla Khomeini, represents an effort to infuse the religion of Islam and its principles into the political life of the state.

The last allusion indicates that the operation of the principle here advocated is not always pleasing to Liberal Religion. The same is true of the Reverend Jerry Falwell, one of America's successful television preachers, who heads the Thomas Road Baptist Church in Lynchburg, Virginia. In September 1979, Falwell decided to go into politics and to hold patriotic rallies all over the country. To this end, he organized Moral Majority, Inc. As a born-again fundamentalist, he believes the Jews to be the chosen people and he is an ardent Zionist. At the rallies he proclaims, against a backdrop of massed American flags, that the Bible is the inerrant "Word of God" and condemns gay rights, feminism, excessive welfare programs, Communists, and a disarmament treaty with Russia. He denounces the Federal Government for promoting socialism and the public school system for fostering humanism. In short, Falwell preaches politics, even as the late Father Coughlin did from his radio station in Michigan. Father Coughlin was eventually silenced by his ecclesiastical superiors. Liberal Religion abjures ecclesiastical superiors. Obnoxious as Reverend Falwell and Father Coughlin may be, adherents of Liberal Religion cannot question their right to preach what they believe.

Paul Tillich has pointed out that the foremost connotation of the phrase "Kingdom of God" is political.[13] Since earliest times, the word "king" has been a symbol in its own right for the highest and most consecrated center of political control. Liberal Religion has a different concept of the Kingdom of God than that employed by Traditional Religion. However, the concept still represents the realization of its high ideals, a realization which can only be achieved by political means.

On his January 1979 visit to Mexico, the pope exhorted priests of Latin America to desist from all political activities and to concentrate on spiritual matters. At the same time, he urged the priests to concentrate their interest on alleviating the situation of the poor and the underprivileged. How the latter aim can be effectively accomplished without political involvement, the pope did not say.

In the course of history, religion and politics have been combined in a variety of ways, frequently not to the credit of religion. A review of these involvements are here considered in seven categories. Additional or different categories may be just as appropriate.

The first category includes events where pure religious passion has been an important factor. The most dramatic contemporary example is Iran. The Thirty Years War in Europe (1618–1648) was a religious war; Catholic nations fought Protestant nations just because they had religious differences. Adherence to a particular faith was not grounded on any consensus of religious conviction, but rather because individual rulers had decided in favor of the new Protestant faith or the old Catholic religion. The slogan *cujius regio ejus religio* (whose region his religion) governed. In the name of religion, the earth of Europe was scorched and about one third of its population killed. In the same category lies the English alliance with France accomplished by Queen Elizabeth I. The traditional English rival came to her rescue because the King of France happened to be a Protestant who desired to prevent Catholic Spain from defeating Protestant England. The slogan cited above applied to England as well. After the death of the renegade Henry VIII, his Roman Catholic daughter, Mary (the bloody Mary) came to the throne and England was promptly drawn into the Catholic orbit once again. The situation was later reversed when Mary died and a Protestant monarch succeeded to the throne.

The massacres between Hindus and Moslems after the partition of India in 1974 were caused by religious antagonism. The killings in Ireland in the late 1970s occurred as result of religious enmity. In the American Colonies the intolerant attitudes of one religious group against all others led to political persecution. In New York, at the time of Peter Stuyvesant, the law prohibited intercourse with members of the Quaker sect. In all of these historical events, religion has been debased and used as a handmaiden of political power struggles.

A second category is exemplified by the Crusades. The Christian crusaders hacked the Turks to pieces unless the latter converted to Christianity. The cruelty was tempered by a desire to make converts; a person who was converted was *literally* saved. While this attitude indicates a heightened religious zeal in the pursuit of foreign policy, it does not bespeak a Christian attitude in the zealots. A similar attitude applied to anti-Semitism in pre-Hitler Europe. Discrimination against a Jew ceased if he converted to a Christian religion. In the immediate past, every Saturday, ultra-Orthodox Jews who proudly acknowledge the appellation of zealots attempt to stone automobiles on the road to Ramot, a suburb of Jerusalem. They engage in this violence as an expression of their anger about what they consider to be a desecration of the Jewish Sabbath.[14]

The third category includes situations where the political power structure demands exclusive devotion and reverence. No other loyalty is tolerated. This is what Calvinism did in the New England colonies. It also happens in the so-called totalitarian societies where Marx and Lenin have become divine figures or where the Führer and *Il Duce* competed with the church. Hitler was not entirely successful in Germany, the churches were persecuted but not abolished. In Italy, Mussolini was unable to succeed against the Church because Traditional Religion was too deeply rooted.

The fourth category of religious involvement with politics encompasses the countries which have an official state religion. The chief example is contemporary England where the monarch is also the head of the Anglican Church. Bishops of the Anglican Church are, in effect, appointed by the British Prime Minister even if he or she personally is not a member of the Anglican Church. The government of the church is a purely political affair. In the Scandinavian countries Lutheranism is the state religion, and in Spain it is Catholicism. The political blight on religion is not limited to Europe. In Malaysia and Iran, for instance, Islam is the state religion.

The fifth category comprises states where a religious group has a domineering strength even though there is no official state religion. This is particularly troublesome for liberals since they always seem to be in the persecuted minority. Israel is in this category. Ever since the state of Israel was established, the small, religious political parties (which adhere to orthodox Judaism) have managed to exert a powerful influence. In consequence, Israel's laws concerning family life, education, and public transportation on the Sabbath day are determined by religious sectarian principles. At this writing, conservative and reform rabbis are not permitted to officiate at weddings, funerals, and conversions. Such rites are only recognized as valid if performed by a rabbi of the orthodox persuasion. If a widow in Israel wants to remarry, she must marry the surviving brother of her former husband, unless she obtains a rabbinical dispensation. This is in accordance with a biblical injunction (Deut. 25:5). The Bible also contains a contrary command (Lev. 20:21) which the orthodox rabbis choose to disregard. These Bible citations were used to support both opposing views when Henry VIII wanted to divorce his first wife, the widow of his brother.

The children of an Israeli Jew, even though brought up as religious Jews, do not enjoy full political rights if their mother was born a non-Jew. Latin American countries frequently fall in the same category because the Roman Catholic Church dominates. As a result, divorce laws are nonexistent in most of these countries, although there are exceptions.

The sixth category of religious involvement with politics includes the countries in which political parties are organized on a religious basis. Outstanding examples are the Christian democratic parties in Germany and Italy. Originally, the Christian Democratic Party in Germany was the party of the Roman Catholics, post-Hitler successor to the former German "Zentrum

Party." The Zentrum Party in Germany carried the Roman Catholic flag in the famous "Kulturkampf" (culture fight) with Bismarck. During the period between the two world wars, the Zentrum Party produced the German Chancellor Brüning. After Hitler, the Christian Democrats grew into a general conservative party opposed to the Socialists. The small kingdom of the Netherlands has numerous political parties, most of them organized on the basis of the religious sectarian affiliation of their members.

The last and seventh of these categories comprises those parts of the world, including the United States, where religion is separated from the body politic. The Constitution of the United States has erected Jefferson's wall between church and state. Every American citizen enjoys freedom *of* religion, as well as freedom *from* religion. Americans are proud of this principle. However, they frequently disregard it when they prepare for an election. The ticket must be balanced—religiously and ethnically—so that no group will feel slighted. Political appointments often depend upon the religious affiliation of the appointee. The president of the United States, and especially the president-elect, often appoints a special assistant whose assignment it is to look after ethnic and religious groups. Governor Alfred Smith, in his unsuccessful campaign for the American presidency, was beset by scurrilous attacks on his Roman Catholic background. All this may be practical politics, but it violates the tenets of Liberal Religion which espouse the dignity and worth of man, regardless of his religious affiliation. The principle of religious freedom does not bar any religious organizations from competing with other religious groups for popular allegiance. Liberal Religion is free to promote its ideals. So is Traditional Religion. An example of this is the political action program of Reverend Jerry Falwell, misleadingly named the Moral Majority. Conservative religionists have founded a group called Christian Voice, aimed at introducing legislation which would declare the United States a Christian nation. This political effort to override the rights of religious minorities is described in detail by Ronald Hegstad in the May, 1980 issue of the Seventh Day Adventist magazine, *Liberty*. Mr. Hegstad adds the following historic comment: "I reminded Senator Hatch, who had spoken of America's religious beginnings, that a 1796 treaty with Tripoli framed under the administration of George Washington, assured the Moslems that the new Government of the United States of America is not, in any sense, founded on the Christian religion. The Senator quickly became preoccupied with another reporter's question." The political effort of the Christian Voice is not a novelty. Several decades ago, the late Senator Flanders introduced the so-called Jesus amendment to the U.S. Constitution. In the chapter on religious liberty, it was pointed out that the framers of the Virginia statute on religious liberty rejected the idea of designating Jesus Christ as representing America's religion.

Pope John Paul II disapproves of the political activity of priests. In 1980, he directed on American priest not to seek re-election to Congress and another to withdraw his candidacy. In Italy and Germany, conservative political parties have adopted the name "Christian Democrats," thus preempting the majority religion for themselves and making political hay by an appeal to religion.

Liberal Religion has not made an adequate effort to make itself felt in the political arena. This is deplorable and calls for remedial action. A number of years ago, Reverend Donald Harrington, the senior minister of The Community Church of New York, mounted an unsuccessful candidacy for Lieutenant Governor of the state of New York. He still endeavors to exert political influence on behalf of Liberal Religion, as did his great predecessor, Reverend John Haynes Holmes. Holmes and his friend, Rabbi Stephen Wise, were powerful voices on behalf of Liberal Religion.

Political activity by its ministers is not only consistent with Liberal Religion, it should be demanded. For instance, most Liberal Religionists (and some Traditionalists as well) are opposed to capital punishment. They must be free to advocate this idea from their pulpits and to oppose, in the name of their religion, any candidate for political office who favors capital punishment. Most Traditional churches are opposed to abortion at any time during a woman's pregnancy. They find it hard—if not impossible—to reconcile their religious beliefs with the decision of the United States Supreme Court which nullified any state law prohibiting abortion during the first three months of pregnancy. Such religious belief is entitled to respect and may legitimately be promoted from church pulpits.

Obviously, such pulpit activity is heartily disliked by proponents of the freedom of choice principle (often misnamed the pro-abortion principle), but it is inconsistent for a Liberal Religious person to restrict or attempt to restrict the voicing of diverse opinions from opposing pulpits. A person who is convinced of some religious truth has the right to proclaim it and to seek its implementation by the body politic. If a group of religious liberals believes that persons who evaded the military draft by escaping from the United States to Canada or Sweden should be pardoned by the United States government, they have the right to advocate pardon legislation. By the same token, the Roman Catholic Church has a right to seek legislation to bar divorce or birth control. Liberal Religionists often resent legislative pressure by Traditional Churches. Such resentment is unjustified and indeed unjustifiable for people who believe in freedom of the marketplace of ideas.

The liberal resentment is generally based upon the thought that it is quite appropriate for a church to make rules for its adherents, but that it is inappropriate to set standards for others or for the entire community. The flaw in this line of thought is the failure to recognize that a church which, for example, condemns birth control as an evil, may consider the evil as one of the absolute evils which it feels bound to stamp out. Believing Satan to be an evil power, a church may want to destroy him rather than leave him free to pollute the world. Religious Liberals who do not believe in absolutes may find this attitude hard to respect, but respect it they must. In consequence, one must recognize the right of Traditional churches to endeavor to translate their teachings into legislation which will be binding on all citizens.

Instead of fuming against such political efforts, it behooves the Liberal Church to make similar efforts and to promote Liberal Religious thoughts through political efforts.

It is well to recall Thucydides' words in Pericles' famous funeral oration: "We differ from other states in regarding the man who holds aloof from public life, not as quiet, but as useless."

19

Worship and Prayer

> Let us worship with our ears and fingertips
> Let us love the world
> Through heart and mind and body
>
> Let us worship not in bowing down
> Not with closed eyes and stopped ears
> Let us worship with the opening of all wisdom
>   of our beings
> With the full outstretching of our spirits.

These lines from a poem by Kenneth Patton,[1] a Unitarian Universalist minister, reflect the spirit of the public worship in the Liberal Church. This chapter deals with public worship in churches, temples, meeting houses, and other public assemblies. Private worship, as the name implies, is an entirely personal matter.

The word "worship" is a contraction of the original "worth-ship" and must be understood as reverence for the values which one cherishes. The celebration of these values may but need not involve reverence for a divinity. Max Weber's thesis that all worship constitutes an attempt to influence or coerce the gods[2] certainly does not apply to Liberal Religion. Public worship is a demonstration of collective engagement or commitment.

And yet, there is no gainsaying that some Liberal Religionists have a deep distrust of any kind of worship service. This distrust and widespread apathy are the reasons why so many pews are empty on Sunday morning.

The distrust which some Liberal Religionists harbor can be attributed to three principle sources:

a) Liberal Religionists are afraid that the worship service will subject them to some unintelligible mumbo-jumbo, remembering that religion was originally practiced as magic by charismatic magicians. Max Weber calls the professional necromancers (magicians) the world's oldest profession,[3] a refreshing departure from the trite American colloquialism.

b) Liberal Religionists fear outdated stereotyping. This fear, unfortunately, is not altogether unfounded. Even some liberal churches adhere to ancient symbols and a rigid liturgy in the Judeo-Christian tradition. Worshippers are told, however, that they need not accept this, that no dogma is being offered and that they are free to put their own interpretation on the use of ancient symbols and words. The trouble is that some people are unwilling to engage in the effort of interpretation and translation because they do not find it conducive to worship.

c) Liberals, being mostly rationalists, dislike the charismatic and even ecstatic elements which are often part of the worship service.

These objections have no real merit. The worship service in a liberal church is paramount proof of it being a free church. Unlike other religions, there is no prescribed liturgy, no required reading, no prescribed prayer, or established order of service. There need not even be a sermon, although almost all congregations prefer a sermon most of the time. Sermons sometimes tend to have the nature of lectures. Some congregations like this approach. Like their conservative contemporaries, most liberal congregations look for a religious experience in the worship service. This is commonly provided by a stimulating sermon which does not offend one's intelligence and yet satisfies intellectual curiosity, or leads to introspection.

Music deepens the reflective mood. There is always music, and most of the time hymn singing, though the music and the hymns are often not of a character commonly thought to be religious. The reading is sometimes from the Bible, but more often than not it is a passage from an essay, a book, a newspaper article, a poem or a passage from the sacred writings of other religions. Diversity is in fact the distinctive feature of a Liberal Religion's service. A Roman Catholic is pleased when, attending mass away from home, he finds that what is heard in a strange church is the familiar liturgy. Liberal Religionists feel the same kind of joy when they visit a strange liberal church; the service may be entirely different from what they are accustomed to, but the open-minded spirit of diversity and freedom is the same.

The absence of symbols is also common among liberal churches. Liberal Religionists live and worship without the aid of symbols. If they wish to address God, they can do so directly without averting their eyes. Some liberal churches choose to display a cross. It symbolizes greatness and love, but also murder and arrogance,[4] a fact which renders the cross inappropriate for the Liberal Church. Unitarian Universalists sometimes display the chalice, the logotype or image of the Unitarian Universalist Service Committee. It is also a cross, though embellished. Some theologians assert that religion cannot exist without symbols.[5] Liberal Religion can and does, as was discussed in Chapter 7.

The worship service of the Liberal Church is permeated with reverence for life. Whether it be the congregation singing the Haydn tune of Psalm 19 ("the spacious firmament on high") or the preacher exploring a specific human problem or condemning some act of violence, it is always a reverence for life that moves the worshipper. The phrase "reverence for life" is, of course, an inspiration of Albert Schweitzer (see p. 252).

The mood of the liberal religious worship is reflected in the following passage from Albert Schweitzer: "Let a man once begin to think about the mystery of his life and the links which connect him with the life that fills the world, and he cannot but bring to bear upon his own life and all other life that comes within his reach the principle of reverence for life, and manifest this principle by ethical world and life affirmation expressed in action. Existence will thereby become harder for him in every respect than it would if he lived for himself, but at the same time it will be richer, more beautiful, and happier. It will become, instead of mere living, a real experience of life."[6]

Schweitzer may not have known or thought of it, but the reverence for life is an echo of the Hebrew blessing, "to Life," which has been set to music in the well-known Broadway show *Fiddler on the Roof*.

In the Traditional Church, the worship service is essentially homage paid to the supernatural God. In the Liberal Church it is essentially a celebration of life. It is unavoidably an emotional experience. The worship service is designed to create such experience. This should not result in ecstasy, if the term is intended to mean irrationality. If, on the other hand, ecstasy means little more than exuberant joy or contentment, no liberal religionist need be ashamed of it. "Worship," writes Henry Nelson Wieman, "means the turning of the appreciative responsiveness of the total personality toward what the individual holds to be supremely worthful for all human living."[7]

Irving Murray prepared a study paper for the Unitarian Universalist Advance about the intent of Unitarian Universalist worship. He regards worship as the Judeo-Christian institutionalization of William Hocking's doctrine of alteration.[8] According to that doctrine, man necessarily functions in alternative cycles: after being awake, he must sleep; after work, he relaxes; after spending time in everyday toil, he needs to turn to worship. If that were correct, the public places of worship would be more crowded than they are, and more than half of the population would not stay away from worship service. Putting aside Dr. Murray's theory and his scorn at Harvey Cox's proposal that religious people should concentrate on the mini-Sabbath of meditation, the study paper contains some excellent observations such as: "The institution of worship . . . requires an organized religious community. A man's church should not interfere with his religion. . . . Musical services should be scheduled from time to time. Our Unitarian Universalist predilection for talk needs occasional rebuke. . . . If the minister is to do his Sabbath presentation well, he must be given adequate time for it." One cannot but agree with Murray's conclusion that the purpose of a worship service is to reach one or more of the following objectives: to help those in attendance put their life experience into focus, to enhance one's awareness, to overcome anxiety, to encourage living, to enlighten the worshipper, to inform him, to stimulate his thinking.

Another Unitarian minister, Alan Seaburg, wrote a much more critical piece on the services in the Liberal Church.[9] He argued that the liberal worship service is in a state of decay, that it has assimilated too much of the traditional order of service, and that it should be scrapped in favor of new designs. Unfortunately, the author does not tell us what should be done except to experiment with "new techniques," which are not described. It is true that some ministers and some congregations cling to the old forms, but many others are interested in experimenting and enjoy it. Some ministers are incapable of new techniques. Others believe that the congregation, however liberal, would not accept it. One never knows until it has been tried.

Preoccupation with techniques must not detract from what many consider the greatest attraction of the worship service, the sense of fellowship among men and women who share the aspiration of Liberal Religion which it engenders and nurtures. Another great value many find in the worship service is that it is an opportunity for solitude and introspection, and a relief from the drudgery and pressure of the work week.

Prayer

Prayer is a difficult topic. Before any criticism can be made, it must be emphasized that religious liberals will not denigrate a person who derives personal comfort from any form of prayer; nor will there be any disparagement of a person who requests a prayer of support for himself or some third person. Any sincerely held religious belief commands respect.

According to Professor Wieman, liberals do not really understand prayer.[10] They know, of course, that not all prayers are thoughtful and sincere. Many are uttered parrot-like and mindlessly. As the praying king in *Hamlet* said:

> My words fly up, my thoughts remain below
> Words without thoughts never to heaven go.

Some people never pray, others pray only occasionally. There is a great diversity regarding questions of when to pray, where to pray, how to pray, to whom to pray, for what to pray, and what response is expected.

Speaking of public prayer in the worship service, Emerson said in his famous Divinity School Address in 1838, "We shrink as soon as the prayers begin, which do not uplift us, but smite and offend us." This applies especially to the hackneyed phrases of supplication ("help us, Oh! God . . .") which are still heard even in the Liberal Church. Emerson shunned public prayer; this is one of the reasons why he resigned his office as a Unitarian minister.

Public prayers are customary at the opening of a legislative session in Congress and in various legislatures. If the praying chaplain is paid with public funds, the constitutional command of neutrality in religious matters is violated. However, a judge in Nebraska recently ruled that the prayer itself serves a secular purpose, which has nothing to do with religion. The alleged secular purpose is to bring the legislators to order.[11] In other words, when the legislators mill around noisily, the prayer will function as a tranquilizer. This is a ludicrous circumvention of the constitutional mandate against governmental involvement in religion, as discussed in Chapter 17. Unfortunately, it reflects the contemporary public mood.

It is difficult to understand why Liberal, as well as Traditional Christian congregations and ministers, pay no attention to the injunction in the Sermon on the Mount against public prayers (Matt. 6:5): "When you pray do not initiate hypocrites, they love to say their prayers standing up in the synagogue and at street corners for people to see them. When you pray go to your closet and when you have shut your door, pray to your Father which is in secret." Even Paul, the zealous and praying Christian, wrote to the Corinthians that they should pray with their minds. And he added, "I would rather say five words that mean something to the listener than ten thousand words in a tongue." The person with the gift of tongues, wrote Paul, speaks for his own benefit, not for the benefit of the community. That is so because "anybody with the gift of tongues speaks to God, not to other people (1 Cor. 14:19).

According to the Gospel of Luke (Chapter 18, verse 1) Jesus told the people always to pray and never to lose heart. He did not mean public prayers but inner prayer or the prayer of the heart which, at a public worship service, would be the silent prayer often called for when the minister asks the congregation for a silent moment of "prayer and meditation." The Liberal Religionist, even if not the praying kind, has no difficulty with this; he or she will concentrate on some matter which is on his or her mind. This is like yoga meditation believed to control the ideas in one's mind. It has been said that such concentration can best be achieved by constant repetition. This is done with the so-called "Jesus prayer" in which the praying person says over and over again, "Lord Jesus Christ, son of God, have mercy on me, a sinner." Perhaps the ceaseless repetition of the Roman Catholic "Hail Mary" is an application of the same technique. The school of transcendental meditation teaches concentration on one's mantra, a special key word. If the Liberal Religionist wants to concentrate, he will probably scorn this technique and think of a different matter each time.

Praying for mercy, as in the Jesus prayer, is common to the liturgy of all Traditional religions. It is based on the belief that man, conceived in sin and living as a sinner, can only survive if the divinity is merciful. Prayers for mercy are related to the prayer of praise which also occurs in the Traditional liturgy. It is based on the notion that God's wrath can be avoided and God's favor can be obtained by fulsome praise and flattery. All these prayers are prayers of supplication, where the supplicant asks the divinity to grant good health or wealth or some other good fortune. This kind of prayer is perfectly natural for those who believe that one cannot have good fortune unless God bestows it. Intercessional prayers are in the same category. Some years ago, a wealthy man in England bequeathed a substantial sum of money to a religious order of nuns whose primary activity was intercessional prayers. The British tax authorities questioned the tax deductibility of such a bequest in connection with the determination of the death duty. The matter was litigated and eventually reached the House of Lords, as the highest legal authority. The Lords ruled that the gift was not tax deductible because there was no legal evidence that the intercessional prayers had any beneficial effect upon the community.

Related to the prayer of supplication is the prayer of confession. In it the devout confess all or some of their sins to God. The praying person also believes that God is omniscient; therefore, he or she is telling what it is believed God already knows. There is, of course, another side to this prayer. It is designed to purge the guilt of the penitent, who believe that by prayerful confession forgiveness is (or will be) obtained.

A peculiar form of prayer, practiced in some Traditional Churches but frowned upon in most, is called "glossalia," the practice of praying in tongues. The following line of gibberish will serve as an illustration: "ulla ulla unga urga garah atta ungaraze." The devotees of this peculiar ritual cite Paul (1 Cor. 12:30) to prove that speaking in tongues is a gift of the Holy Spirit.

Ministers of Liberal Religion do not pray in tongues, but, at times, they find it convenient to use old-time prayer language. Those in the congregation who do not like this practice are expected to translate the old-time language into modern concepts.

Prayers of aspiration are more likely to appeal to Liberal Religionists. Prayers of aspiration are designed to shake us up: "Let us appreciate the beauty of the earth," or "Let us be kind to one another." God is not always, and sometimes never, mentioned by name. Such omission does not denote any absence of reverence. Critics say that this is like having a telephone conversation with no one on the other side. This overlooks that the spiritual self, the inner voice, the soul is on the other side. The following lines from a prayer of Max Gaebler exemplify the prayer of aspiration:

May those of us who are young find inspiration in the poise and grace of
    those who are old
May those of us who are old find comfort in the energy and openness of
    those who are young
And may those of us in between, who feel the burdens of the world heavily
    upon us, find strength and encouragement in both.

Some ministers, in an effort to please everybody who attends public
worship services, might blur the line between prayer of supplication and the
prayer of aspiration. They will use neutral language, as in the old Sioux
Indian prayer, which begins with these words:

> O great spirit
> Whose voice I hear in the wind
> And whose breath gives life to all the world
> Hear me. I am small and weak
> I need your strength and wisdom.

This beautiful prayer then goes on to utter some of the common human
aspirations.

A recent writer attacked the Roman Catholic argument that permissive-
ness in regard to abortion is an interference with the laws of God and
nature. "So is a prayer for rain," the writer commented sarcastically. This
sarcasm is misplaced and fails to comprehend the nature of the traditional
prayer. In a prayer for rain, the supplicant asks God to change the natural course of events which the supplicant believes is controlled by the
Deity. In the case of abortion, the woman or the physician involved takes it
upon herself/himself to interrupt the pregnancy. They do not ask for a
divine decision. The traditional prayer of supplication is based upon the
assumption that God, if it pleases him, will and can change the course of
events.

John M. Morris wrote an article on "Sense and Nonsense About Prayer"
in which he draws a distinction between objective and subjective prayer.[12]
He rejects the objective prayer because the belief that prayer can bring
about changes in external objects is itself a profoundly irreligious conception. It assumes that God is a kind of cosmic bellhop, waiting to do man's
bidding. If God is anything, he is the very laws by which the Universe is governed, and a prayer which demands that these laws be violated is a demand
that God violate himself. It is different with subjective prayers which are
directed to the self; they are either in the form of meditation, affirmation,
or aspiration.

Communion

Max Weber wrote that two essential elements of a worship service are prayer and sacrifice.[13] Sacrifice, as described and prescribed in the Old Testament, has been superseded by the crucifixion of Jesus which, according to Christian teaching, was a vicarious blood sacrifice. The ancients (in the Judeo-Christian tradition as well as in other traditions) offered sacrifices of animals, and often the congregation ate the meat of the sacrificed animal. Christian congregations eat and drink Jesus and call it communion. Very few Liberal churches arrange for communion service. When it is done, the reason is that some people are fond of the old ritual, even if its meaning has been eroded. As one minister describes the ceremony: "It is not necessary to believe in God or Christ in order to experience them anymore than seeing Judy Garland in the *Wizard of Oz* is believing she is Dorothy — experiencing the wine and wafer as the blood and body of Christ may be deeply moving, though I am not a Christian, just as the 1905 Symphony of Shostakovich moves me without forcing me to accept Communist beliefs."[14]

20

Heroes and Saints

The value of a theology may be measured by the individuals who live up to its ideals. If there are no such individuals, one must conclude that the theology is sterile and of little value. Real people who live according to the precepts of a theology illuminate it through their actions. That is why it seems worthwhile to devote a chapter of this work to the heroes and saints of Liberal Religion. They are persons who give it flesh and blood.

Ralph Waldo Emerson, one of our saints, gave a lecture on the "Uses of Great Men," in which he said:

> The world is upheld by the veracity of good men; they make the world wholesome. They who lived with them found life glad and nutritious. Life is sweet and tolerable only in our belief in such society; and, actually or ideally, we manage to live with superiors. . . . The search after the great man is the dream of youth and the most serious occupation of manhood. Our religion is the love and cherishing of these patrons.

And, as Edwin Wilson wrote in the popular liberal hymn:

> Where is our holy one?
> A mighty host respond
> For good ones rise in every land
> To break the captive's bond.[1]

Because Liberal Religion is unfettered by dogmas and, except for its most basic tenets, replete with ambiguity one cannot expect that all its saints and heroes are cast in the same mold. Their common trait is the spirit and the high quality permeating religious liberalism; that spirit has found expression in many forms and in many bodies.

The distinction between heroes and saints in this chapter is somewhat arbitrary and whimsical; it certainly is debatable. The heroes hereafter mentioned are not necessarily heroic figures. They are people who exemplify what Liberal Religion stands for. The saints in this chapter are not necessarily adherents of Liberal Religion. Rather, they are people whom liberal religionists look up to because they have conducted themselves in a manner which commands the respect and veneration of Religious Liberals.

No exhaustive catalogue will be attempted since this chapter is merely intended to illustrate and illuminate what Liberal Religion is all about.

One of the heroes of our times is James Reeb. He was one of the Unitarian ministers of the North who, in 1965, joined the Voter Rights demonstration in Alabama known as the Selma March, organized by Martin Luther King, Jr. Reverend Reeb died as a result of a brutal assault on a group of Unitarian clergymen perpetrated by local rednecks. Clergy of all faiths joined in the Selma march.[2] Reverend Reeb was the only minister to be killed. He is a symbol of the dedication of Liberal Religion's clergymen.

Another hero is Hosea Ballou (1771-1852) who, as a young Universalist minister in New Hampshire, published in 1805 a treatise on atonement. The essay was remarkable because his argument is not based merely on scripture but invokes simple logic and reasoning as well. It has been said that, as one of the founding fathers of Universalism, Ballou moved Universalist thinking from a Calvinistic to a Unitarian base.[3]

Other early leaders of Liberal Religion in America were William Ellery Channing (1780-1842) and Theodore Parker (1810-1860), both Unitarian ministers. They along with Emerson are known as the three great prophets of religious liberalism. Channing's most famous theological pronouncement is his so-called Baltimore sermon which he delivered in 1819 at the ordination of Reverend Jared Sparks. In it Channing called the Calvinist doctrine of election an insult to God and man. He characterized as a dishonorable notion the doctrine that God's wrath was placated by Jesus' death on the cross. He denounced the intolerance of most Christians and their conceit of infallibility as inimical to true religion. Above all, he proclaimed the religious principle of rationality. Channing was also known in his native New England as a social reformer and a promoter of the rights of the laboring man.

Theodore Parker, likewise of New England, is a hero of Liberal Religion because he, too, became deeply involved in social reform. His most famous theological pronouncement is the sermon entitled "The Transient and Permanent in Christianity," which he preached in 1841.

Joseph Priestley (1733-1804) was a cleric and a scientist in Birmingham, England. As a scientist, he is best known as the discoverer of oxygen. As a cleric he was a dissident who enraged the establishment with his agitation against socially restrictive legislation and his nonconformist religious views. At age eighteen he had been refused membership in the established Calvinist Church because he would not state that he shared Adam's sin. In 1791 the torch was put to his home, and in 1794 he moved to America where he was welcomed by fellow Unitarians. He organized and ministered to a Unitarian Church in Philadelphia, Pennsylvania.

One other man of the cloth should be mentioned among the heroes of Liberal Religion. He is Magnus Erikson (1806–1881), a native of Iceland who lived and preached in Copenhagen, Denmark. In the narrow religious atmosphere of Scandinavian Lutheranism he was a voice of free religious thought. He also promoted social reform which he considered a religious duty. He suffered vilification, ostracism, and its ensuing poverty because of his stand against the religious and political establishment.

Lest the false impression be created that heroes and great individuals are necessarily males, the present list cannot be closed without mentioning two great women: Clara Barton (1821–1912) and Susan B. Anthony (1820–1906). Clara Barton, an active member of the Universalist Church, is known as an advocate of child welfare and the founder of the American Red Cross. Susan B. Anthony is so well known as a suffragette and teacher that her reputation speaks for itself. She, too, was a member of the Unitarian Church.

Turning now to the saints of Liberal Religion, it is hardly necessary to emphasize that the reference to saints has no supernatural connotation. The heaven of Traditional Religion seems to be overpopulated with saints who may be implored for favors. According to Will Durant, in the tenth century A.D., already 25,000 persons had been canonized by the Church.[4] In modern times, the Roman Catholic Church has become much more careful regarding the canonization of saints, as is vividly described in Morris West's novel *The Devil's Advocate*. Indeed, a number of old saints have been defrocked by the Traditional Church.

Saints in the Liberal Church have no power to do favors. They are admired and revered because of some special human quality they possess which elevates them above the level of ordinary people. To qualify for sainthood in the Liberal Church, this human quality must have a religious attribute. Since the Liberal Church has its own religious values, it follows that its saints must be people who represent and epitomize the religious values of the Liberal Religion.

If they do, there is no reason why they should not command reverence and adoration. Perhaps Liberal Religionists wince at these words because they associate them with rituals which are alien to them, or merely because they feel that these words do not belong in their vocabulary. It is curious how inhibited many free-thinking liberals are.

Why should one be ashamed of adoration and reverence? These are sentiments which most humans experience from time to time in their human relations. These experiences warm us, teach us, touch us, comfort us, in the family or with friends. Can we not adore and revere ideas or ideals and persons who transmit them to us? Albert Schweitzer's teaching of reverence for life is an integral part of our scripture.

Reverence is not so demeaning as some liberals seem to think. As Emerson has pointed out, it is a very natural human sentiment. One who suppresses such emotions is very likely to be less than a whole person.

There are those, however, who simply cannot accept traditional terminology and therefore will not tolerate saints in the Liberal Church. They may prefer the word "prophet" or more secular still, "exemplar."

Thomas Jefferson (1743-1826) is a saint of Liberal Religion. He was a universal genius of many intellectual attainments. While primarily a statesman, he was a master of philosophy and theology, architecture, natural science, education, agriculture, legal science, and music. When President John F. Kennedy gave a dinner for the American Nobel laureates and other scientists, he remarked that never had there been so much brainpower assembled in the White House, except when Mr. Jefferson dined there alone. We revere him because he applied his brain power to the subject of religion. He established religious liberty in America, and as the author of the bill for establishing religious freedom in Virginia, he proclaimed that no religion must be regarded as superior to others. He was politically denounced as an atheist, but he considered himself a Christian, although not a traditionalist. His attitude toward religion is expressed in a letter of instruction which he wrote to his nephew Peter Carr:

> Religion. Your reason is now mature enough to examine this object. In the first place divest yourself of all bias in favor of novelty and singularity of opinion. Indulge them in any other subject rather than that of religion. It is too important, and the consequences of error may be too serious. On the other hand, shake off all the fears and servile prejudices, under which weak minds are crouched. Fix reason firmly in her seat, and call to her tribunal every fact, every opinion. Question with boldness even the existence of a God; because if there is one, he must more approve of the homage of reason, than that of blindfolded fear. You will naturally examine first, the religion of your own country. Read the Bible then as you would read Livy or Tacitus. Your own reason is the only oracle given you by heaven, and you are answerable, not for the rightness, but the uprightness of the decision.[5]

It is worth reading the foregoing quotation twice. Jefferson expressed the belief that the spread of the Unitarian religion was inevitable.[6] In this, he was of course, mistaken.

One more citation must suffice to recall Thomas Jefferson's attitude to religion. He wrote in a letter to William Short:

> The greatest of all reformers of the depraved religion in his own country was Jesus of Nazareth. Abstracting what is really his from the rubbish in

which it is buried, easily distinguished by its lustre from the dross of his biographers, and as separable from that as the diamond from the dung-hill, we have an outline of a system of the most sublime morality which has ever fallen from the lips of man; outlines which it is lamentable he did not live to fill up.[7]

The so-called "Jefferson Bible," which Jefferson published, contains just such a demythologized outline. Jefferson is also dear to Liberal Religionists because he campaigned vigorously and successfully for what he called the Declaration of Rights. These are the basic civil rights contained in the first ten Amendments to the American Constitution.

Stephen Fritchman, a Unitarian minister, considered it very significant that Jefferson was a layman, not a minister: "As Thomas Jefferson strides across the Virginia hills waging warfare for the rights of man, we can see how important the layman is in religion. No frocked clergyman, no mitred bishop, but a layman carries off top honors from the thrust of Liberal Religion into the life of our nation."[8]

Although descended from a leading Virginia family, Thomas Jefferson detested what he called artificial existency founded upon wealth and birth. He admired a natural aristocracy based upon virtue and talent.[9] He recognized that such existency can be found in white, as well as in black people. His efforts to outlaw slavery were unsuccessful. His original draft of the Declaration of Independence contained a condemnation of slavery, but it was stricken upon the insistence of southern states. Jefferson is one of the most fascinating characters in American history and, as Stephen Fritchman has pointed out, "his life has been more censored in the telling than that of any other American."[10] Jefferson shares this with Abraham Lincoln whose religious liberalism the history books conceal.[11] The lack of outstanding achievement of black people, he wrote to one of them, "is owing merely to the degraded condition of their existence, both in Africa and in America.[12] Jefferson has been criticized for owning slaves, which he had inherited, and for allegedly keeping one of them as his mistress. It must be born in mind that Jefferson was born into a slave economy, and if he alone had freed his slaves, it would have been economic suicide.[13] His saintliness is not impaired by the fact that he inherited some slaves. He did not exploit them or mistreat them. After his death, he set them free. He lived on a modest scale, always.

Saints must be judged in the context of their times and the environment in which they live or lived. Saints need not be all good. A saint in the Liberal Church is still a human being, not a supernatural ghost. For that reason, Albert Schweitzer's stature as a saint is not diminished by the often cited fact that he had a paternalistic attitude toward the African natives, which today is justly regarded as outmoded.

A bust of Albert Schweitzer adorns the sanctuary of the Community Church in New York. He is one of the saints of Liberal Religion. In his memoirs he tells how the phrase "reverence for life" came to mind on a river journey in equatorial Africa.[14] In ancient times, Dr. Schweitzer's inspiration would have been called a divine revelation. He did not use such language. Even while discharging the duties of a young Lutheran pastor in Strassbourg, and of a university lecturer on religion, he was a thoroughly rational person. His researches about the historical Jesus displeased the theological faculty of Strassbourg University, and some of them protested against his appointment as a university lecturer.[15] Later, the missionary society, under whose auspices he went to Africa, questioned the correctness of his belief, and they would allow him to go only after he had promised to refrain from any ministerial activity and to limit himself to the practice of medicine.

Ralph Waldo Emerson was a Unitarian minister who resigned from the ministry because he could not bring himself to pray in public and who would not administer communion. He, too, was a universal spirit who, as a philosopher, writer, and lecturer, spread in America and abroad much of what has become the body of Liberal Religion. One of his most remarkable contributions is the famed Harvard Divinity School Address of 1838, in which he expounded to the graduating young clergymen the errors of Traditional Religion. This is one of the basic writings of Liberal Religion. Emerson described Jesus Christ as a true prophet, a man with a divine message, but a man nevertheless.

In a speech which Emerson delivered in 1869 to the Free Religious Association in Boston, he had this to say about saints:

> We cannot spare the vision nor the virtue of the saints but let it be by pure sympathy, not with any personal or official claim. If you are childish, and exhibit your saint as a worker of wonders, a thaumaturgist, I am repelled. That claim takes his teachings out of logic and out of nature, and permits official and arbitrary senses to be grafted on the teachings.

Emerson was one of the so-called oracles of Concord. Another of these oracles, likewise a Unitarian, was Henry David Thoreau. Because of his essay on *Civil Disobedience,* political liberals adore Thoreau. One may have reservations about that famous essay, but no list of Liberal Religion's saints would be complete without his name. Two anecdotes illuminate Thoreau's theological view. A girl whom he courted asked him to go to church with her. He refused, explaining that the great outdoors was his church. When Thoreau was on his deathbed, an aunt asked him whether he had made peace with God. Replied Thoreau, "I did not know we ever had quarreled." At the funeral, Emerson delivered the eulogy, and in the following passage thereof he seems to canonize Thoreau:

> Whilst he used in his writings a certain petulance of remark in reference to churches or churchmen, he was a person of a rare, tender, and absolute

religion, a person incapable of any profanation, by act or by thought. Of course, the same isolation which belonged to his original thinking and living detached him from the social religious forms. This is neither to be censured nor regretted. Aristotle long ago explained it, when he said, "One who surpasses his fellow citizens in virtue is no longer a part of the city. Their law is not for him, since he is a law to himself." Thoreau was sincerety itself, and might fortify the convictions of prophets in the ethical laws by his holy living.

Thoreau's main occupation was that of a naturalist. In the eulogy Emerson touched upon this in the following charming passage:

> His intimacy with animals suggested what Thomas Fuller records of Butler the apiarist; that "either he had snakes coiled round his leg; the fishes swam into his hand, and he took them out of the water; he pulled the woodchuck out of its hole by the tail and took the foxes under his protection from the hunters.

This is reminiscent of St. Francis of Assisi who, according to legend, preached to "my little sisters the birds," and who tamed the wild wolf of Gubbio by exhorting him. St. Francis felt a sensitive kinship with every living thing. Weber regards St. Francis as an example of aconmistic goodness.[16] Aconmism is a theological theory which denies the physical world. It means in this instance that St. Francis defied or is said to have defied all physical barriers, a feat of which ordinary people are incapable. For that reason, most of us cannot achieve sainthood in any sense. In order that his followers in the Franciscan Order might concentrate on helping the needy, St. Francis postulated poverty for himself and the Order. The following of his sayings, translated from the Latin, is not legendary, "A man has only so much knowledge as he puts to work." What he meant was, knowledge and religious teaching is in vain, unless put into social action—a perfect motto for the Liberal Church.

This is much like the preaching of the Hebrew Prophet Amos, who demanded social action instead of ritualistic performances. This herdsman who lived about 700 B.C., was a thorn in the flesh of the religious establishment. God, he thundered, does not want your sacrifices, he wants justice. Unlike his predecessor prophets, Amos did not work miracles. He was too busy preaching.

It is said that in Traditional Religion, one must perform miracles in order to qualify as a saint. The stories of St. Francis contain a number of miracles.

Reported miracles are often figments of the imagination, or events which, according to modern psychological insight, are not miraculous at all. Some miracle stories are just lovely poetry which we can accept as such without intellectual sacrifice. To take these stories literally is, as Emerson said, childish. Miracles, as Bernard Shaw wrote, are simply events which inspire faith.

John Murray (1741–1815), one of the founders of the Universalist Church in America, arrived in 1770 on the New Jersey shore because the good ship "Hand in Hand," sailing from England to New York, was stranded there. Farmer Potter, a religious dissident, asked him to preach on the following Sunday at his little church, known as Potter's Folly. Murray said he would stay only if there was not sufficient wind for the ship to proceed. And, of course, there was no wind and Murray stayed to preach the first Universalist sermon on American soil, at the place which is today Murray Grove, a Unitarian Universalist conference center. This is Liberal Religion's own miracle story.

Many of the traditional saints—St. Francis included—are reported to have heard voices and to have experienced visions which spurred them on. This business of voices and visions discredits the saints in the eyes of many rationalists. No lesser rationalist and skeptic than Bernard Shaw has debunked this prejudice, in the preface to his play *St. Joan.* Speaking of Joan's voices, Shaw writes:

> If Newton's imagination had been of the same vividly dramatic kind, he might have seen the ghost of Pythagoras walk into the orchard and explain why the apples were falling. Such an illusion would have invalidated neither the theory of gravitation nor Newton's general sanity. What is more, the visionary method of making the discovery would not be a whit more miraculous than the normal method. The test of sanity is not the normality of the method but the reasonableness of the discovery. Joan must be judged a sane woman in spite of her voices because they never gave her any advice that might not have come to her from her mother, exactly as gravitation came to Newton.

Supernatural traits are not essential to sainthood.

Nor is martyrdom essential to sainthood, as some seem to think. One of Liberal Religion's most authentic saints was a martyr. That was Michael Servetus (1511–1553), one of the founding fathers of Unitarianism, and author of the book, *The Errors of the Trinity.* The church, both Catholic and Protestant, persecuted him and, in 1553, Calvin had him burned at the stake in Geneva because he refused to recant.

Francis David (1510–1579) was also a martyr. He was a Roman Catholic bishop in Hungary. He joined the reformation movement and then became the first bishop of the Unitarian Church in Transylvania, a church which survives to this day. David was convicted for heresy, incarcerated and died in prison.

Martin Luther King, Jr., was a modern martyr. He knew he would be assassinated if he did not stop demanding racial justice, even as Jesus knew he was foredoomed when he entered Jerusalem. Jesus and Dr. King stood up for what they believed in. Clearly the saints *in* the Liberal Church are not necessarily *of* the Liberal Church.

Pope John XXIII, Buddha, and Gandhi are persons who deserve the reverence of Religious Liberals as exponents of high religious ideas which transcend the bounds of their particular denomination. Reverence for these individuals accords with the universality of Liberal Religion. This embracing universality is expressed in the following words of a favorite hymn:

> From Sinai's cliffs it echoed
> It breathed from Buddha's tree
> It charmed in Athen's market
> It hallowed Gallilee
> The hammer stroke of Luther
> The pilgrim's seaside prayer
> The oracles of Concord
> One holy word declare.

21

Celebrations

The Community Church in New York is the very model of a Liberal church. It celebrates the holidays of the principal religions in America: Christian, Jewish, Hindu, and Buddhist. Buddhism is celebrated on Buddha's birthday. The Hindu festival of lights, "Diwali," is observed with appropriate ceremonies in mid-November. The high Jewish holidays are observed on the Sunday between Rosh Hashanah and Yom Kippur, generally with a Jewish cantor assisting the minister. In December the festival of Gita Jayanti is occasionally observed, the day on which the truth of life was revealed by the Lord Krishna to Ariuna as recorded in the Bhayvad Gita. The fact that all these observances occur on a Sunday morning indicates that the congregation, while celebrating the peculiar contributions of various religions, still maintains its own stance. However, the annual memorial service for the slain Rabbi Jesus takes place on Good Friday or the eve thereof. The annual Jewish Seder festival for the children of the congregation occurs at the appropriate time on a weekday evening. The exodus from Egypt is celebrated with Jewish food and the customary fun under the direction of the senior minister who has donned a skullcap.

Is this a mindless eclecticism? Hardly. Eclecticism means choosing from various sources without following any one system. Liberal Religion, by its very nature, draws on all available sources without adhering to any one of them. It is a universal religion composed of many strains. Universality is its unifying system and it is therefore quite appropriate to observe the traditions of these various strains.

Celebration and ceremony respond to the deep-seated human desire to elevate special events within the routine of everyday life. This is illustrated

231

by the practice of primitive religions as well as the rituals of Traditional Religions. In Soviet Russia, weddings have been "ceremonialized" and are usually performed in an elegant Palace of Marriage or Palace of Happiness.[1] The Soviet ceremony, like the ceremonies of Traditional churches and synagogues, follows a uniform pattern which reflects the governing doctrine. In contrast, the celebrations of Liberal Religion are unique in that, unlike the celebrations of Traditional Religion, they do not follow a fixed pattern. There is no prescribed ritual. Each celebration may be different from all the others. There are no restrictions placed on innovation, creativity, or ingenuity, except those limitations imposed by the celebrants and the dictates of good taste.

Some ministers of Liberal Religion find the Easter holiday a difficult one to celebrate. This day was originally celebrated because of the alleged bodily resurrection of Christ. This, to these ministers and according to Liberal Religion, is a literal absurdity. It is far too narrow a view of Easter Sunday— a perfect occasion to celebrate the renewal of nature. One does not have to believe that Christ has risen in order to enjoy the crocus flower as a messenger of the things to come, and the myriad other signs of spring. In the words of Goethe's *Faust,* people at Easter feel and celebrate their own resurrection from the darkness of winter. This is expressed in Faust's monologue as he strolls on Easter Sunday about the countryside.[2] It is strange that few ministers seem to know and make use of this Easter morning monologue in the greatest work of Goethe.

Christmas celebrations involve fewer problems. There is, of course, much moaning and groaning about the commercialization that accompanies the yuletide season. It is true that the Christmas season is somewhat diluted by its length if merchants begin to decorate their stores and streets in November, soon after Thanksgiving Day. It is also true that crass advertising with Christmas symbols, and the proliferation of Santa Claus figures on street corners and in stores, tends to demean the holiday. One also deplores the pressure from people for whom this is the season for demanding gratuities, as the garage employees who send Christmas cards reading, "Merry Christmas, second notice." Luckily for most people, nothing can destroy the excitement and the emotion of the season.

In some communities, civil liberty organizations protest the display of creches in public places during the Christmas season. They contend that the display violates the constitutional rights of non-Christians. However, the display should not be regarded as a sectarian symbol. The baby Jesus in the cradle represents the hope and expectation of new life which man entertains in order to be reconciled to the dark of winter. John Hayward, looking at it more broadly, says that the child represents holiness, and he adds, "it is possible for the liberal worshippers to endorse this symbolic message without making Christ an object of idolatrous worship."[3]

On the other hand, devout Christians complain that excessive commercialism has the effect of taking Christ out of Christmas. These people overlook the fact that Christmas is not simply, or exclusively, a Christian holiday. "It is childish," wrote a New York Rabbi, a number of years ago, "to assume that because people are increasingly exchanging gifts and friendly greetings and are making the season of the year a time of unusual business in our stores and marts, that they are, in any way, displeasing God." As a matter of history, the American Puritans condemned any celebration of Christmas as they frowned upon any joyous celebration. Christmas is a folk festival for all people, regardless of their religious outlook, even though no denomination is deprived of adding its particular accent to the celebration. When religious liberals recall that there was no room in the inn for Jesus to be born, they also recall that Jesus grew up to be a critic of the religious establishment and that such critics and dissenters have seldom been welcomed anywhere.

True to their theology of universal religion, religious liberals may enjoy the beauty of the Catholic midnight mass and the variety of Christmas music without being troubled by any sectarian text. This is no different from the enjoyment obtained from the passions of Johann Sebastian Bach, the oratories of Handel and Verdi, or any of the music of modern composers like Benjamin Britten. It is the spirit that counts.

The custom of giving presents symbolizes the affection people have for one another, a feeling which is newly awakened by the Christmas festival. Even though the sending of Christmas cards may have grown to unreasonable proportions, it will warm the heart of many a recipient who hears but once a year from the sender. Universal good will is in the air, so let Liberal Religion partake of it without superintellectual reservation.

Christmas is also the time of the winter solstice when people, since ancient times, have celebrated the fact that from now on the days will grow longer and there will be increasing sunshine on the planet Earth.

Thanksgiving Day is another holiday which may appropriately be celebrated in the Liberal Church. Some praise the Lord or a supernatural deity for the harvest. However, appreciation and gratitude for the blessings of nature do not depend upon one's belief in a supernatural power.

There are other occasions for celebrations of public events, such as the birthday of one of the heroes or saints of Liberal Religion, some of whom are mentioned in the preceding chapter of this book. Other memorable public events include the decision of the United States Supreme Court to institute complete racial desegration of our schools and United Nations Day, celebrated in October of each year on or near the anniversary of the founding of this international organization. The latter celebration was initiated by Frank Frederick when he was general counsel to the American Unitarian Association. In spite of the shortcomings of the United Nations in the field of pure politics, its achievements in the realm of humanitarianism are magnificent and well worth celebrating in the Liberal Church.

Besides the public celebrations, there are the private celebrations — beginning with the dedication of a young child. There is no baptism in the

Liberal Church because Religious Liberals neither believe that a newborn needs to be purified, nor that a particular religious faith can be or should be imposed upon a child. The parents and godparents are merely asked to raise the child as a decent human being. A favorite reading on these occasions is from Kahlil Gibran's *The Prophet,* which so clearly reflects the theology of Liberal Religion:

> Your children are not your children
> They are the sons and daughters of Life's
>   longing for itself.
> They come through you but not from you
> You may give them your love but not your
>   thoughts
> For they have their own thoughts. . .

The Prophet is also a frequent reading resource for ministers in the Liberal Religion when they perform marriages. "Let there be spaces in your togetherness" is the leitmotif of a favorite poem.

Liberal Religion turns even a funeral or a memorial service into a celebration—the celebration of the life of the deceased. Without trying to suppress the tears of the mourners, but also without holding out a better life after death, Liberal Religion seeks to accentuate the good that the deceased achieved during his or her lifetime.

And, of course, the regular worship service of Liberal Religion is a celebration. This has been dealt with in Chapter 19. In the Roman Catholic Church, and in other Traditional churches, it is the priest who celebrates mass or the eucharist. In the Liberal Church, the members of the congregation are the celebrants; they celebrate life.

Celebrations are an opportunity and a means to overcome the "generation gap." Contemporary culture tends to separate the generations. Adults exclude children from their social life; children shun adult parties and do not want adults at their parties. Celebrations can and should be designed to bring adults and children together in a manner that will make both feel comfortable. No harm is done if the content of some reading or statement goes "over the head" of some children. At times, some adults suffer from the same disadvantage. And yet, all will participate joyfully, so long as the celebration reflects the spirit of the occasion and a common understanding thereof.

Such celebration in the Liberal Religious tradition may also help to indoctrinate children. To some Liberal Religionists, the word "indoctrinate" is to be avoided because it violates the belief that religion must not be imposed upon children. However, there is no coercion involved when one acquaints a necessarily ignorant child with what Liberal Religion stands for and how it is celebrated.

22

The Role of the Minister

An experienced cleric and a consultant to liberal religious societies remarked not long ago that "we are at present quite unclear about the crucial and central concept of what parish ministry is."[1] This astonishing observation alone justifies this chapter.

Most state statutes in America provide that the trustees of a religious corporation shall be in charge of its "temporal" matters, which refers specifically to the administration of business or worldly affairs. The word "temporal' signifies a time limitation, not with respect to the trustees' terms of office, but to the transitory nature of worldly matters. One must resist the allure of speculating whether the lawmakers were influenced by eschatological thinking which anticipates an early end of the world. In any event, the opposite of the temporal is the eternal. That is what the minister is in charge of. He is the spiritual leader. Paul knew this distinction. He wrote (1 Cor. 4:18): "The things which are seen are temporal, but the things which are not seen are eternal."

While Liberal Religion is leery about proclaiming eternal values and immutable truth (see Chapter 6), it is not difficult to think of the minister as the spiritual leader of the congregation. It is harder to be a minister of Liberal Religion than to be one in the Traditional mold. The requirements are greater. As was shown in the chapter on worship, the Liberal minister has no prescribed lesson plan. His weekly sermon is expected to be an original creation. The minister of Liberal Religion cannot be just a theologian; he is expected to be knowledgeable in fields such as science or sociology and to impart their new developments to his congregation. In other words, the minister of Liberal Religion must be a well-educated person. Traditional

235

Religion is less demanding in that it often allows a worship service by rote, and uses canned sermons. In 1967 an Episcopal committee headed by the former president of Harvard University Nathan Pusey, reported after an eighteen-month study that one-third of all Episcopal clergymen lacked a complete three-year seminary education and that more than sixty percent of the Episcopal seminarians graduated from college with average grades of C or below. It is, of course, well known that some ministers of Traditional Religion are brilliant intellectuals. One finds them mostly among Jesuits and rabbis.

Some years ago, in an address on "The Role of the Rabbi," delivered at the Jewish Institute of Religion, Rabbi Morton M. Berman pointed out that all of the traditional roles of the rabbi had been invaded, one after another, by the more expert professional. "The Rabbi has become," he said, "an educator among educators, a social worker among social workers, a political reformer among political reformers, an organizer among organizers. The authority which he may claim in these fields, he must share with the more expert. In those functions where he seems to be exercising an old prerogative of his own as, for example, in preaching, he is too often merely the echo of the professionals . . . . But there remains a field that is the special realm of the Rabbi. It is Judaism. . . . The Rabbi thus becomes, for lack of better terms, the Judaizer . . . of Jewish life."

Ministers of Liberal Religion must make the traditions of religious liberalism relevant to the living concerns of their people. This becomes especially apparent among some of the fellowships composed largely of people new to the movement (see Chapter 23). Laile Bartlett, in her book *Bright Galaxy,* speaks of one Unitarian fellowship which described the leadership they needed as a "professional Unitarian." These people want and need interpretations of their own living concerns in terms of the liberal religious heritage they have adopted as their own without fully knowing it. The minister is expected to know it and to be able to make it relevant—to be the "Unitarian-izer Universalizer" of the life of the movement. This requires, in terms of educational experience, that the minister be immersed in the tradition which it will be his or her role to embody and represent.

A Unitarian minister once remarked, whimsically, that his job would be much easier if he had hellfire on his side. What he meant was that he envied those of his colleagues in Traditional Religion whose theology allowed them to threaten their congregation that they would burn in hell if they did not follow the dictates of their religion. The minister of the Liberal Church has no authority but the force of his or her personality. He is only effective if his leadership maintains itself by, to use Reinhold Niebuhr's words, "its intrinsic worth, sans panoply, pomp and power."[2]

Some Methodists consider themselves liberal and yet they are subject to Methodist discipline which calls for trial and possible expulsion of those who disseminate doctrines which are contrary to the Methodists' Articles of

Religion. These articles include, among others, the doctrine of the Trinity, the Virgin Birth, and the inherent depravity of man. The minister in the Liberal Church has no ecclesiastical superiors; there is no hierarchy and no prescribed articles of religion. Nor can the minister of Liberal Religion clothe himself or herself in the cloak of the vicar of God. The title of Pastor, the Latin word for shepherd, is not apt because, in the Liberal Church, the members do not feel like sheep and do not want to be so regarded or treated. The ancient juxtaposition between the minister and his people is likewise an anachronism because it is derived from a monarchial concept. Nor is the minister the servant of the congregation. There is no more appropriate and honorable job description for the minister of Liberal Religion than that of spiritual leader. This may be defined as a leader who has the compassion and care of a shepherd, but not his control; the goodwill and responsibility of the monarch, but not his authority; the unselfish devotion of the servant, but not his abasement; the vision and courage of the prophet, but not his dogmatism.

While functioning as spiritual leader of the congregation, it is sometimes hard for a minister to realize that he/she is still one of the community. In Camus's novel *The Plague,* a noted priest thunders from the pulpit: "My brethren" (females did not count), "you are in trouble, and, my brethren, you deserve it." He might have said, we are in trouble, and we deserve it. But the priest obviously felt that he was above his community, probably halfway between God "out there" and the congregation he was preaching to. In Religious Liberal churches, one also encounters the phrase: "the minister, the trustees, and the member of such and such church," whereas, it would be more appropriate to reverse the order.

Rabbi Stephen Wise was a renowned liberal minister. When in 1905, Temple Emanuel, the famous New York temple of Reformed Judaism, considered calling Wise to its pulpit, Wise demanded that he must become a voting member of the Board of Trustees. He had enjoyed that privilege in his position in Portland, Oregon, although the congregation in Portland did not extend the same right to Wise's successor.[3] And, indeed, the minister in a Liberal church should not expect a vote on a Board which is charged with the administration of the worldly affairs of the congregation.

However, the minister in the Liberal Church must have the freedom of the pulpit. The refusal of Temple Emanuel to grant him this essential attribute of the Liberal ministry was the reason why Stephen Wise did not become its Rabbi. He wanted to be free to criticize the political and business activities of Emanuel's members.[4] Rabbi Wise's definition of the free pulpit is valid for all Liberal churches. It is as follows:

> The Chief Office of the minister, I take it is not to represent the views of the congregation, but to proclaim the truth as he sees fit. How can he serve a congregation as a teacher quicken the mind of his hearers by the

vitality and independence of his utterances? How can a man be vital and independent and helpful if he is tethered and puzzled? A free pulpit, worthily filled, must command respect and influence; a pulpit that is not free, howsoever filled, is sure to be without potency and honesty. A free pulpit may sometimes stumble into error. A pulpit that is not free cannot powerfully plead for truth and righteousness.[5]

The pulpit function is probably the most important activity of the minister of Liberal Religion. This does not mean that the minister must preach every Sabbath. In fact, it is desirable that the regular minister yields the pulpit from time to time to outside speakers, be they ministers or laymen. The regular minister will provide for a well-planned and balanced spiritual and intellectual diet.

Since the Liberal Church has no prescribed lesson plan and no authoritative scripture, it is more difficult for it to hold up its own in the intellectual and spiritual competition with the Traditional churches. In order to assert their uniqueness and independence, Liberal Religionists must know in what respect they differ from Traditional Religion. This means that they must know the dogmas of Traditional Religion and the contemporary theological ferment. Only a full-time professional minister can convey this knowledge adequately to the Liberal congregation. The same is also true of the need for education, information, and inspiration in the fields of current social concern (see Chapter 16). Rabbi Stephen Wise and John Haynes Holmes, the late minister of The Community Church of New York, were friends whose joint and separate achievements epitomized this role of the Liberal minister.[6] Neither of them could have become a famous preacher of national repute if their congregations had not allowed them to spend a great deal of time in civic endeavors not directly connected with their position as clergymen, but which naturally reflected glory on their congregations. This is characteristic of Liberal Religion.

However, it must be admitted that not all Liberal congregations approve of their ministers engaging in such outside activities. Some of them do not even want to hear social questions and politics discussed from the pulpit. This seems to be an exception rather than a rule, because the socially concerned Religious Liberal generally prefers to have this concern put in the kind of perspective which professional ministers can or should be able to supply.

A number of religious movements in America depend entirely on lay leadership: among them the Quakers, the Mormons, and the Christian Scientists. They are all very respectable but they neither have nor seek any strong influence on the spiritual life of our nation—the kind of influence most Liberal Religionists wish to impart. This cannot be achieved without professional leadership.

Not all pulpit occupants are satisfactory. A minister fails the Liberal Church, and those who might otherwise be attracted to its services, if year in and year out he or she travels in the outworn rut of the ancient Judeo-Christian order of service, if the only novelty in the liturgy is an unknown hymn which frustrates one's desire to participate in the singing, and if the minister utters shopworn prayers in hackneyed phrases which evoke no response and are intellectually unacceptable. The complaint is not new. In 1832, when he addressed the graduating class of the Harvard Divinity School, Emerson warned: "Whenever the pulpit is usurped by a formalist, the worshipper is defrauded and disconsolate. We shrink and wince as soon as the prayers begin . . . ."

If ministers of Liberal Religion are disappointing in the matter of liturgy, it is generally not because they are unable to conduct a more imaginative or more exciting form of service. More likely, the reason for the shortcoming is that the minister is too busy with his many concerns and duties to devote enough time to the planning of other than a routine liturgy. Some ministers rationalize that it is good for the congregation to have the same standard diet every Sunday. No minister can perform his or her function properly if his or her other personal preferences and those of the congregation are not shared. If these preferences are incompatible, minister and congregation are mismatched.

There is a certain amount of anti-clericalism in the Liberal Church. This is not based upon a dissatisfaction with the minister's pulpit performance. The reason for it appears to be what, for lack of a better phrase, may be called "fear of bossism." The 1963 report of the Unitarian Universalist Association on "The Free Church in a Changing World" summarized the situation thus:

> Suspicion of professional leadership arises in churches as anti-clericalism. As a denomination, we are singularly free from this malaise. At present, it occurs almost entirely in the newer fellowships, the ministry of the pulpit and pew are in practice completely fused. Like the Quaker meetings, which they in some respect resemble, they are often characterized by an unusual sense of fervency even a mystical spirit of communion of the members with one another. The members fear lest the calling of a minister which their growth has made necessary *will threaten their treasured sense of community.*[7]

It is undoubtedly true that some ministers tend to be domineering in that they strive to impose their will on the congregation. Often they take on tasks which laypeople should perform. The problem here is that laypeople are not always reliable. They come and go and grow tired. Often, things do not get done unless the minister does them. This is not a desirable situation, but the laypeople must be held primarily responsible. Lay leaders of the Liberal Church are delinquent to the degree to which they push administrative decisions onto the ministers. A minister who allows this to happen, fails in his role as the spiritual leader.

It is perfectly true that many, if not most, administrative decisions in the life of the church have, or should have, spiritual attributes. This applies to such diverse matters as the discharge of a janitor; the manner in which funds are solicited, collected, and spent; or the method of publicity. The minister must observe but not direct all these activities. He must be ready with spiritual guidance. At committee meetings, he should be available as a resource person and as a sparkler. However, he should exercise restraint in imposing his views and preferences, lest he stifle individual and collective initiative in the congregation.

The minister should not interfere in congregational elections. Group meetings should not be attended unless by invitation. And above all, no attempt should be made to become an administrative chief. If the administrative burden in a church becomes heavy, a secretary or office manager should be employed. A minister who spends any appreciable amount of time with administrative work invariably neglects his ministerial function— the sermons and the liturgy suffer.

So far, nothing has been said about the minister's pastoral services which include counseling and visitation, as well as the performance of weddings and funerals. It is a telling commentary on the culture of our times that people who never in their lives cared about any religious affiliation suddenly look for a minister when a wedding or a funeral is to be performed. As such people are not adherents of a particular tradition; they often seek out a minister of Liberal Religion on such an occasion.

Many members of the Liberal Church do not want parish calls (another name for private ministerial visits). Ministers do not wish to impose their presence. However, there are still quite a few people to whom a minister's visit in time of distress or illness means a great deal. The hectic tempo of present day life, our crowded schedules, and the obstacles of traffic make the lives of some people lonelier than ever. A sympathetic minister can fill a much-needed void, especially a Liberal minister who has other resources than simply kneeling in prayer. When it comes to the need for sympathy, companionship, and comfort, religious liberals are no different from other people, except that their demands may be greater. The pastoral services are, therefore, a very important aspect of the minister's role. It is one of the strongest arguments in favor of professional versus lay leadership.

Many adherents of Liberal Religion are fugitives from Traditional Religion. They sometimes carry over from their early days an excessive deference for the minister. Also, female parishioners sometimes have a less than healthy regard for a male minister. He becomes a father figure or even a yearned-for lover. There is as yet an insufficient number of female minister to allow for a general statement about the attitude of male parishioners towards them. Suffice it to say that neither undue deference nor unhealthy affection have a proper place in the Liberal Church. A good minister must nip it in the bud when it becomes noticeable. The danger is not as great as in Traditional Religion where anti-rational devotionalism is more likely to have a latent or even manifest "tinge of eroticism."[8]

The unique position of the minister in the Liberal Church is threatened with dilution if directors of religious education and music directors demand the title of "Minister." Some of them want to be "Minister of Education" or "Minister of Music." Both fill important roles in the life of a church. But, these are specialized functions in which the individuals excel and, one expects, have greater skills than the minister. However, these specialists do not have, and are not expected to have, the general skills of the minister. It is, therefore, not reasonable for them to aspire to the title of "Minister," or for a congregation to bestow such title upon them.

Some congregations expect the minister's wife to serve them in a variety of ways, without pay. This often borders on, and in some cases actually becomes, exploitation. It violates the tenet of the dignity of man (see Chapter 13) which must also be applied to the wife of the minister.

Max Weber makes an interesting distinction between priests and prophets. The priest, according to this sociologist, is the teacher of religious ethics. The prophet is a charismatic and exciting preacher and visionary of new religious values.[9] In the words of Jeremiah, God puts his words in the mouth of the prophet (Jer. 1:9). Historically, most prophets have been untrained laymen. The following founders of new religious groups are in that category: Buddha, Paul, Mohammed, George Fox, Joseph Smith, and Mary Baker Eddy. Jesus and Amos also were of the laity. Most modern cult leaders are laymen as well. According to the Reverend Stephen Fritchman, top honors for the thrust of Liberal Religion go to Thomas Jefferson, a layman.[10]

The ministers in a denomination may be likened to the bureaucracy of any establishment. As such, they are indispensable to the maintenance of the structure. On occasion, the prophetic pulpit is needed in order to infuse the structure with new values and to lift religion to new heights.

Liberal Religion does not allow its ministers to preach a canned sermon which can be easily cribbed from a book. The congregation expects a fresh and new creative effort each week. It is, therefore, important that the ministers have sufficient free time to recharge their mental batteries and to read at leisure. That is why there is no reason to complain if a minister is free of duties during the summer.

Also, a minister should not live in strained financial circumstances. In Liberal Religion, a cleric is not bound by any vow of poverty in the expectation that he or she will be rewarded in the afterlife. The minister must be enabled to lead a full and fulfilled life so that this life can be communicated to the congregation. In blunt terms, the minister should receive a good salary. A person may be so dedicated to the cause of Liberal Religion that he or she may be willing to accept an inadequate salary. However, it is unconscionable for any congregation to take advantage of such willingness and dedication. There are, of course, circumstances in which funds for payment of a decent salary are not available. More often than not, such circumstances exist because the members of the congregation do not possess the degree of dedication which they have come to expect from their minister.

23

Is Organized Religion Necessary?

Liberal Religion is an intensely personal religion, as distinguished from institutional religion. It is, therefore, understandable that free-wheeling Religious Liberals sometimes disdain the need for organized religion. Anything that smacks of "organized church" is anathema to them. This is a shortsighted view.

Albert Schweitzer, who joined the Unitarians late in life, was able to proclaim his message single-handedly through his exemplary life, his noble deeds, and his lucid writings. Few of us (probably none of us) are in that class. Our aspirations would falter, our liberal energy would collapse, and our zeal would cease if we were not organized as a band of brothers and sisters who uphold, strengthen, and inspire each other.

There are persons who are wholly self-centered. Religiously, they are like hermits. Whether religiously oriented or not, they do not care about the world and the people around them. No doubt they are entitled to this attitude. It is not the attitude of a religious liberal who, almost by definition, is a member of a caring community and therefore needs organization. A community, also by definition, must be able constantly to renew itself by receiving new members. This requires organization.

Liberal Religious ideas cannot be spread except by organization. The communities in which we live and the elected representatives at the national, state, and local levels constantly hear the loud voices of Traditional Religion, and of the new evangelicals. They are highly organized and each is capable of making its influence felt. Therefore, only as an organized church can liberals hope to supply the much needed antidote for our body politic.

This attitude has historic reasons. An organization tends to be authoritarian. Through its organization, the Roman Catholic Church acquired spiritual and secular power. The Reformation loosened the strings but did not abolish them. Traditional Religion, whether Judeo-Christian or otherwise, distrusts anyone who seeks to think for himself/herself. Organization is conceptually inhospitable to independence. And yet, unorganized independence is apt to die on the vine. Therefore, Liberal Religion needs organization.

Most of all, no matter how intellectual or even elitist Liberal Religionists sometimes feel themselves to be, they still share the common human need for fellowship and the need to belong. Membership in an organized society fills these needs. The sense of belonging to a religious community and the fulfillment that one receives from a commitment to its goals and values satisfies the basic yearning of almost all individuals.

There is another practical aspect to the need for organization. It is required to train ministers, educators, and other religious leaders. Groups or congregations seeking a minister, religious leader, or director of religious education must be able to turn to a central place for guidance unless they prefer to leave the search to a haphazard process. This is not to suggest an authoritarian method for training and recruitment of religious leaders. There need not be any restraint on individual initiative. What is suggested is that in the absence of, or in addition to, individual initiative, there is a need for organized activity. This also applies to teaching material for religious education.

Furthermore, an advantage of organization is that a larger group can assist or sponsor a smaller or incipient group. For instance, the All Souls Unitarian Church in Washington, D.C. sponsored a number of satellite congregations in the suburbs. Today these congregations are healthy, self-sustaining churches. The combined Unitarian Universalist Churches maintain a political lobbying and information office in Washington, something none of them could have done alone. The United Nations Office of the Unitarian Universalists could not exist were it not for an organized effort of many smaller units.

Even the Buddhist monks, who are not interested in organized religion because their only concern is personal achievement of Nirvana, maintain training schools which would not be possible without organization.[1] The devotees of transcendental meditation cannot do without the International Meditation Society where they consult about their practice and purchase their mantras.

Churches and temples have been criticized for being mere social clubs. In the words of one critic, they are primarily interested in such matters as "therapy, politics, pottery, and bellydancing." When such activities cease to be of a peripheral nature, the organization is no longer a religious society. Social clubs have their justification; they need no disguise as religious organizations. On the other hand, an organization which is centered on religion does not lose its character as a religious organization if its members do enjoy a pottery class or a bellydancing show.

Religious edifices are often impressive and pleasing. Traditional Religion refers to these edifices as houses of God. But, as Paul told the Athenians, God does not make his home in shrines made by human hands (Acts 17:24). Religion can flourish without such edifices. This is fortunate because stone and mortar are often out of the financial reach of organized and organizing religionists. In 1948, the Unitarians initiated a fellowship program which has since spread and prospered in various parts of the world. Fellowships are small organizations which frequently have no professional leadership. They meet in public school rooms or other rented quarters. If Liberal Religion is to spread, fellowships are its best hope for effective grassroots organization. The following is an apt description by an observant member: "A fellowship is an island of liberalism in a sea of orthodoxy; it is a group of people sitting on borrowed chairs in preference to padded pews. It is a state of religious satisfaction amidst financial despair. A fellowship consists of people with horrified relatives and precocious children, and develops tremendous *esprit de corps* by arguing violently among themselves. A fellowship has sourdough pancakes for Easter breakfast, jazz for the processional, and Mark Twain for the benediction. It borrows furniture from its members, hymns from the orthodox, and ideas from everyone. It is composed of three parts exhilaration and two parts exasperation, and glues everything together with coffee. It is at once a risky enterprise and a great adventure, and without it I would be a lost soul."

The quest of religious organizations for new members poses the question: How does one become a member? In some organizations, one can become a member by simply "signing the book," meaning the membership book. This is supposed to indicate the openness and the free spirit of Liberal Religion, even though one does not know whether and to what extent the signer believes in the principles of Liberal Religion. To raise any question in that regard is considered an inappropriate form of establishing a creedal test. The present author does not share this view for two reasons. First, the unquestioning admission policy opens the door for members of the Ku Klux Klan, anti-Semites, racists, and other individuals who do not share the faith of Liberal Religion. Secondly—and this applies only to organizations that have accumulated some property—there is the danger of infiltration by strangers who join for nonreligious reasons. It is one thing to have strangers as visitors who are welcomed and made acquainted with the ways of Liberal Religion. It is quite another to promote the visitor to membership.

Instances have been known where people have confused the visitors' book with the membership book. This is another reason why the membership book should not be made readily accessible. Membership in a Liberal Religious group should not be a casual affair. It should be a carefully considered commitment.

Some of those who commit themselves seek participation in the activities of the organization. Others shy away from it. Usually, there is room for both types. This requires a thoughtful approach to new members.

It must be admitted that all organizations tend to harden into bureaucracies. The chief evil of a religious bureaucracy is that its practices may be thoughtlessly perpetuated just because "we always did it that way." This is inappropriate for an organization of Liberal Religion which prides itself on the insight that "new occasions teach new duties." It therefore bears repeating what this author wrote some twenty years ago: "all organizations should be built on and around the principles which are the cause for their existence."[2]

Finally, mention should be made of a legal reason justifying organized religion. The constitutional protection of religious liberty does not extend to a religious belief which is not shared by an organized group.[3]

24

The Virtues—A Summary

This last chapter is an attempt to summarize the general concepts of Liberal Religion and some of their practical applications, which have been set forth in the preceding chapters. This is done by suggesting some virtues which Liberal Religion prizes. These virtues are not necessarily unique to Liberal Religion. But the ones enumerated here seem indispensable to a person of Liberal Religion. Indispensable, not in the sense that a Liberal Religionist must possess these virtues, but in the sense that he or she must recognize these attributes as virtues worthy of attainment. Human as we are, we cannot be virtuous all of the time. But, we should be virtuous some of the time and, indeed, much of the time.

The word "virtue" may have an old-fashioned scent, but Liberal Religion can and should clothe it with fresh fragrance. As Channing said in his famed Baltimore sermon: "We believe that all virtue has its foundation in the moral nature of man, that is, in conscience, or his sense of duty, and in the power of forming his temper and life according to conscience."[1]

Plato believed that virtue is inborn by nature and cannot be taught.[2] This is not true. Precepts of good conduct and ethical living can be instilled in young people and even in older persons. Liberal Religion is uniquely qualified for this task because it involves no bargains, no promises, no threats; no precepts are taught which are irrational, mythical, or otherwise incomprehensible.

Like the biblical commandments, the sequence in the enumeration of these virtues does not denote a scale of descending values. The following sequence, therefore, is of no particular significance.

247

Truth

Truth is the most difficult of the virtues. It is not enough to refrain from lying. Of course, not to lie is part of the virtue. It is the easiest part, and it is a universal command. To know the truth and to adhere to it is harder.

When William Jennings Bryan testified under oath at the Scopes Trial of his belief that God made the sun stand still in aid of Joshua as related in the Bible, he was not lying. He was not telling the truth either, even though he knew it. He was under the influence, not of alcohol, but of the equally intoxicating Traditional Religion. When Galileo was forced by the Inquisition to recant his scientific discoveries, he betrayed the truth, and the Church knew it.

Peter Putnam of Princeton once said that the Unitarian Church, which was to him the archetypical Liberal Church, was the only church in which he did not have to deposit his intelligence at the door, like a hat or a coat. Intellectual honesty is part of the virtue of truth. The opposite thereof is hypocrisy, the false pretense of virtue. Hypocrisy is frequently condemned in the Bible. This condemnation is of little avail among Traditional Religionists. The foremost example is the widely disregarded injunction against public prayer. Jesus said, "When you pray do not imitate the hypocrites who do it in public." Mention was made in Chapter 3 of Blaise Pascal's advocacy of false pretense in regard to religious observance. Contemporary experience leads one to believe that Pascal still has many followers. One is reminded of Hamlet's advice to his mother, "Assume a virtue if you have it not." Thomas Paine's statement, which was cited in Chapter 6, bears repeating, "Infidelity does not consist in believing, or in disbelieving—it consists in professing to believe what one does not believe." Shakespeare's exhortation "To thine own self be true" is scripture in the Liberal Church. It means that one should not pretend to be what one is not, nor pretend to believe what one does not believe. Jefferson wrote that it is not necessary to be always right, but one must always be upright.[3]

Searching for the truth is an activity of which some are incapable and others deliberately attempt to avoid. Albert Einstein came to regret the publication of his research because it led to the development of the atomic bomb. In Chapter 6, mention was made of a theology student who refused to read certain books because it might unsettle his religious beliefs. Liberal Religion demands that we search for truth regardless of the consequences. It demands that we have the courage and integrity to face the unvarnished, straight, unveiled truth without mythical clothing. It teaches that no truth is permanent because new insights and new developments may make untrue what was true yesterday. Beloved phrases such as "eternal truth" and "timeless truth" are deceptive. Many preachers have deluded themselves and their listeners with such phrases. Moreover—and this is the hardest part of the virtue—Liberal Religion recognizes that its truth is not the only truth, that some different truth may also exist.

Knowledge

That knowledge is a virtue may be questioned. Criminals may be knowledgeable persons. Some people are insufferable because of a constant habit of displaying their knowledge, reminding one of Paul's phrase: "knowledge puffeth up" (1 Cor. 8:1). Nevertheless, knowledge is valuable and its absence (ignorance) is hard to tolerate. Some people do not want to know; they close their ears or avert their eyes. Especially in the field of religion, many prefer belief to knowledge. If the president of the United States acts upon the advice of an intelligence agency which ought to, or pretends to, but does not have knowledge, the consequences can be disastrous. In his novel *The Plague,* Camus demonstrates the evil which occurs when a city administration does not want to know that an epidemic is threatening.

When a bewildered youth says he or she wishes to find himself or herself, it means that the youth seeks to know what he or she is like and what life is all about. The youth is unsettled by the lack of knowledge. Blessed are those who have gained knowledge of life, and who can impart it to others. Duncan Howlett, forester and outstanding leader of Liberal Religion, wrote: "A new picture of the human creature is emerging today . . . the results are neither certain nor final . . . the resulting picture . . . represents albeit in a limited fashion, a picture of the reality we are seeking when we speak of the pursuit of knowledge."[4]

Traditional Religion claims knowledge of God and the Creation without troubling with the teachings of science. Liberal Religion has no use for the God of Genesis who forbade Adam and Eve to eat from the tree of knowledge. It disapproves of religious leaders who wish to keep man ignorant in order to make them more pliable. However, it must be recognized that there is more to know than anyone can absorb. Only a fool will try to know everything. But that is no excuse for sticking one's head in the sand. What is called for is selectivity in acquiring knowledge and concentration on what one's life requires. This includes, not only knowledge of one's craft, business, or profession, but also knowledge of all facets of the state and community in which one lives. Without such knowledge, one cannot be a useful and participating member of society. It violates this standard if one avoids, as humans are inclined to, the knowledge of the unpleasant, sad and seedier side of life.

On the other hand, too many people do not know what they are talking about. Others do not talk because they have no knowledge. This is particularly true in the field of religion. It is striking how little is known about

Abraham and David, about Jesus and Paul, and about the contents of the Bible in general. Religious Liberals do not regard the Bible as a holy book, or as the supreme source of religious inspiration. But Traditional Religion does, and the ignorance of its followers, therefore, is an absence of virtue. This is also true of Religious Liberals as, irrespective of one's religious affiliation, one must know the Bible as it is ingrained in Western culture. The majority of the people in the West are religiously illiterate. They may parrot phrases and engage in traditional exercises without knowing their meaning. Religious Liberals cannot afford such illiteracy. In the preceding pages (especially in Chapter 4), Religious Liberals have been urged to propagate and publicize their faith. This cannot be done without knowledge of what Religious Liberalism stands for and the positions to which it is opposed. Unfortunately, some Sunday schools of Liberal Religion fail to impress their students with this knowledge.

As was said in Chapter 4, the use of reasoning power is the keystone to Liberal Religion. Reasoning power and rationality presupposes knowledge.

Compassion

In one of his most famous passages, Paul extols love as the greatest of all virtues (1 Cor. 13). Christianity is said to be based on love. Christian love is much preached about but hardly ever encountered. It is alien to human nature. Compassion, however, is an attainable virtue. One can have compassion for one's neighbors and one's fellow man without loving him or loving oneself. Compassion propels most if not all of the actions which were discussed in the chapter on social concern. To Liberal Religion the life of the community is more important than the life of the individual. The religious devotion of the hermit is stale and worthless (see Chapter 16). James Luther Adams says in a pithy albeit a flippant way, "We deny the immaculate conception of virtue and affirm the necessity of social incarnation."[5]

Compassion makes it impossible to disregard the dignity of the most loathesome individual (see Chapter 13). Compassion is also an attribute of many of the heroes and saints who were mentioned in Chapter 20, even though not all of them attained the degree of compassion characterized by St. Francis.

Compassion has a divine quality. As Portia said in the famous address on the quality of mercy, "It is an attribute to God himself." The virtue of compassion embraces kindness. Kindness to those whom one loves or likes is no real kindness. Kindness is a virtue if practiced in relation to those for whom one has no or little sympathy. It pertains to personal as well as to public relationships. The command "Walk humbly with your God" implies that your God need not be my God, and that, in the words of Ethel S. Smith, there is God and there are other gods, all of whom rank alike. This is a fundamental precept of Liberal Religion.

Social Service

Traditional Religion imposes certain religious obligations on its adherents, consisting mostly of the duty to observe certain religious rites, attend certain ceremonies and/or be in church at stated times. Liberal Religion does not obligate its people to observe rituals or for that matter to attend worship services at any time. However, Liberal Religion requires the performance of social service. This virtue can be practiced in a variety of ways. One can be a volunteer worker in the church or temple, become involved with a larger religious organization, serve in a hospital, or actively participate in the work of an organization that cares for the social, physical, or political environment. In the wider sense, one can actively participate in the political activities of the town, the county, the state, or the nation. The important thing is that one cannot be a good Religious Liberal and confine one's activities to that of breadwinning and recreation. Personal piety will not do, unless one benefits the community.

If such service is rendered not for personal gain or glory, but solely out of sense of religious obligation, pure religion is manifested. But even if public service is rendered with a view to personal gain or glory, and if no corruption is involved, the cause of religion is served.

Let no one denigrate the virtue by saying, "What you are doing is just a drop in the bucket." This drop-in-the-bucket argument is frequently used to excuse total inactivity. Some service and some participation is preferable to none. It takes many drops to fill the bucket. Without the drops, it may never be filled.

Religious Liberals sometimes overdo it. They belong to too many organizations. They fragment their efforts and their resources. This is a common human frailty which most of us have not learned to overcome. Sometimes it is the result of a nonvirtuous vanity or conceit. A liberal person may think that his or her outlook is so different from that of existing liberal organizations, that a different group must be created. The outcome is a plethora of organizations which tend to overlap in many respects. Inevitably this fragmentation weakens the impact and the effectiveness of Liberal Religion. One must try to avoid this and to suppress excessive individualism.

The corollary of duty is right. The American Constitution has a Bill of Rights (Jefferson called it the Declaration of Rights) but not a Bill of Duties. This is the reason why one hears so much of civil and human rights, but little of civil duties and human duties. It is the function of religion to emphasize these duties.

Commitment is another word for the virtue of social service, commitment to one or more social causes all of which spring forth from the commitment to Liberal Religion.

Integration

Integration is generally understood as referring to the relationship between human races. That certainly is one of the tenets of Liberal Religion (see Chapter 13). However, as a religious virtue, integration has a wider meaning; it refers to the integration of the individual into his environment. The individual is part of nature and of the Universe. Chapter 1 deals with this aspect of Liberal Religion in some detail. The Liberal Church does not accept the biblical command that man should subdue the earth and dominate nature. To the contrary, Liberal Religion teaches the integration of man with nature.

In his encyclica "Dives in Misericondia" ("On the Meaning of God"), Pope John Paul II stated that man has the choice between controlling the environment or being enslaved by it.[6] Liberal Religion wants neither. It aspires to integration.

And yet, we have learned that nature can be improved upon by such activities as reforestation, intensive agriculture, birth control, and irrigation. Integration does not preclude scientific research directed toward the improvement of the quality of life. Human beings are naturally, primarily, and selfishly interested in the quality of human life. The virtue of integration is that it strives for improvement of all life. Body and soul are integrated; there is no separate life of the soul.[7] The secular and the sacred are integrated; all life is sacred.[8] Integration also denotes a balancing of rationality and emotion in one person. Indeed, such integration is the mark of the Religious Liberal.

Reverence for Life

Albert Schweitzer describes how the phrase "Reverence for Life" came to his mind while he was on a river journey in Equatorial Africa.

Late on the third day, at the very moment when, at sunset, we were making our way through a herd of hippopotamuses, there flashed through my mind, unforeseen and unsought, the phrase "Reverence for Life." The iron door had yielded: the path in the thicket had become visible. Now I had found my way to the idea in which world and life affirmation and

ethics are contained side by side. Now I knew that the world-view of ethical world and life-affirmation, together with the idea of civilization is
founded in thought.[9]

Reverence for life is a virtue of great scope. It ranges from the abhor-
rence of killing insects, which was practiced by Schweitzer and is part of the
Jain religion in India, to an uncompromising repudiation of war and any
form of violence. "The ethical mysticism of Reverence for Life," writes
Schweitzer, "is rationalism thought to a conclusion."[10]

While all religious liberals profess reverence for life, they are not united
in the application of the principle and the adherence to this virtue. Many of
them "draw the line" somewhere. This applies also to the question of capital
punishment.

The contemporary American "Right to Life" groups are not, as a rule,
of a Religious Liberal persuasion. They are not interested in a general reverence for life. They advocate the preservation of the life of an unborn fetus.
Their religious concern for the right to life of an unborn fetus rarely extends
to the victims of war. Right to life is strictly a single issue, anti-abortion
movement. In contrast, Liberal Religion's reverence for life is an all-
encompassing tenet, as discussed under the headings, "Dignity of Man"
(Chapter 13), "Justice" (Chapter 14), and "Social Concern" (Chapter 16).

Patriotism

Patriotism is regarded with a jaundiced eye by many liberals, especially
after the American war in Vietnam. There are always facets to criticize and
to dislike in anyone's relations and surroundings. To overcome such dislike
and to accentuate the positive is a virtue which is born of the reverence for
life in its totality. Patriotism denotes love of one's country which is as simple.
and fundamental as love of one's family. Such love is not uncritical. As
George Santayana wrote, "To love one's country, unless that love is quite
blind and lazy, must involve a distinction between the country's actual condition and its inherent ideal; and this distinction in turn involves a demand
for changes and for effort."[11] Santayana also points out in his essay on
patriotism that it has two aspects: "it is partly sentiment, by which it looks
back upon the sources of culture, and partly policy, or allegiance to those
ideals which . . . animate the better organs of society and demand further
embodiment."[12] Liberal Religion asserts that its tenets are the sources of
American culture and represent not what most Americans believe, but what
most Americans really want.

In the United States, we experienced a great surge of patriotism when the
tall ships sailed up the Hudson River in 1976, in celebration of the bicentennial

anniversary of the Republic, and again in 1980 when the hostages came home from Iran. The bicentennial celebration reminded Americans of their history of progress in the world; the return of the hostages brought to the fore the commonality which Americans enjoy even if they come from very different backgrounds and walks of life.

Patriotism does not conflict with the mundialism advocated by most Religious Liberals. Mundialism is a program of subscribing to world citizenship. The defeated Republican presidential candidate Wendell Wilkie wrote in 1943, "It is inescapable that there can be no peace for any part of the world unless the foundations of peace are made secure throughout the world."[13] This is the essence of mundialism and it demonstrates why it is compatible with patriotism. Patriotism also does not conflict with sympathy for the United Nations. The Community Church of New York, the Unitarian Church of Phoenix, Arizona, and other liberal churches display the blue United Nations flag next to their national flags.

Just as one who marries into a large family and learns to love its members need not thereby foreswear the love for the family into which one was born, so a person can become a citizen of the world without losing affection for the homeland.

Patriotism ceases to be a virtue if it develops into that unintelligent zealotry which is known as chauvinism. Chauvinists are individuals who, without apparent provocation, proclaim support of their country in a loudmouthed and bellicose manner. Chauvinism is irrational and alien to Liberal Religion.

In the Liberal churches of America, the song: "America the Beautiful" is not infrequently sung as a hymn, and sung with lusty fervor. The Declaration of Independence and the Gettysburg Address, both written by devout Religious Liberals, are part of the scripture of Liberal Religion.

Liberal Religion's rationality, as expounded in Chapter 4 is compatible with love of country. It does not abjure emotion (see Chapter 5). Martin Luther King, Jr., in his famous "I have a dream" speech in Washington in 1963 said, "I have a dream that one day this nation will rise up, live up to the true meaning of its creed—that all men are created equal." This indeed is the American creed to which Religious Liberals subscribe fervently, and it is part and parcel of their patriotism.

Listening

Some years ago, the Reverend James Hutchinson announced that next Sunday's sermon topic would be the Eleventh Commandment. The congregation was mystified but learned on that Sunday that the Eleventh Commandment consists of one word "LISTEN."

Seemingly, nothing has been said about this virtue in the preceding pages. But that is not quite correct. There have been repeated urges to communicate. People are often prepared to communicate by talking. However, there can be no communication unless someone listens to what is said. Often, listeners are sadly lacking. The person who uses intervals between his or her utterances in order to think of what to say next, is not listening. It is important to listen to what the other person has to say, otherwise truth and knowledge will escape us.

Older people who speak to youngsters or bosses who talk to subordinates are frequently not communicating because they make no effort to listen to what the younger person or subordinate has to say or would like to say if given the chance. In order to achieve a satisfactory or a creative relationship, it is necessary to establish an atmosphere in which one can listen. One must seek the opportunity to listen.

A good listener must have an open mind. He/she will not respond until the speaker has finished his or her statement. It is a common failing to allow skillful rhetoric to make up for questionable logic. In religious terms this means that Liberal Religion does not allow its adherents to be seduced by vague preachings, unverifiable teaching, or beautiful rituals. Liberal Religion can thrive only in a climate that encourages the free exchange of ideas. To this end, the virtue of listening is indispensable.

There is another aspect to the virtue of listening: silence and quietude must be sought. It will enable one to listen to the inner voice. The inner voice comes to man in a variety of ways: as inspiration, as a call of conscience, or even through dreams or visions. The psychiatrist Carl Jung taught that dreams and visions are the only means by which God has ever communicated with men. One may, but need not, take this literally.

Liberal Religion does not object to dreams so long as they are not confused with, or represented as, reality. One recalls the famous speech of Martin Luther King, Jr., at the Washington Civil Rights Rally (1963) in which he spoke of his dream and vision of America's future. Flights of fancy and dreams are often the germ of innovation which Liberal Religion treasures. Artists and other creative spirits dream before they create. Langston Hughes wrote these beautiful lines:

> Hold fast to dreams
> For if dreams die
> Life is a broken winged bird
> That cannot fly

> Hold fast to dreams
> For when dreams go
> Life is a barren field
> Frozen with snow

In his essay on "The Oversoul," Emerson alluded to this inner voice, "Jesus speaks always from within." And in the same essay: "Let men then learn the revelation of all nature and all thought to his heart; this namely, that the sources are in his mind, if the sentiment of duty is there. But, if he would know what the great God speaketh, he must go into his closet and shut the door, as Jesus said. . . . He must greatly listen to himself, withdrawing himself from all the accents of other men's devotions."

Consistency

This is a difficult virtue for the human being. Emerson called it the hobgoblin of a little mind, thus rationalizing what most of us cannot attain.[14] Consistency means: "Do as you preach." And that is what most humans find so difficult.

Religious Liberals stand for the free mind. But many of them will not be tolerant of a mind which chooses the Ku Klux Klan or some other movement that exalts racial or ethnic superiority. It is consistent to combat an ideology or religion that does not permit Religious Liberals to live according to the dictates of their free minds. It is not consistent to condemn others who, in the exercise of their convictions, hold beliefs which we do not share or even condemn. A chauvinist or a warmonger may be perfectly honest in his belief and therefore entitled to the respect of a Religious Liberal.

Religious Liberals postulate the separation of church and state as a basic ingredient of the principle of religious liberty. And yet, many of them claim exemption from municipal taxes which pay for the services the state makes available through the municipal police, fire, and sanitation departments. This is an inconsistency.[15]

The church schools of Liberal Religionists often act on the belief that children cannot be taught religion's truth except through the medium of myths. The children are taught myths, not as myths, but as religious truths. This is also inconsistent with Liberal Religion's devotion to the exaltation of truth.

Participation

As a religious virtue, participation is unique to Liberal Religion in several aspects.

Liberal Religion teaches that the creation is not finished, that all humans are called upon to help perfect the creation and, in particular, to improve all animate life on the planet Earth.

In Traditional Religion, the Universe and religion itself are closed systems; that is, those who adhere to Traditional Religion, and especially to authoritarian religion, are told what to believe, what to do, when to do it, and how to do it. It reminds one of the conduct of a squad of soldiers who are trained under the command of a drill sergeant. They often execute the drill with enthusiasm and with the satisfaction gained from a duty well performed. This kind of religion may invoke a sense of religious fulfillment, contentment, or even happiness, but it is not a participatory religion; it is not creative.

The devout hermit, like the Buddhist who strives for Nirvana, turns away from the world. He or she is not a participant.

Liberal Religion wants its adherents to participate in life and all its manifestations. Its followers are expected to take an active part in all concerns of Liberal Religion. This includes its organization: the church, the temple, or the meeting house, and the larger organization by whatever name it may be known. This concern, while not negligible, is less important than the concern with the community at large. Liberal Religion demands participation in the affairs of the larger community, as alluded to in the chapters on "Social Concern," "Politics," and in the other chapters of this book.

Some stern Presbyterians in the north of Scotland have banned the use of organ music in order to induce a better participation in the worship service of their kirk. This type of Sunday participation is far less important to Liberal Religion than participation in the workaday life and the concerns of the larger community.

Obedience to the Law

Most of us are law abiding, whether by habit or because we fear the consequence of breaking the law. This involves no virtue. Obedience to the law becomes a virtue when an opportunity to break the law exists and the temptation is resisted. Such temptations occur in a variety of ways, for instance, when stealing food for a hungry stomach, smashing a window or hurling rocks in a protest action, smuggling imported articles past a customs inspector, or cheating. The opportunity to cheat is at times almost irresistible, for example, while taking an examination, filing a tax return, or in business. Resistance on these occasions is virtuous.

The phrase "law and order" is unpopular because it has been misused, and it sometimes is understood as a code phrase for oppression, which is a vice and not a virtue. Law and order are necessary for any free society; that is, any society in which every member is free to exercise what are known as human rights and is free from arbitrary governmental interference. Law and order create the climate in which Liberal Religion can live and flourish.

Liberal Religion values the democratic process in human relations, a process which includes the right of the majority to make the laws and an obligation on the part of the minority to obey these laws. We must reject the theory that there is a higher law than that promulgated by the democratic process (see the discussion of natural law on page 164). The law protects the minorities of which, unhappily, Liberal Religion is one. Disregard for the law is likely to lead to anarchy and destruction of the social fabric. To uphold the rule of law requires a judiciary guided only by legal principles. It was, therefore, inappropriate for the Republican platform of 1980 to demand that judges must have prescribed political beliefs.

Picture a deserted street crossing at night. A traffic light above alternatively emits red and green signals. An automobile approaches. There is no on-coming traffic, nor does the driver observe any car coming from the left or the right. Nevertheless, the driver stops at the red light and waits until it changes. This is a perfect demonstration of what is meant by obedience to the law.

In a political revolution, the existing law and order are overthrown. Citizens cease to abide by the overthrown law. Such monumental events occur rarely, but when they do they create a new set of values and virtues. Ordinarily, ideological, political, and religious disputes or eruptions must be dealt with within the existing framework of law and order. When the followers of Jesus became restive because of his attacks on the establishment and its outworn values, he admonished them to stay within the existing law which, he said, he had come to fulfill (Matt. 5:17).

Henry Thoreau, one of the saints of Liberal Religion (see Chapter 20) was not law abiding. He was an ardent abolitionist, like most Liberal Religionists of his time. He was also opposed to the 1840 war against Mexico. He refused to pay the poll tax which he said was used to finance the extension of slavery and the war. He was arrested and he spent a night in jail. Thereafter, he wrote the famous essay on *Civil Disobedience*. In it, he calls for disobedience of any law which one holds unjust or wrong. It was (and is) unrealistic to expect that the majority which makes the laws in a democratic society would necessarily make just laws. The primary purpose of the legal order, as was pointed out above (in Chapter 14), is not justice, but the smooth operation of society. Thoreau's demand that everybody should be allowed to disobey any law he/she considers wrong, is bound to result in disorganization and chaos. The essay is written in a querulous style. It is an expression of sophomoric idealism and naive selfishness. ("I came into this world not chiefly to make this a good place to live in, but to live in it, be it good or bad. . . . It is not a man's duty to devote himself to the eradication of any, even the most enormous wrong. . . . I cast my vote perchance, but I am not vitally concerned that right should prevail.") Thoreau served as a role model for the men who refused to serve in the Vietnam War, although they were not opposed to all wars. Unlike Thoreau, these men desired to avoid jail.

Gandhi was strongly influenced by Thoreau. His name for civil disobedience was "satyagraha" which, as we know, broke the back of British colonial rule in India. While Thoreau called for disobedience of all "unjust" laws, Gandhi wrote that it is not "necessary for voluntary obedience that the laws to be obeyed must be good. There are many unjust laws which a good citizen obeys, so long as they do not hurt his self-respect, or the moral being . . . ."[16]

Thoreau's theory was often invoked in the civil rights demonstrations of the 1960s. However, as Professor Harry Jones has pointed out, the civil rights movement was far less a challenge to law than an appeal to law.[17] Martin Luther King, Jr., the late leader of the civil rights movement, had great respect for the law;[18] he merely advocated disobedience of such laws as were not democratically enacted by the majority of the citizens and which, therefore, are unjust (lawyers regard such laws as unconstitutional—one example being the segregation law of Alabama). All laws which are democratically enacted by a majority of the citizens are just and must be obeyed by all. This is a far cry from Thoreau's call for civil disobedience. Martin Luther King, Jr., agreed with the principle of democratic procedures in human relations, one of the tenets of Liberal Religion (see Chapter 12). To be law abiding is a postulate which flows from this principle.

Humility

As a young man, this writer went to listen to a lecture by Albert Einstein which was designed to instruct people in the intricacies of the theory of relativity. What the great man said is forgotten, but not how he said it. Dr. Einstein explained his work without a single time using the pronoun, "I." This was not only an absence of vanity, but impressed the young man as true humility. The lecturer conveyed the impression that it was the force and the genius of mathematics and physics which had developed the new theory, and not any one individual. Liberal Religion shows this humility by not claiming that it is the sole possessor of truth. Liberal Religion believes certain things to be true and it adheres to its beliefs and proclaims them. However, Liberal Religion concedes that truth is transient. In this, it differs from Traditional Religion.

Religious wars were (and are still) fought on the basis of one premise: if you do not consent to be my brother, I will kill you. In many instances, the animosity has so hardened that the killing proceeds without a prior attempt to convert the potential victim to the killer's faith. History books abound with examples. Only two will be mentioned here: the massacre between Hindus and Moslems after Britain withdrew from India (1946), and the ongoing warfare between Protestants and Catholics in Ireland. The leitmotif in these instances is that one religious group considers itself superior to the other, and that killing or being killed is glorious. This is the opposite of humility. Lack of humility can also be observed in group as well as personal relationships. Anti-Semites are not humble because they think their race is superior. Those who profess Christianity are rarely humble, particularly if they believe that their faith excels all others and that Jesus is the hope of the world—which, of course, he was not and he is not. The Jews, who think of themselves as the chosen people, are not humble, nor are the Calvinist elects. The adherents of Liberal Religion often regard themselves as an intellectual or spiritual elite and, thus, lack the virtue of humility.

It is a virtue not easily achieved. Pride goes before destruction, says one of the Proverbs of the Bible (Prov. 16:18). In ordinary language this means that a conceited person is likely to fall in the abyss of failure and misery. Two other Proverbs contrast humility with honor (Prov. 15:33 and 18:12). This points to the fact that a person lacks humility when something is done to establish honor. In religious terms, the proud warrior says or thinks that he/she is battling for the greater glory and honor of God. This generally means that one battles for one's own imagined honor.

Humility does not mean meekness. Jesus told the crowd listening to the Sermon on the Mount that the meek will inherit the earth. This was music to the ears of the meek, but it is just that, music. Meekness means submission. It may be doubted that men like Einstein or Darwin would have achieved any success if they had meekly submitted to existing teachings. We do not expect contemporary scientists to be meek in their research at the frontiers of learning. The meek person shys away from interfering. Liberal Religion encourages innovation which comes only from interfering with existing concepts. Upsetting the applecart is not a sin; but it should be done not only with prudence, but also with humility.

Humility does not preclude firmness. There is nothing wrong with Paul's admonition to hold firmly to "whatever things are just, pure, lovely and of good report" (Phil. 4:8).

Religious gestures such as prostrating towards Mecca, genuflexion, kneeling, and downcasting of one's head in prayer are supposed to indicate humility. Such gestures do indeed debase and humiliate the bodies of those who are born to stand straight and to face the Creation. One is entitled to question whether these gestures reflect or even induce spiritual humility. The posture of stretching out one's arms and to gaze out on the world seems more reverent, especially for those who have a reverence for life and for the Creation.

Unlike Traditional Religion, Liberal Religion does not regard people as inherently sinful and depraved, born in sin and living in sin, or saved only by the mercy of God. The persons who debase themselves by proclaiming their sinfulness in public worship services and who ask for God's forgiveness, often do not really mean it. It sounds very humble, but the sound reflects memorized phrases and taught dogma, rather than true inner conviction. It is not honest humility. Liberal Religion encourages people to cultivate what is inborn in them, to develop their potential, and to enjoy life in all its manifestations without a guilty conscience or the fear of an invisible God. The virtue of humility consists of being aware that such achievements as we enjoy are owing to the genes and the life force with which we were born and which surrounds us, and that the opinions which we hold so firmly and so dear, are not necessarily true and everlasting.

In Shakespeare's play *Henry VI* the soldier king exhorted his troops not to be humble in battle but

> In peace there's nothing so becomes a man
> As modest stillness and humility.

John Haynes Holmes regarded humility as the first mark of a Religious Liberal. He said: "The true liberal matches himself against the vastness of the world, and recognizes how little he can hope to know of the secrets of reality. . . . He never pretends that he knows everything. . . . This does not dissuade him from convictions. He has his ideas and defends them stoutly. But he has no pride of opinion, and no finality of judgment. . . . Contrast this with the orthodox who turns truth into dogma. This man has no humility about this matter of knowledge and belief. Karl Marx's famous book, *Das Kapital* is for millions of communists, the world around, "the final word of wisdom . . . as infallible as any bull that was ever published by a pope. . . . The Communist is the typical orthodox of our time. He is like the Mormon, with Joseph Smith and his golden Tablets of the Law. . . ." The Liberal can have nothing to do with this point of view. The last thing of which he would be guilty is this arrogance of mind which is the denial of that humility which is basic to his soul.[19]

Respect

If a child respects its parents, it probably does so out of fear or out of habit. That conduct cannot be called virtuous, because it is based on fear or, in any event, it involves no conscious effort. Even obedience to the fifth commandment ("Honor thy father and mother") does not merit the word virtue because that rule is a command. Unlike any of the other commandments, it is coupled with the promise of a reward or bribe—"that thy days may be long upon the land which the Lord thy God giveth thee." In Traditional Religion, morality is often achieved through fear of God and with bribes. Any morality induced by fear and bribery is not a virtue.

Respect is a virtue when it is given voluntarily, by a conscious effort.

Liberal Religion requires respect for the beliefs and opinion of others. It also postulates respect for those people whom one finds loathesome and cannot love. Such respect follows from the basic tenets of the dignity of man, and it is another aspect of the reverence for life.

This, presumably, is the meaning of the Biblical phrase "God is no respecter of persons" (Acts 11:34). In the Jerusalem Bible, this passage reads "God does not have favorites," which affirms the Liberal principle that the concept of a religious elite, of elects, or of a chosen people is not tenable. Traditional Religion does not accord equal respect to all human beings. Paul says that God is no respecter of persons (Rom. 2:11), but in the same connection, he draws a distinction and writes (Rom. 2:10), "Glory, honor and peace to every man that worketh good, to the Jew first and also to the Gentile."

The late Unitarian leader Frederick May Elliott, bemoaning the fact that Unitarians are generally thought of as opposing all tradition, pointed out that Unitarians have traditions of their own, such as having respect for the mind.[20] Liberal Religion respects rationality; it respects religion. In its worship services, that respect is apparent. Respect for the mind makes Liberal Religionists skeptical because they are aware of the changing content of truth, for which they also have a high respect. Skepticism must be distinguished from cynicism. The skeptic questions with respect, the cynic belittles without respect.

In the essay entitled "Intellect," Ralph Waldo Emerson says that God offers to every mind the choice between truth and repose. One cannot have both. "He in whom the love of repose predominates will accept the first creed, the first philosophy, the first political party—most likely his fathers."[21] The religious liberal does not choose repose; he or she chooses truth, and, therefore, in Emerson's words, "submits to the inconvenience of suspense and imperfect opinions, but he is a candidate for truth, as the other is not, and respects the highest law of his being." In the same essay, Emerson speaks of the intelligence and the wisdom of the common man who merits our respect. "Do you think the porter or the cook has no anecdotes, no experience, no wonders for you? Everybody knows as much as the savant."[22] The difference is that some have a superior skill in expressing what they know. And, then, there is the confusion of sentiments which beclouds intelligent thinking and, especially, religion. To quote Emerson's essay once more: "In the fog of good and evil affections, it is hard for man to walk forward in a straight line. Intellect is void of affection and sees an object as it stands in the light of science, cool and disengaged." Respect for scientific truth is at the heart of Liberal Religion.

Postscript

The manuscript of this book was completed in the early summer of 1981. Of the events bearing on the subject matter of this book, which have occurred since that time, a few appear significant.

A test tube baby has now been born in the United States (see pp. 161 and 177).

In January 1982, the U.S. Government overruled the 1980 decision against Bob Jones University, which was mentioned at the end of Chapter 17 (p. 109). Bob Jones is a religious institution which believes in racial segregation and expels students who engage in interracial dating. The Internal Revenue Service had ruled that the religious views of Bob Jones violated the public policy of the United States and, for that reason, had withdrawn the tax exemption of the university. The government now holds that courts should not deal with such matters (a legally dubious proposition), and it forbade the Internal Revenue Service to consider public policy matters when dealing with tax exemption applications. Ostensibly, this is a broadening of the religious liberty principle. Actually, the opposite is true. By removing the restraints imposed by the public interest, the government dilutes the integrity of religious liberty. Liberal Religion cannot approve it.

Sonia Johnson, who was excommunicated from the Mormon Church because of her zealous promotion of the Equal Rights Amendment (see p. 51), has published an autobiographical book.[1] In this book, she denounces the male dominance and the servitude of women in the Mormon Church. She organized a public demonstration in Washington against the prophet, as the Mormon president is called. She was supported in this by Roman Catholic nuns, in return for her participation in a public demonstration against the visiting pope. The book criticizes the Mormon Church only for interfering with her political rights. In December 1981, Mrs. Johnson stated on television that she would not rejoin the Mormon Church, even if she would be invited to do so. In a recent letter to *The New York Times Book Review*[2] she criticized the Mormon religion for its rigidity and its closed system of thought. She expresses exhilaration and embraces the open-minded approach of liberal religion.

A Pennsylvania court case involved an association called MOVE, whose members are opposed to any kind of pollution and eat only raw food. A convict complained that the prison did not supply him with this diet and, therefore, violated his religious freedom. A lower court denied his claim and the judges of the Federal Appeals Court in Philadelphia were, therefore, called upon to determine whether MOVE was a religion. This obviously embarrassed the judges, especially since the Seeger decision of the U.S. Supreme Court (see p. 190) did not allow them to define religion simply as faith in a supernatural, personal God. Nevertheless, the court concluded that MOVE was not a religion protected by the Constitution, since it was only concerned with pollution and a raw food diet. A religion, the court held, must have deeper, broader, and comprehensive concerns. It must be a system of belief. Liberal Religion can agree with the foregoing. However, it will not agree with the following pronouncement which may be correct from a legal point of view, but which is difficult to reconcile with the outlook of Liberal Religion: "it is crucial to realize that the free exercise clause does not protect all deeply held beliefs, however 'ultimate' their ends or all-consuming their means. An individual or group may adhere to and profess certain political, economical or social doctrines, perhaps quite passionately. The umbrella of the first amendment, though, has not been extended to shelter strongly held ideologies of such a nature, however all encompassing their scope."[3]

The Iranian revolution, under the leadership of the Ayatolla Khomeini, was discussed not only as an indication of a growing orthodoxy in the Eastern world, but also as an example of the interaction of religion and politics (see Chapter 17). Recent events in Turkey are further evidence of this. The *New York Times* reported that since 1977, attendance at mosque services has noticeably increased. More and more Turkish men wear the traditional Islam beard, and an increasing number of females cover their faces with kerchiefs. In December 1981, the government of Turkey cracked down on this growing orthodoxy and, among other measures, imposed a ban on the wearing of head kerchiefs by female students and teachers. Schoolboys are forbidden to wear skullcaps.[4] The get-tough policy of the Turkish military government is reminiscent of the policy of Ataturk in the 1920s. Ataturk was determined to make Turkey a modern nation. That, in the view of Ataturk and the present rulers, requires suppression of traditional religious customs. "Since Ataturk's revolution," wrote the *New York Times*, "Turkey has taken the lead among Moslem countries in separating religion from government and in giving women equal rights with men—something not provided for under Islamic law."[5] The Turkish fundamentalists protest that they obey God's command and the Koran, and they fight the government through the National Salvation party.[6] While the separation of traditional religion from public life may be pleasing to us, it must be noted that the forcible suppression of religious traditions is repugnant to Liberal Religion.

The doctrines of evolution and Darwinism have increasingly irked the fundamentalist believers in traditional religion. Evolution and Darwinism are regarded as wicked devices of Satan. In 1928, Arkansas made it unlawful to teach evolution in the public schools and colleges, but that law was declared unconstitutional in 1968. Arkansas then enacted a new statute which requires science teachers who teach evolution to also present the biblical cosmology called creation science, according to which the world and all human beings were created, as the statute says, at a "relatively recent" time, meaning about 6,000 to 10,000 years ago. Evolution science and creation science must be given equal time.

Creationism (see p. 109) has made no headlines. In December 1981, a trial took place in the Federal District Court of Little Rock, Arkansas, in which the statute was attacked as unconstitutional and, hence, void. The plaintiffs contended that the so-called creation science is not science at all but merely Bible-based religion, which may not be taught in public schools. The judge held for the plaintiff and ruled that creationism is not science, thus rendering the statute unconstitutional. Liberal Religion agrees, but this is not the last word on the matter, since the judge's ruling will be reviewed by an appellate court and, possibly, the Supreme Court of the United States.

The trial in Little Rock has been compared to the Tennessee "monkey trial" in 1925. However, this time there was no circus atmosphere. It has been said that this was due to the sophistication and thorough preparation of the trial judge.[7] There was probably a deeper reason. The proponents of literal Bible belief regard the evolution doctrine as a formidable menace and they do not want any hoopla to dilute their earnest promotion of creationism. The idea that man should have developed from a lower form of animal life and that the earth should be older than 10,000 years is blasphemous to them and a threat to good morals. Liberal Religionists may shake their heads about such irrationality, but they must recognize that they are up against a popular mood which is impervious to reasoning. It may be, as one scholar recently wrote, that anti-intellectualism is latent in American society, and has been throughout our history. However, it is not without significance that the creationists try to convince the world that they are teaching science. This homage to science is a step in the direction which Liberal Religion proclaims. It justifies the belief that the strangle-hold of Traditional Religion is loosening. Liberal religious fervor and moral passion for the principles of Liberal Religion must ultimately liberate our society from the yoke and the irrationality of Traditional Religion.

Notes

Chapter 1

Introduction to Liberal Religion

1. *New York World Telegram,* 11 April 1959, p. 9.
2. Henry Nelson Weiman, *Religious Experience & Scientific Method,* p. 48.
3. Hans Küng, *The Church,* preface, p. 14.
4. John F. Hayward, *Existentialism and Religious Liberalism,* p. 3.
5. Frank G. Opton, "Creed is Not a Dirty Word," *Register Leader,* December, 1967.
6. James Luther Adams, *On Being Human—Religiously,* p. 12.
7. Frederick M. Eliot, "The Essence of Liberalism," *Christian Register,* vol. 3 no. 18 (16 May 1935), reprinted in *An Anthology,* p. 71.
8. Max L. Stackhouse, Introduction to J. L. Adams's essays, *On Being Human—Religiously,* p. xv.
9. John F. Hayward, *Kairos* no. 8 and 10 (1978).
10. Henry N. Wieman, *The Growth of Religion,* p. 238.
11. Robert M. Hemstreet, *Identity and Ideology,* Unitarian Universalist Advance study paper, no. 3 (1977), p. 3.
12. Paul Carnes, *The Free Church in a Changing World,* p. 162.
13. John A. T. Robinson, *Honest to God,* p. 7.
14. Lewis Carroll, *Through the Looking Glass,* Chapter VI.
15. James L. Adams, op. cit., p. 26.
16. Peter Fleck, *The Mask of Religion,* p. 16.
17. Ibid., p. 9.
18. Ibid.

Chapter 2

Religion

1. Psalm 100.

2. *Hymns for the Celebration of Life* No. 390.

3. Arthur Schlesinger, ed., *History of American Life*, Vol. II, Chapter XI.

4. Frances Trollope, *Domestic Manners of Americans,* edited by Donald Smalley, p. 209.

5. Stephen H. Fritchman, "The Irrational Fear of Happiness," *Unity* vol. 150 no. 1, (1964), p. 5.

6. Alan W. Watts, *Myth and Ritual in Christianity,* p. 208.

7. Dietrich Bonhoeffer, *Letters and Papers from Prison,* p. 163.

8. Joseph Fletcher, "An Odyssey from Theology to Humanism," *Religious Humanism* vol. XIII (1979), p. 146.

9. Duncan Howlett, *The Fourth Faith,* p. 210.

10. Colleen McCullough, *The Thornbirds.*

11. *Davis v. Beeson,* 133 U.S. 333 (1890).

12. Henry N. Wieman, *Seeking a Faith for a New Age,* p. 139.

13. Henry N. Wieman, *The Wrestle of Religion with Truth,* p. 135.

14. Ibid., p. 3.

15. Henry N. Wieman, *Man's Ultimate Commitment,* p. 5.

16. Benjamin Cardozo, "The Choice of Tycho Brahe," from *Selected Writings,* p. 4.

17. Felix Adler, *Our Part in this World,* p. 47.

18. Victor Murray, *How to Know Your Bible,* p. 47.

19. I. B. Hormer, "Buddhism," in *The Concise Encyclopedia of Living Faiths,* p. 267.

20. Hans Küng, *On Being a Christian,* p. 93.

21. Robert Ellwood, *Religious and Spiritual Groups in America,* p. 4.

22. Ibid., p. 5.

23. See Chapter 7.

24. Harold Berman, *The Interaction of the Law and Religion,* p. 31.

25. William James, *Varieties of Religious Experience,* p. 35.

26. Ibid., p. 36.

27. Berman, op. cit., footnote 3 to Chapter 1.

28. Peter Fleck, *The Mask of Religion,* p. 150.

29. Harvey Cox, *The Secular City,* revised ed., p. 166.

30. Duncan Howlett, *The Critical Way in Religion,* p. 166.

31. Henry N. Wieman, *The Growth of Religion,* p. 193 seq.

32. "A Secular Humanist Declaration," *Free Inquiry* vol. 1 no. 3 (1980).

33. Sidney Hook, "The Ground We Stand On," *Free Inquiry* vol. 1 no. 3 (1980).

34. Paul Beatty, "Humanism: Secular or Religious?" *Free Inquiry* vol. 1 no. 3 (1980).

35. *Unitarian Universalist World,* 15 November 1980, p. 11.

36. Will and Ariel Durant, *The Reformation,* p. 370; Vol. VI of *The Story of Civilization.*

37. Irwin Polishook, *Roger Williams, John Cotton and Religious Freedom,* p. 6.

38. Robert Mueller, *Prayer and Meditation at the United Nations,* p. 4.

39. Henry Steele Commager, *The American Mind,* pp. 162 and 164.

40. Robert Bellah, "Civil Religion in America," *Proceedings of American Academy of Arts and Sciences* vol. 96 no. 1.

41. Ralph Waldo Emerson, "The Oversoul."

42. Robert Mueller, op. cit., p. 3.

43. Ibid., p. 4.

44. Hans Küng, *The Church,* p. 43.

45. Paul Tillich, *Systematic Theology,* Vol. III, p. 51.

46. Pierre Teilhard de Chardin, *The Phenomenon of Man,* p. 296.

47. Carl Sagan, *Broca's Brain,* p. 312.

48. Exodus 19:5; Deuteronomy 7:6 and 14:2; Psalms 133:13 and 135; Isaiah 49:7.

49. Victor Murray, op. cit., p. 53.

50. Herman Wouk, *This Is My God,* p. 32.

51. Ibid., p. 35.
52. George Orwell, *Animal Farm,* p. 112.
53. Donald S. Harrington, *The Faith Behind Freedom.*
54. Victor Murray, op. cit., p. 23.
55. II Kings 3:27; see also Durant, "Caesar and Christ," p. 588 footnote, Vol. III of *The Story of Civilization.*
56. Max Weber, *The Sociology of Religion,* p. 68.
57. James L. Adams, *On Being Human—Religiously,* p. 102.
58. Max Weber, op. cit., p. 69.
59. Paul Tillich, *Systematic Theology,* Vol. I, p. 102.
60. *The New York Times,* 9 June 1970.
61. Unitarian Universalist World, 15 October 1980, p. 6.
62. Wieman, *The Growth of Religion,* p. 287.
63. Wieman, *The Wrestle of Religion with Truth,* p. 132.
64. Felix Adler, "Essay on the Ethical Culture Movement," in *Our Part in this World,* p. 57.
65. James L. Adams, *On Being Human—Religiously,* p. 11.
66. Wieman, *The Wrestle of Religion with Truth,* p. 138.
67. *Smithsonian,* 1979, p. 167.
68. Rene Wormser, "The Legal System of Islam," *The American Bar Association Journal* vol. 64 September 1978, p. 1939.
69. *Lee v. U.S.,* U.S. District Court, 7/15/80.
70. *Holy Spirit Association v. Harper & Row,* N.Y. Supreme Ct. 1/12/79, 47 L.W. 2460.
71. *United States v. Ballard,* 322 U.S. 78 (1944).
72. Gibbon, *The Decline and Fall of the Roman Empire,* p. 50.
73. *The New York Times,* 8 June 1980.
74. Paul Tillich, *Systematic Theology,* Vol. II, p. 179.
75. *The New York Times,* 10 January 1981, p. A14.
76. *The New York Times,* 25 February 1968, p. 3.
77. *Christian Register,* April 1956.
78. Samuel Eliot Morison, *The Oxford History of the American People,* p. 152.
79. *Time,* 15 September 1980, p. 54.

Chapter 3

God

1. Max Weber, *The Sociology of Religion,* p. 10.
2. *Institutes* II & XVI as quoted by Walker.
3. *The New York Times* advertisement 17 January 1979; *idem.* 18 January 1979.
4. Max Dimont, *Jews, God and History,* p. 29.
5. Ibid., p. 30.
6. Weber, op. cit., p. 16.
7. Donald S. Harrington, "The Faith Beneath Freedom," p. 7.
8. Dimont, op. cit., p. 16.
9. A. R. Gibb, "Islam," in *The Concise Encyclopedia of Living Faiths,* p. 199.
10. Weber, op. cit., p. 103.
11. Dietrich Bonhoeffer, *Letters and Papers from Prison,* p. 218.
12. Ibid., p. 219.
13. Paul Tillich, *Theology of Culture, p. 21; William James, Varieties of Religious Experience,* p. 598.

14. Harvey Cox, *The Secular City*, p. 235.
15. Thomas Paine, *Age of Reason*, in *Basic Writings*, p. 42.
16. Mary Daly, *Beyond God the Father*, p. 13.
17. Weber, op. cit., p. 105.
18. W. V. Goethe, *Faust*, "Prologue in Heaven."
19. Robert Mueller, *Most of All, They Taught Me Happiness*, p. 115.
20. James L. Adams, *On Being Human—Religiously*, p. 13.
21. Ibid., p. 13.
22. Henry E. Barnes, *An Intellectual and Cultural History of the Western World*, p. 802.
23. Ibid., p. 791.
24. Ibid., p. 793.
25. Thomas Paine, *The Age of Reason*, in *Basic Writings*, p. 66.
26. Carl Sagan, *Broca's Brain*, p. 287.
27. Milton Konvitz, *Religious Liberty and Conscience*, p. 70.
28. Erich Fromm, *You Shall Be as Gods*, p. 19.
29. William James, *The Varieties of Religious Experience*, p. 32.
30. Carl Sagan, *The American Scholar 1978*, p. 460.
31. Ibid.
32. Thomas Paine, op. cit., p. 44.
33. Milton Konvitz, op. cit.
34. John A. T. Robinson, *Honest to God*, p. 126.
35. Erich Fromm, op. cit., p. 228.
36. James L. Adams, op. cit., p. 14.
37. Erich Fromm, op. cit., p. 19.
38. William James, op. cit., p. 32.
39. "A Secular Humanist Declaration," *Free Inquiry*, vol. 1 no. 1 (1980), p. 3.
40. Paul Beatty, "Humanism: Secular or Religious?" *Free Inquiry*, vol. 1 no. 1 (1980), p. 11.
41. *Crowley v. Smithsonian Institution*, 636 F.2d (1980).
42. *The New York Times*, 27 January 1981.
43. *The New York Times*, 28 January 1981.
44. Charles Darwin, *Autobiography*, p. 87.
45. Ibid., p. 93.
46. Ibid., p. 94.
47. Ibid., p. 95.
48. James L. Adams, op. cit., p. 98.
49. Ibid., p. 99.
50. Paul Tillich, *Systematic Theology*, Vol. I, p. 264.
51. Pierre Teilhard de Chardin, *The Phenomenon of Man*, p. 295.
52. Quoted by M. Stackhouse, editor of James L. Adams, op. cit., p. 224.
53. Durant, *The Life of Greece*, Vol. II of the *Story of Civilization*, p. 78.
54. Victor Murray, *How to Know Your Bible*, p. 133.
55. Tillich, op. cit., Vol. I, p. 25.
56. Ibid., Vol. I, p. 263.
57. Ibid., Vol. III, p. 323.
58. Ibid., Vol. I, p. 228.
59. Harold Berman, *The Interaction of Law and Religion*, pp. 75–76.
60. Erich Fromm, op. cit., pp. 23 and 87.
61. Tillich, op. cit.
62. St. Augustine, *City of God*, Chapter 26, p. 235.
63. Tillich, op. cit., Vol. III, p. 149; Hans Küng, *On Being a Christian*, p. 475.
64. Hans Küng, *The Church*, p. 323.

65. Rulff Otto, *The Idea of the Holy*, p. 147.
66. Ibid., Chapter 5.
67. Hans Küng, *Does God Exist?*, p. 633.
68. Ibid., p. 625.
69. Ibid., p. 626.
70. See footnote 2, Chapter 4.
71. Fleck, *The Mask of Religion*, p. 16.
72. Hans Küng, *Does God Exist?*, p. 626.
73. Ibid., p. 645.
74. Ibid., p. 646.
75. Ibid., p. 630.
76. Ibid., p. 647.
77. Hans Küng, *The Church*, p. 56.

Chapter 4

Reason and Faith

1. William James, *The Varieties of Religious Experience*, p. 433.
2. Max Weber, *The Sociology of Religion*, p. 84.
3. Durant, *The Reformation*, p. 370, Vol. VI of the *Story of Civilization*.
4. *The Sayings of Mohammed*, p. 55.
5. Ibid., p. 35.
6. Carl Jung, *Man and His Symbols*, p. 94.
7. Ibid.
8. W. V. Goethe, *Faust*, Act I, Scene I.
9. Exodus Chapter 20 and Deuteronomy Chapter 5.
10. Durant, *The Age of Faith*, p. 1082, Vol. IV of the *Story of Civilization*.
11. Durant, *The Age of Louis XIV*, p. 64, Vol. VIII of the *Story of Civilization*.
12. Ibid., p. 65.
13. Ibid.
14. Alan W. Watts, *Myth and Ritual in Christianity*, p. 208.
15. Quoted from Duncan Howlett, *The Fourth Faith*, p. 42.
16. Albert Camus, *The Myth of Sisyphus*.
17. Hans Küng, *The Church*, p. 56.
18. Ralph Waldo Emerson, "The Oversoul."
19. *Parker v. Commissioner of Internal Revenue*, 365 F. 2d 792 (1966).

Chapter 5

Emotion and Mysticism

1. Frances Trollope, *Domestic Manners of the Americans*, Chapter 29, footnote 4.
2. Ralph Waldo Emerson, "The Oversoul."
3. Ibid.
4. Edith Hamilton, *The Greek Way*, p. 296.
5. William James, *The Varieties of Religious Experience*, p. 8.
6. Ibid., p. 24.
7. Ibid., p. 17.
8. Albert Einstein, "What I Believe," *Forum* (October 1930).

9. Pierre Teilhard de Chardin, *The Phenomenon of Man,* p. 283.
10. Erich Fromm, *You Shall Be as Gods,* p. 19.
11. Durant, *The Life of Greece,* p. 96, Vol. II of *The Story of Civilization.*
12. Henry Elma Barnes, *An Intellectual and Cultural History of the Western World,* p. 790, seq.
13. Bertha Stevens, *Miracles Abound,* p. 13.
14. Duncan Howlett, *The Fourth American Faith,* p. 214.
15. Carl Sagan, *Broca's Brain,* p. 309.
16. Samuel Eliot Morison, *The Oxford History of the American People,* p. 526.
17. Peter Fleck, *The Mask of Religion.*

Chapter 6

Truth

1. Peter Fleck, *The Mask of Religion,* p. 9.
2. Ibid., p. 16.
3. Ralph Burhoe, address reprinted in *Unitarian Universalist World,* 15 October 1980, p. 6.
4. Hans Küng, *The Church,* p. 52.
5. *Crowley v. Smithsonian Institution,* 636 F. 2d 738 (1980).
6. *The New York Times,* 27 May 1978.
7. Carl Sagan, *Broca's Brain,* p. 284.
8. Julian Huxley, Introduction to Teilhard de Chardin, *The Phenomenon of Man,* p. 23.
9. *Time,* 31 July 1978.
10. Lewis Thomas, *The Medusa and the Snail,* p. 73.
11. Ibid., p. 26.
12. Carl Sagan, op. cit., p. 286.
13. Ruth Zimmerman, *Smithsonian,* June 1979, p. 52.
14. Jacob Bronowski, *The Ascent of Man,* p. 353.
15. James L. Adams, *On Being Human—Religiously,* p. 11.
16. The Unitarian Church of Princeton, New Jersey.
17. Thomas, op. cit., p. 114.
18. E. F. Schumacher, *A Guide for the Perplexed,* p. 110.
19. Ibid., p. 114.
20. Ibid., Chapter 9, footnote 12.

Chapter 7

Myths and Symbols

1. Alan W. Watts, *Myth and Ritual in Christianity,* p. 6.
2. Hans Küng, *On Being a Christian,* p. 451.
3. Rudolf Bultmann, *New Testament and Mythology,* p. 10, footnote 3.
4. Thomas Bulfinch, *The Age of Fable,* p. ix.
5. Ibid., p. 12.
6. Hans Küng, *On Being a Christian,* p. 450, seq.
7. Paul Tillich, *Theology of Culture,* p. 60.
8. Hans Küng, op. cit., p. 412.
9. Edith Hamilton, *The Greek Way,* p. 284.

10. Ibid., p. 285.

11. Durant, *The Life of Greece,* p. 192, Vol. II of *The Story of Civilization.*

12. Mircea Eliade, *Myth and Reality,* pp. 7, 19, and 92.

13. Plato, *The Republic,* Book III, p. 74.

14. *Hymns of the Spirit,* No. 297.

15. Dietrich Bonhoeffer, *Letters and Papers from Prison,* p. 167 (letter dated 5 May 1944).

16. Rudolf Bultmann, *New Testament and Mythology,* p. 3.

17. John A. T. Robinson, *Honest to God,* p. 24.

18. William James, *The Varieties of Religious Experience,* p. 485.

19. Ibid., Chapter 20.

20. Charles H. Long, *Alpha, The Myths of Creation,* p. 10.

21. Robert B. Tapp, *Religion Among the Unitarian Universalists,* p. 198.

22. Leviticus 12:3.

23. Hans Küng, op. cit., p. 412.

24. Donald Harrington, *The Curse, Cruelty, Comfort, and Challenge of the Cross.*

25. *Anderson v. Salt Lake City Corporation,* 475 F. 2d 29 (1973).

26. *Fox v. City of Los Angeles,* 150 Cal. 876, 878 (178).

Chapter 8

Jesus and Christianity

1. *Unitarian Universalist Association Bylaws,* Article II, Section 2.2(b).

2. Albert Schweitzer, *Out of My Life and Thought,* p. 68.

3. Ibid.

4. Ibid.

5. Ibid., p. 74.

6. Max Weber, *The Sociology of Religion,* p. 51.

7. Alan W. Watts, *Myth and Ritual in Christianity,* p. 208.

8. *The New York Times,* 5 December 1978.

9. James L. Adams, *On Being Human—Religiously,* p. 5.

10. Paul Tillich, *Theology of Culture,* p. 66.

11. Max Weber, op. cit., p. 105.

12. Durant, *The Life of Greece,* p. 13, Vol. II of *The Story of Civilization.*

13. Harry E. Barnes, *An Intellectual & Cultural History of the Western World,* Vol. I, p. 791.

14. Max Weber, op. cit., p. 261.

15. G. E. Lessing, *The Religion of Christ.*

16. Ralph Waldo Emerson, "The Divinity School Address."

17. Peter Fleck, *The Mask of Religion,* p. 55.

18. Max Weber, op. cit., p. 115.

19. Ibid., p. 116.

20. Ibid.

21. *Smithsonian,* November 1978, p. 50.

22. Albert Schweitzer, op. cit., p. 65, seq.

23. *Dayton Journal Herald,* 27 December 1980, p. 26.

Chapter 9

Satan, Heaven, and Hell

1. Alan W. Watts, *Myth and Ritual in Christianity,* p. 82.
2. Sterling North and C. B. Boutell, *Speak of the Devil.*
3. George B. Shaw, *Man and Superman,* Act III.
4. Robert Ellwood, *Religious and Spiritual Groups in America,* p. 211.
5. Durant, *The Reformation,* p. 363, Vol. VI of *The Story of Civilization.*
6. Charles Beaudelaire, "The Generous Gambler," reprinted in North and Boutell *Speak of the Devil,* p. 48.
7. *The New York Times,* 5 December 1978.
8. Ellwood, op. cit.
9. Durant, *The Life of Greece,* p. 192, Vol. II of *The Story of Civilization.*
10. Herman Wouk, *This Is My God,* p. 167.
11. Shaw, op. cit.
12. Ralph Burhoe, "Proposal to Establish CASIRAS," *Zygon,* vol. 7 no. 3, p. 169.
13. Hans Küng, *On Being a Christian,* p. 369.
14. Andrew Greeley, *Everything You Wanted to Know About the Catholic Church But Were Too Pious to Ask,* p. 99.

Chapter 10

Sin, Redemption, and Salvation

1. James L. Adams, *On Being Human—Religiously,* p. 7.
2. Erich Fromm, *You Shall Be As Gods,* p. 87.
3. Chapter 2, footnote 2.
4. John Hayward, *Existentialism and Religious Liberalism,* p. 70.
5. Ibid., p. 86.
6. Sohaku Ogata, *Zen for the West,* p. 18.
7. Ibid., p. 16.
8. Max Weber, *The Sociology of Religion,* p. 116.
9. Rudolf Otto, *The Idea of the Holy,* p. 86.

Chapter 11

Death, Immortality, the Soul, and the Last Judgment

1. Herman Wouk, *This Is My God,* p. 16.
2. Hans Küng, *On Being a Christian,* p. 356.
3. Ethel Sabin Smith, *God and Other Gods,* p. 4.
4. Ibid., p. 5.
5. Küng, op. cit., pp. 356–357.
6. II Kings 4:32 seq; II Kings 8:5.
7. William James, *The Varieties of Religious Experience,* p. 514.
8. Carl Sagan, *Broca's Brain,* p. 310.
9. Küng, op. cit., p. 357.
10. Ibid., p. 360.
11. Ibid., p. 357.

12. Max Weber, *The Sociology of Religion,* p. 110 seq.
13. Albert Camus, *The Myth of Sisyphus and Other Essays,* preface.
14. James, op. cit., p. 125.
15. Ibid., Lectures VI and VII.
16. Ralph Waldo Emerson, "The Oversoul."
17. James L. Adams, *On Being Human—Religiously,* p. 18.

Chapter 12

The Democratic Process in Human Relations

1. Durant, *The Life of Greece,* p. 126, Vol. II of *The Story of Civilization.*
2. Ibid., p. 254.
3. Ibid., p. 519.
4. Ibid., p. 531.
5. Harold J. Laski, *The American Democracy,* p. 432.
6. Henry Steele Commager, *Living Ideas of America,* p. 148.

Chapter 13

The Dignity of Man

1. Edith Hamilton, *The Echo of Greece,* p. 151.
2. John Courtney Murray, S.J., "America's Four Conspiracies," in *Religion in America* edited by John Cogley, p. 33.
3. *De Franco v. De Franco,* Ill. App. Ct. 26 December 1978.
4. *Jarrett v. Jarrett,* Ill. App. Ct. 13 January 1979.
5. *In re Dalesandro,* Pa. Sup. Ct. 12 January 1979.

Chapter 14

Justice

1. Martin Luther King, Jr., "Address to the New York City Bar Association."
2. Paul Tillich, *Systematic Theology,* Vol. III, p. 267.
3. Harold Berman, *The Interaction of Law and Religion,* p. 52.
4. *U.S. v. MacIntosh,* 283 U.S. 605 (1931).

Chapter 15

Freedom of Belief

1. See Chapter 6, p. 108.
2. Durant *The Reformation,* p. 485 seq. Vol. VI of *The Story of Civilization.*
3. *Hymns for the Celebration of Life,* No. 420.
4. Donald Harrington, "The Faith Beneath Freedom," *Community Pulpit* 1967.
5. *The New York Times,* 19 December 1979, p. A8.
6. Albert Schweitzer, *Out of My Life and Thought,* p. 55.
7. *Roe v. Wade,* 410 U.S. 113 (1973).

Chapter 16

Social Concern

1. Charles E. Fager, *Selma 1965,* p. 113.
2. Ibid., p. 158.
3. Ibid., p. 124.
4. Ibid., p. 130.
5. Ibid., p. 145; see also Chapter 20.
6. *The New York Times,* 26 October 1969, p. 65.
7. Max Weber, *The Sociology of Religion,* p. 51.
8. *U.S. v MacIntosh,* 283 U.S. 605 (1931), and see above Chapter 14, footnote 4.
9. Pierre Teilhard de Chardin, *The Phenomenon of Man,* p. 282.
10. *Roe v. Wade,* 410 U.S. 113 (1973).
11. *The New York Times,* 20 May 1978.
12. George B. Shaw, *Major Barbara,* preface.
13. James L. Adams, *On Being Human—Religiously,* p. 10.

Chapter 17

Religious Liberty

1. Haynes Trebor, *The Flushing Remonstrance,* p. 11.
2. Ibid., p. 4.
3. Joseph L. Blau, *Cornerstones of Religious Freedom in America,* p. 36.
4. Ibid., p. 74.
5. Thomas Paine, *The Age of Reason,* in *Basic Writings,* p. 7.
6. William Walker, *John Calvin,* p. 421.
7. Irwin H. Polishook, *Roger Williams, John Cotton and Religious Freedom,* p. 4 seq.
8. Thomas Jefferson, "Notes on Virginia," Chapter 18, *Basic Writings,* p. 158.
9. *Thomas V. Review Board of Indiana Employment,* U.S. Sup. Court, 6 April, 1981.
10. *Zorach v. Clauson,* 343 U.S. 306 (1952).
11. *Lemon v. Kuntzman,* 403 U.S. 602 (1971).
12. *Chambers v. March,* Federal District Court Nebraska (1980) 49 LW 2477.
13. Robert Nixon, "Up in the Air Over Airport Chapels," *Liberty,* July–August, 1980, p. 8.
14. *U.S. v. Reynolds,* 98 U.S. 148 (1878).
15. *Heffron v. International Society for Krishna Consciousness, Inc., et al.,* 101 S. Ct., 917 (1981).
16. U.S. v. American Friends Service Committee, 419 U.S. 95 (1974).
17. *Prince v. Massachusetts,* 321 U.S. 158 (1944).
18. *Stone v. Agraham,* 101 S. Ct. 192 (1980).
19. *Sequoyah v. Tennessee Valley Authority,* 620 F. 2d 1159 (1980) affirming 480 F. Supp. 608 (1979), cert. denied 101 S. Ct. 357 (1980).
20. *U.S. v. Seeger,* 380 U.S. 163 (1965).
21. *U.S. v. Shacter,* 293 F. Supp. 1057 (1968).
22. *Harris v. McRae,* 100 S. Ct. 2671 (1980).
23. *Crowley v. Smithsonian Institution,* 636 F. 2d 738 (1980).
24. *U.S. v. Seeger,* op. cit., note 23.
25. *Wisconsin v. Yoder,* 406 U.S. 205 (1972).
26. *Thomas v. Collins,* 323 U.S. 516.

27. *Braunfeld v. Brown,* 366 U.S. 599 (1961).

28. *Brandon v. Board of Education,* 635 F. 2d 971 (1980).

29. *The New York Times,* 30 November 1980.

30. Leo Pfeffer, "The Right of Religious Liberty," in N. Dorsen, *The Right of Americans,* p. 339.

31. Ibid., p. 341.

32. *Hall v. Bradshaw,* 640 F. 2d. 1018 (1980).

33. Blau, *Cornerstones of Religious Freedom in America,* p. 74.

34. *The New York Times,* 8 July 1978.

35. *The New York Times,* 19 July 1981, p. A14.

36. *The New York Times,* 28 June 1980.

37. Heller TC Memo 1978-149 and Haak DC Mich. 21 March 1978.

38. *Bob Jones University v. U.S.,* 639 F. 2d 147 (1980).

Chapter 18

Politics

1. William James, *The Varieties of Religious Experience,* postscript footnote 1, p. 512.

2. Carl Sagan, *Broca's Brain,* p. 283.

3. Max Weber, *The Sociology of Religion,* p. 90.

4. Hans Küng, *On Being a Christian,* p. 90.

5. Franz Fanon, *The Wretched of the Earth.*

6. Samuel E. Morrison, *The Oxford History of the American People,* pp. 513–514.

7. Thomas Jefferson, *Basic Writings,* p. 432.

8. Edward Gibbon, *The Decline and Fall of the Roman Empire,* Chapter II.

9. Thomas A. Owen Fowle, Advance Newsletter, January 1978.

10. Weber, op. cit., p. 225.

11. Ibid., p. 226.

12. A. Powell Davis, *America's Real Religion,* p. 72.

13. Paul Tillich, *Systematic Religion,* Vol. IV, p. 358.

14. *International Herald Tribune,* 12 September 1979.

Chapter 19

Worship and Prayer

1. *Hymns of the Spirit,* No. 372.

2. Max Weber, *The Sociology of Religion,* pp. 14 and 28.

3. Ibid., p. 3.

4. Donald S. Harrington, *The Curse, Cruelty, Comfort and Challenge of the Cross.*

5. Charles Long, *Alpha, The Myths of Creation,* p. 10 and see Chapter 7.

6. Albert Schweitzer, *Out of My Life and Thought,* p. 268.

7. Henry N. Weiman, *The Growth of Religion,* p. 391.

8. Irving R. Murray, *Unitarian Universalist Worship* (1978), p. 1.

9. Alan Seaburg, "Worship," *Unity,* vol. 150, p. 118 (November-December 1965).

10. Weiman, op. cit., p. 373.

11. *Chambers v. March,* Federal District Court Nebraska, 24 December 1980.

12. John M. Morris, "Sense and Nonsense About Prayer," *Unity,* vol. 148, p. 110 (December 1961).

13. Weber, op. cit., p. 26.
14. Vern Barnet in Unitarian Universalist Association pamphlet on sacraments, p. 5.

Chapter 20

Heroes and Saints

1. *Hymns of the Spirit,* No. 412.
2. Charles E. Fager, *Selma 1965,* p. 107.
3. David B. Parke, *The Epic of Unitarianism,* p. 80.
4. Durant, *The Age of Faith,* p. 743, Vol. IV of *The Story of Civilization.*
5. Thomas Jefferson, *Basic Writings,* p. 561.
6. Parke, op. cit., pp. 99–100.
7. Thomas Jefferson, *The Morals of Jesus.*
8. Stephen H. Fritchman, *Men of Liberty,* p. 86 footnote.
9. Jefferson, *Basic Writings,* op. cit., p. 764.
10. Fritchman, op. cit., p. 86.
11. A. Powell Davies, *America's Real Religion,* p. 67.
12. Jefferson, *Basic Writings,* op. cit., p. 601, Letter to Benjamin (1791).
13. Claude G. Bowers, *The Young Jefferson,* p. 174.
14. Albert Schweitzer, *Out of My Life and Thought,* p. 185.
15. Ibid., p. 117.

Chapter 21

Celebrations

1. Blackman, "The Civil Sacrament: Law and Practices in the Soviet Wedding," 28 *American Journal of Comparative Law,* 555 (Fall 1980).
2. J. W. Goethe, *Faust,* Scene II.
3. John F. Hayward, *Existentialism and Religious Liberalism,* p. 123.

Chapter 22

The Role of the Minister

1. Josiah Bartlett, Unitarian Universalist Advance, *Newsletter Supplement,* January 1978.
2. Reinhold Niebuhr, *Leaves from the Notebook of a Tamed Cynic,* p. 149.
3. Carl Hermann Voss, *Rabbi and Minister,* p. 59.
4. Ibid., p. 55.
5. Ibid., p. 57.
6. Ibid., p. 13.
7. *The Free Church in a Changing World* (1963), p. 19.
8. Max Weber, *The Sociology of Religion,* p. 200.
9. Ibid., p. 46.
10. Stephen H. Fritchman, *Men of Liberty,* p. 86, footnote.

Chapter 23

Is Organized Religion Necessary?

1. Harold Berman, *The Interaction of Law and Religion*, p. 79.
2. Frank G. Opton, "Freedom v. Efficiency," *Unity*, vol. 148, p. 29, (March 1962).
3. *Wisconsin v. Yoder*, 406 U.S. 205 (1972).

Chapter 24

The Virtues: A Summary

1. Conrad Wright, *Three Prophets*, p. 79.
2. Plato, *Meno*, in *Dialogues*, p. 68.
3. Thomas Jefferson, *Basic Writings*, p. 562, Letter to Peter Carr (1787).
4. Duncan Howlett, *The Critical Way in Religion*, p. 259.
5. James L. Adams, *On Being Human—Religiously*, p. 18.
6. *The New York Times*, 3 December 1980, p. A12.
7. See Chapter 11.
8. See Chapter 2.
9. Albert Schweitzer, *Out of My Life and Thought*, p. 185.
10. Ibid., p. 235.
11. George Santayana, *Reason in Society*, p. 164.
12. Ibid., p. 153.
13. Wendell Wilkie, *One World*, p. 84.
14. Ralph Waldo Emerson, "The Oversoul."
15. See Chapter 17.
16. Mahatma Gandhi, *Selected Writings*, p. 83.
17. Harry Jones, *The Efficacy of the Law*, p. 98.
18. Martin Luther King, Jr., *Why We Can't Wait*, p. 83.
19. John Haynes Holmes, "Are We Losing Our Liberal Spirit?" *The Community Pulpit* (1947) No. III.
20. Frederick M. Eliot, *An Anthology*, p. 3.
21. Emerson, "Intellect."
22. Ibid.

Postscript

1. Sonia Johnson, *From Housewife to Heretic* (New York: Doubleday, 1981).
2. *The New York Times Book Review*, 7 February 1982, p. 35.
3. *Frank Africa v. The Commonwealth of Pennsylvania*, CA3d 30 October 1981.
4. *The New York Times*, 29 December 1981.
5. Ibid.
6. Ibid.
7. *The New York Times*, 9 December 1981.

Bibliography

Adams, James Luther. *On Being Human—The Liberal Way.* Pamphlet from The American Unitarian Association.

———. *On Being Human—Religiously.* Edited by Max L. Stackhouse. Boston: Beacon Press, 1976.

Adler, Felix. *Our Part in This World.* Edited by Horace Friess. New York: Kings Crown Press, 1946.

Barnes, Henry Elma. *An Intellectual & Cultural History of the Western World.* Vol. 2. 3rd. ed. New York: Dover Publications, 1965.

Bartlett, Josiah R. and Laile E. *Moment of Truth.* Berkeley, California, 1968.

Bartlett, Laile E. *Bright Galaxy.* Boston: Beacon Press, 1960.

Beaudelaire, Charles. "The Generous Gambler." Reprinted in *Speak of the Devil,* edited by Sterling North and L. B. Boutell. Garden City, New York: Doubleday 1945.

Berman, Harold J. *The Interaction of Law and Religion.* New York, 1974.

Bible. The King James Version.

———. The Jerusalem Bible. Garden City, New York: Doubleday, 1966.

———. American Translation by Smith and Goodspeed. Chicago: University of Chicago Press, 1937.

———. *The Lost Books of the Bible.* New York: Dell, 1979.

Blau, Joseph L. *Cornerstones of Religious Freedom in America.* Boston: Beacon Press, 1950.

Bonhoeffer, Dietrich. *The Cost of Discipleship.* 2nd rev. ed. Trans. by Reginald H. Fuller. New York: Macmillan, 1973.

———. *Letters and Papers from Prison.* Edited by Eberhard Bethge. Trans. by Reginald H. Fuller. New York: Macmillan, 1962.

The Book of Common Prayer.

Bowers, Claude G. *The Young Jefferson.* Boston: Hougton Mifflin, 1945.

Bratton, Fred. G. *A History of the Bible.* Boston: Beacon Press, 1969.

Bronowski, Jacob. *The Ascent of Man.* Boston: Beacon Press, 1969.

Bultmann, Rudolf. "New Testament and Mythology." Reprinted in *Keryema and Mythy,* edited by Bartsch. London, 1954.

Burhoe, Ralph. "Proposal to Establish CASIRAS." *Zygon,* 7:168.

Call, Lon Ray. "The Faith Behind Freedom." Mimeographed pamphlet.

Camus, Albert. *The Myth of Sisyphus and Other Essays.* New York: Vintage, 1955.

Cardozo, Benjamin. "The Choice of Tycho Brahe." Reprinted in *Selected Writings of Cardozo.* New York: Fallon, 1947.

Carnes, Paul. "Commentary in the Free Church." In *A Changing World in the U.S.A.* Boston: Beacon Press, 1963.

Cogley, John, ed. *Religion in America.* New York: Meridian, 1958.

Commager, Henry S. *The American Mind.* New Haven: Yale University Press, 1950.

Conze, E. "Buddhism: The Mahayana." In the *Concise Encyclopedia of Living Faiths.* Boston: Beacon Press, 1959.

Cox, Harvey. *The Feast of Fools.* Cambridge: Harvard University Press, 1969.

———. *The Secular City.* rev. ed. New York: Macmillan, 1967.

Daly, Mary. *Beyond God the Father: Towards a Philosophy of Women's Liberation.* Boston: Beacon Press, 1973.

Dante, Allighieri. *The Divine Comedy.* Trans. by Lawrence Grant White. New York: Pantheon, 1958.

Darwin, Charles. *Autobiography.* Edited by Nora Baslow. New York: Harcourt Brace Jovanovich, 1959.

Davies, Powell A. *America's Real Religion.* Boston: Beacon Press, 1953.

———. *The First Christian.* New York: New American Library, 1959.

Dimont, Max I. *Jews, God and History.* New York: New American Library, 1962.

Dorsen, Norman, ed. *The Rights of Americans.* New York: Pantheon, 1971.

Durant, Will. *The Story of Philosophy.* New York: Simon & Schuster, 1953.

Durant, Will and Ariel. *The Story of Civilization.* Vols. 1–11. New York: Simon & Schuster, 1939–1975.

Eliade, Mircea. *From Primitives to Zen.* San Francisco: Harper & Row, 1977.

———. *Myth and Reality.* New York: Harper & Row, 1963/1975.

Eliot, Frederick M. *An Anthology.* Edited by Alfred P. Stiernotte. Boston: Beacon Press, 1959.

Ellwood, Robert S. *Religious & Spiritual Groups in Modern America.* Englewood Cliffs, New Jersey. Prentice-Hall, 1973.

Emerson, Ralph W. *The Complete Works of Ralph Waldo Emerson.* Boston: Houghton Mifflin, 1891.

Fager, Charles E. *Selma 1965.* New York: Charles Scribner's Sons, 1964.

Fleck, Peter G. *The Mask of Religion.* Buffalo: Prometheus, 1980.

Fritchman, Stephen H. *Men of Liberty.* Boston: Beacon Press, 1945.

Fromm, Erich. *You Shall Be Like Gods.* New York: Holt, Rinehart & Winston, 1966.

Gandhi, Mohandas. *Selected Writings.* Edited by Ronald Dugan. Boston: Beacon Press, 1951.

Gibb, H. A. R. "Islam." In *The Concise Encyclopedia of Living Faiths.* Boston: Beacon Press, 1959.

Gibbon, Edward. *The Decline and Fall of the Roman Empire.* Reprinted in *The Portable Gibbon.* New York: Viking Press, 1952.

Gibran, Kahlil. *The Prophet.* New York: Alfred A. Knopf, 1953.

Goethe, Johann W. *Faust.* Trans. by Bayard Taylor. New York: Modern Library.

Graves, Robert. *Adam's Rib.* New York: Yoseloff, 1958.

Grunebaum, L. H. *Philosophy of Modern Man.* New York: Horizon, 1970.

Haining, Peter. *The Satanist.* New York: Taplinger Press, 1969.

Hamilton, Edith. *The Echo of Greece.* New York: W. W. Norton, 1957.

———. *The Greek Way.* New York: W. W. Norton, 1942.

Harrington, Donald S. "The Curse, Cruelty, Comfort, and Challenge of the Cross." An address published in the *Community Pulpit,* 1963.

———. "The Faith Beneath Freedom." An address published in the *Community Pulpit,* 1967.

Hayward, John F. *Existentialism and Religious Liberalism.* Boston: Beacon Press, 1962.

Hemstreet, Robert M. *Identity and Ideology.* A pamphlet issued by the Unitarian Universalist Advance c. 1977.

Heschell, Abraham J. "The Religious Message." In *Religion in America,* edited by John Cogley. New York: Meridian, 1958.

Hocking, William Ernest. *The Meaning of God in Human Experience.* New Haven: Yale University Press, 1912.

Horner, I. B. "Buddhism: The Theravada." In *The Concise Encyclopedia of Living Faiths.* Boston: Beacon Press, 1959.

Howlett, Duncan. *The Critical Way in Religion.* Buffalo: Prometheus, 1980.

———. *The Fourth American Faith.* Boston: Beacon Press, 1964.

Huizinga, Johan. *Erasmus and the Age of Reformation.* Trans. by F. Hopman. New York: Harper Torchbooks, 1957.

Hymns for the Celebration of Life. Boston: Beacon Press, 1967.

James, William. *The Varieties of Religious Experience.* New York: Modern Library, 1902.

Jefferson, Thomas. *Basic Writings of Thomas Jefferson.* Edited by Philip S. Foller. New York: Haleyon House, 1944.

———. *The Morals of Jesus.* (The Jefferson Bible). New York, 1904.

Jones, Harry W. *The Effigy of Law.* Evanston: Northwestern University Press, 1959.

Jung, Carl G. *Man and His Symbols.* Garden City: Doubleday, 1964.

Kaufmann, Walter. *The Faith of a Heretic.* Garden City: Doubleday, 1961.

———. *Hegel.* Garden City: Doubleday, 1965.

Kelly, Henry A. *Towards the Death of Satan.* London: Chapman Publishers, 1968.

King, Jr., Martin Luther. *Why We Can't Wait.* New York: Segel Books, 1964.

Kierkegaard, Søren. *Fear & Trembling.* Trans. by Walter Lowry. Princeton: Princeton University Press, 1941.

Konvitz, Milton R. *Religious Liberty and Conscience.* New York: Viking, 1968.

Küng, Hans. *The Church.* New York: Doubleday, 1976.

———. *Does God Exist?* New York: Doubleday, 1980.

———. *On Being a Christian.* New York: Wallarby, 1978.

Laski, Harold J. *The American Democracy.* New York: Viking, 1948.

Long, Charles H. *Alpha: The Myths of Creation.* New York: George Braziller, 1963.

McCullough, Colleen. *The Thornbirds.* New York: Avon, 1981.

Mehta, Ved. *The New Theologian.* New York: Harper & Row, 1963.

Mendelsohn, Jack. *Why I Am a Unitarian Universalist.* Boston: Beacon Press, 1963.

Sayings of Mohammed. Mount Vernon: Peter Pauper, 1958.

Morrison, Samuel E. *The Oxford History of the American People.* New York: Oxford University Press, 1965.

Mueller, Robert. *Most of All They Taught Me Happiness.* New York: Doubleday, 1978.

———. *Prayer and Meditation at the United Nations.* Jamaica, New York, 1977.

Murray, John Courtney, S.J. "America's Four Conspiracies." In *Religion in America,* edited by John Cogley. New York: Meridian, 1958.

Murray, Victor A. *How to Know Your Bible.* Boston: Beacon Press, 1952.

Niebuhr, Reinhold. *Leaves from the Notebooks of a Tamed Cynic.* New York: Meridian, 1957.

North, Sterling, and Boutell, L. B. *Speak of the Devil.* Garden City: Doubleday, 1945.

Du Nouy, Lecomte. *Human Destiny.* New York: Longmans Green Publishers, 1947.

———. *The Road to Reason.* New York: Longmans Green, 1949.

Ogata, Sohaku. *Zen for the West.* New York: Dial, 1959.

Orwell, George. *Animal Farm.* New York: Harcourt Brace Jovanovich, 1946.

Otto, Rudolf. *The Idea of the Holy.* Trans. by John Harvey. London: Oxford University Press, 1923.

Paine, Thomas. *The Age of Reason.* Reprinted in *The Basic Writings of Thomas Paine.* New York: John Wiley & Sons, 1942.

Papini, Giovanni. *The Devil.* New York: E. P. Dutton, 1954.

Parke, David B. *The Epic of Unitarianism.* Boston: Beacon Press, 1957.

Pfeffer, Leo. "The Right of Religious Liberty." In *The Rights of Americans,* edited by Norman Dorsen. New York: Simon & Schuster, 1953.

Plato. *The Republic.* Trans. by B. Jowett. New York: Modern Library, 1892.

Polishook, Irwin H. *Roger Williams, John Cotton and Religious Freedom.* Englewood Cliffs: Prentice-Hall, 1967.

Radin, Paul. *Primitive Religion: Its Nature and Origin.* New York: Dover Publications, 1957.

Rhodes, H. T. F. *The Satanic Mass.* London: Jarrold Publishing, 1955.

Robinson, John A. F. *Honest to God.* Philadelphia: Westminster, 1963.

Roston, Leo. *A Guide to the Religions of America.* New York: Simon & Schuster, 1955.

Runnes, D. D., ed. *Dictionary of Philosophy.* 15th ed. New York: Philosophical Library, 1960.

Sagan, Carl. *Broca's Brain.* New York: Random House, 1979.

Saint Augustine. *The City of God.* New York: Image, 1959.

Schumacher, E. F. *A Guide for the Perplexed.* New York: Harper & Row, 1977.

Schweitzer, Albert. *Ausgewahlte Werke* Vols. 1–5. Berlin: Union Publishing, c. 1976.

———. "The Ethics of Reverence for Life." *Christendom* Vol. 1 (1936), p. 255.

———. *Out of My Life and Thought.* New York: Henry Holt, 1933.

Shaw, George B. "Man and Superman," "St. Joan," and "Major Barbara." In *The Selected Plays of George Bernard Shaw.* New York: Dodd, Meed & Co., 1948.

Smith, Ethel Sabin. *God and Other Gods.* New York: Exposition Press, 1973.

Sophocles. *Antigone.* In *The Complete Greek Dramas.* New York: Random House, 1938.

Stevens, Bertha. *How Miracles Abound.* Boston: Beacon Press, 1941.

Tapp, Robert B. *Religion Among the Unitarian Universalists.* New York: Seminary Press, 1973.

Teilhard de Chardin, Pierre. *The Phenomenon of Man.* New York: Harper Torchbooks, 1961.

Thoreau, Henry David. *Civil Disobedience.* New York: New American Library, 1960.

Thucydides. *The History of the Peloponnesian War.* Edited and trans. by Livingstone. London: Oxford University Press, 1943.

Tillich, Paul. "Freedom and Ultimate Concern." In *Religion in America,* edited by John Cogley. New York: Meridian, 1958.

———. *Systematic Theology.* Vol. 1 (1959), Vol. 2 (1957), Vol. 3 (1963). Chicago: University of Chicago Press.

———. *Theology of Culture.* New York: Oxford University Press, 1959.

Trebor, Haynes. *The Flushing Remonstrance.* Distributed by Bowne House, Flushing, New York.

Trollope, Frances. *Domestic Manners of the Americans.* Reprint of the 5th ed. New York: Alfred A. Knopf, 1949.

Unitarian Universalist Association. *The Free Church in a Changing World.* Report, 1963.

———. *Sacrament.* (a pamphlet).

Voss, Carl Hermann. *Rabbi and Minister.* Cleveland: World Publishing Co., 1964.

Walker, William. *John Calvin, The Organizer of Reformed Protestantism.* New York: G. P. Putnam's Sons, 1906.

Watts, Alan W. *Myth and Ritual in Christianity.* Boston: Beacon Press, 1968.

Weber, Max. *The Sociology of Religion.* Boston: Beacon Press, 1964.

Weigel, Gustave. "The Present Embarrassment of the Church." In *Religion in America,* edited by John Cogley. New York: Meridian, 1958.

Wertenbacker, Thomas J. *The First Americans* (Vol. 2 of *A History of American Life*). New York: Macmillan, 1927.

Wieman, Henry Nelson. *The Growth of Religion.* Chicago: Willett Clark, 1938.

———. *Man's Ultimate Commitment.* Carbondale: Southern Illinois University Press, 1958.

———. *Religious Experience and Scientific Method.* New York: Macmillan, 1926.

———. *Seeking a Faith for a New Age.* Edited by Cedric Hepler. Metuchen, New Jersey: Scarecrow, 1975.

———. *The Wrestle of Religion with Truth.* New York: Macmillan, 1927.

Wilkie, Wendell. *One World.* New York: Simon & Schuster, 1943.

Wilson, Edmund. *The Scrolls of the Dead Sea.* New York: Oxford University Press, 1955.

Wouk, Herman. *This Is My God.* London: Cape Publishers, 1960.

Wright, Conrad, ed. *Three Prophets of Religious Liberalism.* Boston: Beacon Press, 1961.

Index of Names

287

Index of Subjects